[英] E.M.福斯特 著

刘文荣 译

小说面面观

中英合订·最新译本

ASPECTS
OF THE NOVEL

文汇出版社

图书在版编目（CIP）数据

小说面面观：汉英对照／（英）E.M.福斯特著；刘文荣译．—上海：文汇出版社，2022.2
ISBN 978-7-5496-3700-3

Ⅰ.①小… Ⅱ.①E… ②刘… Ⅲ.①小说评论—英国—现代—汉、英 Ⅳ.①I561.074

中国版本图书馆CIP数据核字（2022）第008903号

小说面面观

著　　者／［英］E.M.福斯特
译　　者／刘文荣

责任编辑／陈今夫　王　骏
封面装帧／薛　冰

出版发行／**文匯**出版社
　　　　　上海市威海路755号
　　　　　（邮政编码 200041）
经　　销／全国新华书店
排　　版／南京展望文化发展有限公司
印刷装订／启东市人民印刷有限公司
版　　次／2022年2月第1版
印　　次／2022年2月第1次印刷
开　　本／889×1194　1/32
字　　数／220千字
印　　张／12
ISBN 978-7-5496-3700-3
定　　价／58.00元

译者前言

关于本书作者和本书背景已在"作者简介"和"本书简介"中说了,在此不必重复。此处仅对作者在本书中所探讨的小说的七个"面"(aspect)——即:故事、人物、情节、幻想、启示、图形和节奏——稍作解释,以供初识小说理论的读者参考。

第一个"面",故事。这可说是小说中的"时间面"。按作者的说法,"故事就是按时序对事件所作的叙述——早饭之后是晚饭,星期一之后是星期二,死了之后是腐烂,如此等等"。也就是说,故事的核心是时间,或者说,时间顺序,即先与后。所以,听故事的人总是在问:"后来呢?后来呢?"虽然故事是所有小说的基本要素(没有故事,不成小说),但它却是小说中最原始、最低级的一面,仅仅满足读者的好奇心而已。

第二个"面",人物。这可说是小说中的"心理面"。按作者的说法,虽然小说中的人物往往和现实生活中的人很相像，似乎也有生有死，也吃饭睡觉、谈情说爱、生儿育女，但小说中的人物和现实生活中的人之间的本质区别就在于：他们的内心是完全袒露的。他们的所有心理活动都呈现在读者眼前。这是他们之所以存在的必要条件，也是他们之所以存在的价值所在。否则，读者又何必去了解小说中的人物？如果小说中的人物和现实生活中的人一模一样，那读者不是天天看到现实生活中的人吗？何必还要去看小说？也就是说，看小说中的人物，可以看到在现实生活中的人身上看不到的东西。这就是他们的价值所在，也是他们的魅力所在。至于小说家笔下形形色色的人物，按作者的说法，大致可以分为两种，即"扁平人物"和"圆形人物"。所谓"扁平人物"，就是简单人物，可以用一句话甚至一个词将其说明，譬如勇敢、胆小、慷慨、吝啬，等等（注意：现实生活中的人很少是这样的）。所谓"圆形人物"，就是复杂人物，很难用一个词或者一句话将其说明，因为他们有时勇敢，有时胆小；有时慷慨，有时吝啬，如此等等（注意：现实生活中的人大多是这样的）。这两种人物本身无所谓好坏，能使读者感兴趣的，就是好的；不能使读者感兴趣的，就是坏的。

第三个"面"，情节。这可说是小说中的"逻辑面"。按作者的说法，"情节也是对事件的叙述，只是重点放在因果关系上"。所以，说"国王死了，后来王后也死了"，是故事；而说"国王死了，后来王后因为伤心过度也死了"，则是情节；因为前者仅说出时间顺序（先与后），后者虽然也有时间顺序，但强调的是因果关系——因为国王死了，所以王后伤心过度；因为伤心过度，所以她也死了。"因为……所以……"即因果律，即逻辑。情节和故事一样，也是小说的基本要素，但情节要比故事高级一点，按作者的说法，"情节就是小说中合乎逻辑和理性的一面"。正因为如此，情节和人物往往处于对立状态：小说家若注重情节，人物往往就要被忽视；反之，若注重人物，情节往往就要被忽视（其中原因非常复杂，在此不便详说）。这是小说家面对的最大难题。既要情节生动，又要人物鲜明，几乎是不可能的。所以，实际情况是小说家似乎分成了两派：一派注重情节；一派注重人物。至于谁好谁坏，那就由读者来决定了；因为读者也似乎分成了两派：一派喜欢情节；一派喜欢人物。

第四、第五个"面"，幻想与启示。这可说是小说中的"神秘面"。按作者的说法，幻想与启示"同样相信神灵，但它们相信的神灵却有所不同"。幻想是把一系列"超自然事物"，如精灵、鬼魂、天使、猿猴、怪物、侏儒、女巫等，引入小说；或者，把读者引入无人之地、未来、过去、地球内部、四维空间，等等。启示则是以神的名义、上帝的名义，表达一种全人类的理想，或者梦想。幻想与启示都具有神话性质，都赋予小说以神秘色彩，因而都可使小说似乎具有某种"深度"；不过，这仍是小说的一种艺术手法，不是什么"思想"（注意：本书作者在本书中从未提到小说中的"思想"，即人们常说的"主题"，因为他要探讨的是"小说艺术"）。幻想小说以其离奇而吸引读者，启示小说则以其（貌似）崇高而感动读者。

第六、第七个"面"，图形与节奏。这可说是小说中的"形式面"。图形与节奏都是比喻。"图形"一词是从绘画艺术中借用来的,指的是小说的情节结构;"节奏"一词是从音乐中借用来的,指的也是小说的情节结构。所谓小说中的图形,就是由小说情节线索构成的某种形状,譬如钟漏形、长链形;所谓小说中的节奏,用作者的话来说,就是情节的"重复加变化"。无论是图形,还是节奏,都可能给小说带来美感,但弄得不好,反而会使小说变得狭隘或者僵化。就如作者所言,固定的图形"也许可以使小说氛围具体化,而且从情节中自然产生,但是它关掉了生活之门,使小说家往往只能在客厅里施展才能①";节奏也一样,"弄得不好,节奏是最令人厌烦的,它僵化为一种符号,不但不引领我们,反而绊倒我们"。所以,他认为,小说家在处理图形或者节奏时要慎之又慎;否则,读者很可能会说:"美是美的,但不值得。"

以上便是我对本书中关于小说的七个"面"所作的解释,不能保证完全正确,只能说大致就是这样——权且当作读者享用正餐前的一道开胃菜吧!

刘文荣

2021年2月于上海

---

① 意即图形(即某种人为的情节结构)可使小说具有某种审美形态("小说氛围具体化"),但很可能会使小说太"人为"而不像是真实的生活,小说家只是在自己设定的图形内写小说(这里的"客厅"即喻小说家自己设定的图形)。

目录

译者前言	1
第一章　导言	1
第二章　故事	25
第三章　人物	44
第四章　人物（续）	67
第五章　情节	87
第六章　幻想	109
第七章　启示	130
第八章　图形与节奏	155
第九章　结语	178

第一章 导　言

本讲座和三一学院①研究员威廉·乔治·克拉克的名字相关联②，是他使我们今天聚在一起，因而我们就从他开始说起。

据我所知，克拉克是约克郡人。他出生于一八二一年，在塞德伯和什鲁斯伯上学③，一八四〇年作为本科生进入三一学院，四年后成为研究员，此后近三十年间，他一直以学院为家，直到去世前不久，才因为健康问题而离开学院。他以研究莎士比亚的学者而最为人知，但也出版过两本其他方面的书，在此有必要提一下。他年轻时去过西班牙，并写了一部生动有趣的度假札记，叫作《格斯巴乔奥》。"格斯巴乔奥"是一种冷汤，他在安达卢西亚的农民家里喝过而且显然很喜欢；其实，他对那里的一切都很喜欢。八年后，他到希腊去度假，结果是出版了第二本书——《伯罗奔尼撒》。这本书写得比较庄

---

① 三一学院：剑桥大学中规模最大、名声最响的学院。
② 此讲座由威廉·乔治·克拉克创办，称为"克拉克讲座"。
③ 这两所学校都始建于16世纪，皆属英格兰最古老、最著名的学校。

重，也比较沉闷。那时的希腊是个严肃的地方，比西班牙要严肃得多；再说，克拉克那时已获得圣职①，而且还是学院的发言人，最为重要的是，他是和当时的院长汤普森博士一起去的，后者可不是那种会对冷汤感兴趣的人。所以，关于骡子和跳蚤之类的玩笑是几乎没有的，我们接二连三看到的不是古迹遗址，就是古战场。当然，这本书里除了学识，还有对希腊乡村的深切感受。克拉克还去过意大利和波兰。

再来说说他的学术生涯。他曾先后和格罗弗以及阿尔迪斯·赖特（两人都是三一学院的图书管理员）合作，计划出版了那套经典版的《剑桥莎士比亚全集》，后来又在阿尔迪斯·赖特帮助下出版了那套普及版的《环球莎士比亚全集》。他曾为新版《阿里斯托芬全集》收集了大量资料。他还曾出版过一些布道书，但在一八九六年，他辞去了圣职——这样，顺便提一下，我们也就不必再去谈论教会里的那些事了。他和他的朋友、传记作家莱斯利·斯蒂芬②以及亨利·西奇威克③和那一代人中的其他一些人一样，觉得自己不可能再待在教会里了；对此，他还写了一本题为《当前英国教会之危机》的小册子加以解释。继而，他又辞去了学院发言人职务，仅作为教师留在学院里。他五十七岁时去世，认识

---

① 三一学院属剑桥大学，由教会主办，故而其教师也是教会的神职人员。
② 莱斯利·斯蒂芬：19世纪英国传记作家、散文家、评论家，弗吉尼亚·伍尔夫的父亲。
③ 西奇威克（Henry Sidgwick，1838—1900），英国作家、哲学家。

他的人都尊他为可亲、博学、坦诚之人。想来你们也都知道，他是剑桥大学的人。他不是世界名人，甚至都不是牛津大学的人，但他代表了剑桥大学各学院的独特精神，这种精神或许只有你们这些愿意追随他的人才能真正赏识，即：笃学精神。依照他的遗愿，三一学院举办了每年一次的"自乔叟以来某一或某些阶段的英语文学"系列讲座，这就是为什么我们现在要在这里相聚的缘由。

虽然祈祷已经过时，但我还是想做个小小的祈祷，为两件事。首先，我要祈求克拉克的笃学精神在本次讲座中与我们同在；其次，我要祈求他不要对我们太认真！因为我要讲的并不完全符合讲座的主题——"某一或某些阶段的英语文学"。这个限定听上去很宽泛，似乎也相当自由，但字面上还是和我们的话题不相符的；所以，我在这第一讲中就要把这一点讲清楚。下面提出的几点或许有点琐碎。但是这几点能引导我们占据有利位置，然后我们便可以从那里发起主攻①。

我们需要有利位置，因为小说多得令人难以应付，而且又是那样杂乱无章——那里没有高山可以攀爬，没有帕纳塞斯山或赫利孔山②，甚至没有毗斯迦山③。毫无疑问，那是一片文学沼泽地——有一百条溪流在那里流淌，时而还会搅成一潭泥浆。所以，我毫不奇怪，诗人有时偶然进入其中会嗤

---

① 发起主攻：喻进入主题。
② 帕纳塞斯山、赫利孔山：古希腊神话中太阳神和文艺女神居住的灵山。
③ 毗斯迦山：《圣经》中的圣山，摩西从此山上眺望上帝赐给亚伯拉罕的迦南地。

之以鼻。我也毫不惊讶，历史学家偶尔涉足那里会懊恼不已。或许，我们在开始前应该对什么是小说先下个定义。这不需要一秒钟。因为阿贝尔·舍瓦莱先生已经在他那本出色的论著①里给出了定义，而若一位法国批评家不能定义英国小说，还有谁能？他说，小说就是"具有一定长度的散文虚构作品"②。这对我们来说已经完全可以了，或许要补充的仅仅是长度不应少于五万字。任何五万字以上的散文虚构作品，在本次讲座中都被视为小说③，如果你们觉得这不够精确，那不妨想一个可以替代它的定义，看看能不能把《天路历程》《享乐主义者马里乌斯》《幼子历险记》《魔笛》《瘟疫年纪事》《朱莱卡·多布森》《拉塞拉斯》《尤利西斯》和《绿厦》④都包括在内。如果有的不能，能不能说明为什么不能。确实，在小说这个海绵状地带，有的地方比其他地方更具虚构性：就在靠近当中的地方，奥斯汀小姐带着她的人物爱玛站在一个绿草茵茵的小丘上，而萨克雷也在那里，带着他的艾斯芒德⑤。不过，据我所知，还没有哪个高明之人对

---

① 即《当代英国小说》(*Le Roman de Notre Temps*)，阿贝尔·舍瓦莱著（Milford，伦敦）。

② 原文为法文：Une fiction enprose d' une certaine etendue。

③ 小说：原文是 novel，长篇小说。本书中所说"小说"，绝大多数是指长篇小说，仅少数泛指小说（即除长篇小说之外，还包括中短篇小说）。

④ 这些均为英国文学史上的著名作品，写法各不相同，题材千差万别，但一般都被认作是小说（novel）。

⑤ 艾斯芒德：萨克雷历史小说《亨利·艾斯芒德》中的主人公。这句话的意思是，简·奥斯汀和萨克雷的作品都被称作小说，但简·奥斯汀作品的虚构性要比萨克雷强一些。

这一地带下过完整的定义。我们所能说的是，这是个两边有山的地带，而两边的山又不是很陡峭①——一边是诗歌，一边是历史——还有一边有海——就是我们读《白鲸》时看到的那片海②。

先让我们来探讨一下讲座限定的"英语文学"。既然是"英语"，我们当然理解为是用英语写的作品，而不一定要在特威德河以南或大西洋以东或赤道以北③出版的：地理问题我们不必关心，那是政治家的事情。但是，即便这样理解，我们是不是就能像我们希望的那样自由探讨了吗？在探讨英语小说时，我们可以对其他语言中的小说——尤其是法语小说和俄语小说——不予理会吗？就影响来说，我们可以不予理会，因为我们的作家从未受到欧洲大陆的太多影响。不过——理由稍后再作解释——我虽然在讲座中会尽可能地少谈影响，我谈论的却是用英语写的一种特别种类的书④的方方面面。既然这样，我们能对欧洲大陆的同类书的方方面面不予理会吗？当然不能。因为有个令人不愉快而且有伤爱国热情的事实必须面对。没有哪个英语小说家像托尔斯泰那样伟大——也就是说，没有哪个英语小说家像他那样完整地描写人类生活，既描写平凡人生，又描写英雄主义。没有哪个英语小说家像陀思妥耶夫斯基那样深

---

① 不是很陡峭：意为和夹在中间的小说地带并没有明确的界限。
② 此处的"海"喻自然，意即小说与自然也很接近。
③ 特威德河以南或大西洋以东或赤道以北：意指英格兰。
④ 一种特别种类的书：指小说。

度探索人类灵魂。也没有哪个小说家像马塞尔·普鲁斯特①那样成功分析现代人的意识。在这些成就面前，我们必须停下来想一想。英语诗歌，不论是数量，还是质量，都不逊色于人。然而，英语小说却少有成就，至今还没有写出极品佳作。如若不承认这一点，我们就成了乡土习气的牺牲品。

说到乡土习气，这对作家来说倒是无所谓的，说不定还会成为他的魅力所在：只有自以为是的人或者没头没脑的人才会指责笛福是伦敦佬，托马斯·哈代是乡巴佬。但是，乡土习气对于批评家来说却是个严重问题。虽然偏执时常是艺术家的特权，但批评家是无权偏执的。他必须视野开阔，否则他就什么都不是了。小说家可以夸大对象，批评家是绝对不可以的，然而还是有许许多多英国小说中的小小庭院被夸大成了宏伟宫殿。随便取四部小说为例：《克兰福德》《中洛辛郡的心脏》《简·爱》和《理查德·费沃里尔的考验》②。出于各种个人的或地方的原因，我们可能很喜欢这四部小说。《克兰福德》散发出那种内地城镇的气息；《中洛辛郡的心脏》充分描绘了爱丁堡；《简·爱》是一个纯洁而未成熟的女子的激情梦想；《理查德·费沃里尔》洋溢着田园风情

---

① 马塞尔·普鲁斯特：19世纪和20世纪之际法国小说家，以长篇意识流小说《追忆似水年华》闻名于世。
② 《克兰福德》《中洛辛郡的心脏》《简·爱》和《理查德·费沃里尔的考验》：分别是19世纪英国小说家盖斯凯尔夫人、瓦尔特·司各特、夏洛蒂·勃朗特和乔治·梅瑞狄斯的长篇小说。

而且闪烁着那时流行的机智。然而，这四部小说都是小小庭院，而非宏伟宫殿，只要把它们放在《战争与和平》的立柱之间或者《卡拉马佐夫兄弟》的穹顶之下，我们马上就能看出而且看清它们究竟是什么。

我在本次讲座中不会时常提及外国小说，更不会摆出专家的架势，用专门术语来大谈特谈外国小说。但是在正式开始之前，我还是要强调外国小说的伟大；也就是说，我事先在我们的话题之上投下这道阴影，这样当我们最后回过头来时，或许能更好地认识到这一话题的真实含义。

关于讲座限定的"英语文学"，就讲这些。接下来要讲的一点更为重要，就是讲座限定的"某一或某些阶段"。这种时间上的某一阶段或者某种发展的观念，以及由此而对影响和流派的强调，恰恰是我在本次简短的讲座中要想避免的，而且我相信《格斯巴乔奥》的作者①不会计较。在本次讲座中，时间始终是我们的敌人②。我们要把那些英国小说家看作不是随时间之流一代一代漂浮而下的，而是全都坐在一个圆形房间里，坐在一个就像大英博物馆阅览室那样的房间里，同时在写小说。他们坐在那儿，并不是在想："我生活在维多利亚女王时代③。""我生活在安妮女王时代④。""我继承的是特罗洛普⑤

---

① 即威廉·乔治·克拉克，此讲座创始人。
② 意即他就是要摆脱时间和时代的限制来讲小说的要素。
③ 维多利亚女王时代：即19世纪。
④ 安妮女王时代：即18世纪初期。
⑤ 特罗洛普：19世纪英国小说家。

的传统。""我是和阿尔都斯·赫胥黎①背道而驰的。"而是他们手里都拿着笔这一事实,对他们来说更为重要。他们都是半着魔的,他们的忧伤与喜悦随墨水一起倾注,他们都因创作而彼此相像,而当奥利佛·埃尔顿教授说"一八四七年后激情小说已难以为继"时,他们谁也不明白他是什么意思。这就是我们对我们看待他们的方式,并不完美,但和我们的能力相符,而且可使我们避免一个重大的危险——假学问的危险。

真正的学术是人类所能达到的最高成就之一。没有人比这样一个人更有成就了:他选择一个有价值的课题,不仅掌握其全部知识,还掌握了相关领域的重要知识。所以,他可以做他想做的事情。如果他的课题是小说研究,那只要他愿意,就可以按年代讲述小说的历史,因为他不仅把过去四个世纪的所有重要小说都读过了,还读过许多不太重要的小说,同时又充分掌握了与英语小说相关的各种知识。已故瓦尔特·莱利②爵士(他曾主持过这个讲座)就是这样一个学者。他的知识如此之多,故而他能进一步施加影响:他对英国小说的专题论述采用分期论述法,这是学力不足的后继者避之不及的。学者,像哲学家一样,也能纵观时间长河。他虽不能纵观一切,但却能看清从他身边漂过的事物、人物,

---

① 阿尔都斯·赫胥黎:20世纪初期英国小说家。
② 瓦尔特·莱利:19世纪与20世纪之际英国批评家、散文家。

并对它们之间的关系作出评价，而若他的结论对我们能像对他自己一样有价值，那他早就使全人类文明化了。但就如你们所知，他失败了。真正的学术是不可传授的，真正的学者是罕见的。在今天的听众之中会有几个学者，实在的或潜在的学者，但就那么几个，而在讲台上是肯定没有的。虽然我们大多是假学者，我却要对我们的本性表以同情与敬意，因为我们人数众多而且都属权势阶级，在教会和政府里身居要职；我们掌管帝国①的教育，我们左右报界的好恶，我们还是晚宴上受欢迎的贵宾。

假学问，就其好的一面来说，是无知者对学问的尊崇。此外，假学问还有经济的一面②，对此我们不必苛责。我们大多在三十岁前必须工作，否则就要靠亲友为生了，而很多工作是要通过考试才能得到的。假学者往往对考试很在行（真学者倒是不大在行的），就是失败了，仍然很敬仰考试固有的权威性。考试即就业的大门，考试拥有生杀大权。一篇关于《李尔王》的论文或许也有用处，尽管《李尔王》这部戏剧本身与此不太相干。那篇论文或许是进入地方政府机关的一块垫脚石。对此，假学者通常不会坦率地对自己说："这就是知识的用处，可以助你一臂之力。"他所感受到的经济压力往往是无意识的，而他去参加考试也仅仅是因为他觉得，写一篇关于《李尔王》的论文固然很有意思，也更有用

---

① 帝国：即大英帝国。
② 还有经济的一面：意为靠做假学问来赚钱。

处，但实在太艰难、太可怕了。不管他是油滑也好，还是幼稚也好，反正他是无可厚非的。既然认知（learning）和工资（earning）缠在一起，既然某些工作只有通过考试才能得到，我们当然只能严肃对待考试制度。如果另设求职之路，大部分所谓的教育就会消失，但没有人会因此变得愚蠢一点。

不过，如果他去从事文学批评——就如我们现在所做的——那他就成了害人精，因为他没有真学者的本事，却要去学真学者的样。他一开始就胡作非为，书还没读懂或者根本没读过，却想把书分门别类。譬如，按时间分类：一八四七年前写的书、一八四七年后写的书；或者，安妮女王时期的小说、前小说①、原始小说、未来小说。再譬如，按题材分类——这更加愚蠢：始于《汤姆·琼斯》②的客栈文学、始于《谢利》③的女权运动文学、从《鲁滨孙漂流记》到《蓝色珊瑚岛》④的荒岛文学、流浪汉文学——这最无聊，其次是大路文学；还有苏塞克斯文学（大概伦敦周围的几个郡中苏塞克斯郡对文学最热心）；还有离经叛道书——这类书看似可怕，其实属于严肃的社会调查，只有上了年纪的假学

---

① 前小说：the pre-novel，即"小说之前"，未正式形成小说的叙事形式。
② 《汤姆·琼斯》：18世纪英国小说家菲尔丁的长篇小说。
③ 《谢利》：19世纪英国女作家夏洛蒂·勃朗特（《简·爱》作者）的长篇小说。
④ 《蓝色珊瑚岛》：20世纪初英国小说家亨利·德弗尔·斯塔克普尔的浪漫小说，出版于1908年。

者才会关注；此外，还有与工业有关的小说、与航空有关的小说、与手足病有关的小说、与天气有关的小说。我把天气也包括在内是有根据的，那是我多年前读到的一部最令人吃惊的关于小说的权威论著。那本书来自大西洋彼岸①，这我不会忘。那是一本文学参考书，书名是《小说的材料与方法》。作者的名字姑且保密。他是个假学者，而且是个不错的假学者。他按日期、长度、地区、性别、观点对小说加以分类，一直分到似乎不能再分。但他的袖子里还藏着"天气"，而当他把它拿出来后，它竟然还有九项。每一项下面他都举例说明，看来他一点也不懒惰，下面我们就来看看他的分类。第一，天气可以是"修饰的"，譬如在彼埃尔·洛蒂②的作品中；第二，"实用的"，譬如在《弗洛斯河上的磨坊》③中（没有弗洛斯河，就没有磨坊；没有磨坊，就没有塔利弗一家）；第三，"解释的"，譬如在《利己主义者》④中；第四，"预设的"，譬如在菲奥娜·麦克利奥德⑤的作品中；第五，"对照的"，譬如在《巴伦特雷的少爷》⑥中；第六，"决定的"，譬如在吉卜林的一个短篇小说中，沙尘暴使一个男子求婚求错了人；第七，"支配的"，譬如在《理查

---

① 大西洋彼岸：意为美国。
② 彼埃尔·洛蒂：19世纪法国小说家，其作品充满异国情调。
③ 《弗洛斯河上的磨坊》：19世纪英国女作家乔治·艾略特的长篇小说。
④ 《利己主义者》：19世纪英国小说家乔治·梅瑞狄斯的长篇小说。
⑤ 菲奥纳·麦克利奥德：19世纪苏格兰小说家，其作品充满神秘主义色彩。
⑥ 《巴伦特雷的少爷》：19世纪英国小说家斯蒂文森的长篇小说。

德·费沃里尔的考验》①中；第八，"主角的"，譬如《庞贝城的末日》②中的维苏威火山；第九，还可以是"不存在的"，譬如在一篇童话故事里。我很高兴他竟然撞到不存在里去了。他把一切都弄得那么科学、那么整齐。但他自己仍有点不满意，在作了上述分类后还说：是的，当然还有一项，那就是天才；如果小说家没有天才，那就是知道了这九种"天气"也是没什么用的。出于同样的想法，他还按语调对小说分类。但仅分出两种：个人语调和非个人语调，而且在举例说明这两种语调后，他更加忧心忡忡地说："是的，你必须要有天才，否则的话，没有哪种语调是有用的。"

动不动就说天才，也是假学者的标志。他喜欢说天才，因为他只发这个词的音而不深究其意义。文学作品是天才写的。小说家是天才。既然这样，那就让我们分分类吧。他这么做了。他说的每件事或许都很精确，但全是无用的，因为他只是绕着那些书兜圈子，而不是深入其中；他不是没有读过那些书，而是没能正确地读那些书。书是要读的（不幸的是，需要很长时间）；这是发现其中含义的唯一途径。有些野蛮部落吃书③，但对西方社会来说，读书是理解书的唯一方式。读者必须独自坐下来与作者较量，而这却是假学者不愿意做的。他宁

---

① 《理查德·费沃里尔的考验》：19世纪英国小说家乔治·梅瑞狄斯的长篇小说。
② 《庞贝城的末日》：19世纪英国小说家布尔沃-林顿的历史小说。
③ 吃书：意即吞符，把写有咒语的纸条吞入腹中。

愿关心一本书的历史背景,关心作者生前的事情,关心书中讲到的事件,最后关心某种趋势。一旦说到"趋势"一词,他就精神百倍,而听众呢,虽然可能没精打采,这时往往还是会拿出铅笔来做笔记,因为他们相信记下某种趋势总是有用的。

所以,在我们将要讲的那松松散散的几讲中,我们不能按年代来讲述小说;我们肯定不能考虑时间顺序。另一种想法比较合乎我们的能力,即:把所有小说家都想象为是同时在写小说。虽然他们来自不同的时代和阶层,虽然他们各有各的个性和目的,但他们手里都握着笔,都在创作。让我们从他们背后张望,看看他们在写什么。这样也许可以祛除时间鬼魅的作祟;这鬼魅正是我们的敌人,(下星期我们就会讲到)有时也是他们的敌人。"哦,这是怎样一种永无止境的世仇,时间与人类之子!"赫尔曼·麦尔维尔曾感叹道。这世仇不仅存在于生与死之间,同时也存在于文学创作与文学批评之间。那就让我们避开它,把所有小说家想象为是同时在一个圆形房间里写作。我不会提到他们的名字,直到我们听到他们说话为止,因为一提到名字,就会带出和名字有关的日期、传闻,就会带出那一套我们要抛弃的东西。

他们被安排为两人一对。我们走到第一对边上,看到他们分别是这样写的:

(一)我不知道做什么,我不知道!——上帝宽恕我,可我无法忍受!我希望——可我不知道希望什么,才是无罪的！——然而我仍然希望这会使上帝愉悦而赐福于我！——我在这儿见不到一个人——这是什么世界！——在这儿还有什么可求？我们盼望的善，那么惊人地被玷污了，现在谁也不知道还能希望什么！一半人在折磨另一半人，而折磨别人的人自己也在受折磨！①

(二)我恨的是我自己——因为我想到，一个人要想幸福就要从别人的生活中攫取那么多东西，而且就是这样，那个人也不见得幸福。那个人这么做是在欺骗自己，是在堵自己的嘴——但是，至多也就那么一会儿。那个被骗的自我始终在那儿，始终使我们莫名地感到焦虑。结果得到的呢，不是幸福，绝对不是，什么幸福都不是。唯一可靠的是给予。这最不会使你上当受骗。②

显然，坐在这儿的两个小说家是从相同的角度看待生活的，其中的第一个是塞缪尔·理查生；第二个呢，你们可能已经认出来了，是亨利·詹姆斯。两人除了都很焦虑，还都是热切的心理学家③。两人对痛苦都很敏感而且都很崇尚自我牺牲；两人都不擅长悲剧，但都想和悲剧沾点边。在他们洋洋洒洒的行文中都有一种怯懦的傲气——那是他们的精神

---

① 此段引文引自18世纪英国小说家塞缪尔·理查生的小说。
② 此段引文引自20世纪与作者同时代的英国小说家亨利·詹姆斯的小说。
③ 热切的心理学家：意为热衷于心理描写。

支柱——哦,他们写得多好啊!——没有一个词用得不恰当。他们相隔一百五十年,但他们在其他方面不是很接近吗?他们的相邻性不是对我们很有利①吗?当然,我这么说时,我听到亨利·詹姆斯开始表示不满——不,不是不满,而是惊讶——不,甚至不是惊讶,而是觉察到有人把相邻性强加于他,而且——他肯定会补充说——强迫他和一个店老板②为邻。我也听到理查生表示不解,他同样心怀疑虑地说,不是出生在英国的作家③算不算正统。但这些都是表面上的区别,其实根本不是区别,只是额外涉及的几点而已。让他们客客气气地坐在那里吧,我们接着来看下面的一对。

(一)葬礼的准备工作在约翰逊太太熟练的双手下进行得顺利而愉快。在那悲伤一刻到来之前的那天晚上,她把准备好的黑棉缎、厨房梯子和一盒大头钉取出来,用黑饰带和蝶形结尽可能有品位地布置起来。她在门环上扎了黑皱纱,在加里波第④的一幅钢版肖像的一角上挂了一个大大的蝶形结,并用黑布把死者生前拥有的那尊格莱斯顿先生⑤的胸像包起来。她把两个绘有意大利提沃利和那不勒斯海湾风景的花瓶转了个身,这样

---

① 因为他的这次讲座就是要超越时代来讲小说。
② 塞缪尔·理查生曾做过印刷商。
③ 亨利·詹姆斯出生于美国,后移居英国。
④ 加里波第:19世纪意大利民族英雄。
⑤ 格莱斯顿:19世纪英国政治家,曾四次出任英国首相。

颇为鲜艳的一面就藏到后面去了,前面只见纯蓝色的瓷釉,此外她还早作准备,已经为客厅预先买好了一块新桌布,于是就用这块紫罗兰色的桌布换下了那块原本花花绿绿、但用到现在已经破旧不堪的旧桌布。凡是出于爱的考虑而能为她这个小小的家增添一点庄严肃穆气氛的事情,她都做了。①

(二)客厅里荡漾着一阵淡淡的甜食的气味,我举目四望,想找出那张放糕点的桌子;好不容易等眼睛习惯了屋内的阴暗光线,才看见有张桌子上放着一个切开的葡萄干蛋糕,还有几个切开的橙子、一盘三明治、一盘饼干,此外还有两个大酒瓶,我很明白这两个酒瓶一向是用来装装门面的,从不曾见使用过,而这一回却是一个装着葡萄酒,一个装着雪利酒。我走到这张桌子旁站定,才看见那个卑躬屈节的彭波丘克,穿一身黑外套,帽子上系一根长达数码的帽带,一边糕点酒水不停地往嘴里送,一边做出种种谄媚举动,引我的注意。他一看见自己这种举动有了作用,就马上走到我跟前(满嘴的酒气和糕饼味),压低声音说:"可以吗,亲爱的先生?"说着伸出手来。②

---

① 此段引文引自 20 世纪与作者同时代的英国作家 H. G. 威尔斯的小说《波利先生的历史》。
② 此段引文引自 19 世纪英国小说家狄更斯的小说《远大前程》。

这两个葬礼当然不是同一天举行的。一个是《波利先生的历史》(1910)中波利先生父亲的葬礼,另一个是《远大前程》(1861)中葛吉瑞太太的葬礼。但威尔斯和狄更斯有相同的视角,甚至使用相同风格的技巧(比较:那两个花瓶和两个酒瓶)。他们两人都是幽默家和观察家,都用罗列细节和快速转换来制造某种效果。他们都很有气度;他们都憎恨虚伪,常对虚情假意表示愤慨;他们都是难得的社会改革家;他们都不想让自己的书只放在图书馆的架子上。有时,他们都会写得很马虎,就像一张廉价的唱片,显然没有什么质量,而且作者的脸也凑得离读者太近。换句话说,他们都没有什么品位:对狄更斯来说,美的世界大部分是关闭的,而对威尔斯来说,则是完全关闭的。还有其他相似之处——譬如,描画人物的方式。他们都曾是贫寒而有天赋的少年,他们之间的主要区别或许是他们一个在一百年前、一个在四十年前所遇到的机会有所不同。在这方面,威尔斯比较有利。他比他的前辈狄更斯受到较好的教育;尤其是科学知识,强化了他的心智,克制了他的狂躁。他见证了社会的改良——道瑟博斯学堂①已为普雷斯顿工艺学院②所取代——在小说艺术方面,却没有任何改进。

接下来的一对怎样?

---

① 道瑟博斯学堂:Dotheboys Hall,狄更斯的小说《尼古拉斯·尼克尔贝》中塑造的一所摧残儿童身心的学校。
② 普雷斯顿工艺学院:20世纪初英国新建学院,代表现代教育。

（一）但是，我还是弄不清那个斑点到底是什么；我又想，它不像是钉子留下的痕迹。它太大、太圆了。我本来可以站起来，但是，即使我站起身来瞧瞧它，十之八九我也说不出它到底是什么；因为一旦一件事发生以后，就没有人能知道它是怎么发生的了。唉！天哪，生命是多么神秘；思想是多么不准确！人类是多么无知！为了证明我们对自己的私有物品是多么无法加以控制……和我们的文明相比，人的生活带有多少偶然性啊……我只要列举少数几件我们一生中遗失的物件就够了。就从三只装着订书工具的浅蓝色罐子说起吧，这永远是遗失的东西当中丢失得最神秘的几件——哪只猫会去咬它们，哪只老鼠会去啃它们呢？再数下去，还有那几个鸟笼子、铁裙箍、钢滑冰鞋、安妮女王时代的煤斗子、弹子戏球台、手摇风琴……全都丢失了，还有一些珠宝，也遗失了。有乳白宝石、绿宝石，它们都散失在芜菁的根部旁边。它们是花了多少心血节衣缩食积蓄起来的啊！此刻我四周全是挺有分量的家具，身上还穿着几件衣服，简直是奇迹。要是拿什么来和生活相比的话，就只能比作一个人以一小时五十英里的速度穿过隧道……①

（二）至少有十年了，我父亲天天都下决心把它修理

---

① 此段引文引自20世纪与作者同时代的英国女作家弗吉尼亚·伍尔夫的小说《墙上的斑点》。

修理——可至今还没有修理；——除了我们家，别的人家一个小时都忍不下去——最令人惊奇的是，世上没有一个话题能使我父亲像对门上的铰链这般滔滔雄辩——可与此同时，在铰链问题上，我想他肯定是有史以来最大的空想家，他讲出来的道理和他干出来的事情总是对不上号。只要客厅的门一开——他的哲学也好，原则也罢，统统都成了铰链的牺牲品——其实，只要用一根鸡毛沾三滴油，用一把锤子敲一敲，他的名誉也就永远保住了。

——人是多么地自相矛盾啊！明明可以治疗，却甘愿受创伤的折磨！——他的整个一生和他的知识正相矛盾！——他的理智，那上帝给他的珍贵礼物——（非但没有为他加油）反而加剧了他的神经过敏——增加了他的痛苦，使他更加忧郁、更加不安！——可怜的不幸之人，他竟然这样！——难道生活中需要承受的苦难还不够多，还要这样自寻烦恼吗？——邪恶当然是要抵制的，但听从他人，那不过是一点点小委屈，为什么就是不能不放在心上？

以所有的美德起誓，只要在项狄府十英里范围内还能弄到三滴油，还能找到一把锤子——客厅门上的铰链是可以就地修好的。①

---

① 以上三段引文均引自18世纪英国小说家斯特恩的小说《项狄传》。

没错，这三段引文引自《项狄传》。另一段出自弗吉尼亚·伍尔夫。她和斯特恩都是幻想家。他们都从小事情着手，由此加以发挥，再以此结束。他们都幽默地欣赏生活的混浊，同时又敏锐地感受到其中之美。甚至他们的语气也是一样的——故作困惑，以此向世人表明，他们不知道他们要往何处去。毫无疑问，他们的价值标准是不一样的。斯特恩是个感伤主义者，弗吉尼亚·伍尔夫则是绝对冷淡的（她最近的作品《到灯塔去》或许是个例外）。他们的成就也不是同等的。但他们的手法很相似，所获得的效果也一样：客厅的门永远修不好，墙上的斑点原来是蜗牛，生活是如此混浊，哦，天哪，意志是如此脆弱，感觉是如此多变……哲学……上帝……哦，天哪，看那个斑点……听那扇门——生存真是太……我们在说什么？

以上，我们设想了六个正在写作的小说家，年代不是就不那么重要了吗？就算小说是发展的，它的发展路线大概也不同于跟英国宪法，甚至不同于女权运动，是不是？我说"甚至不同于女权运动"，是因为十九世纪的英国小说正好和女权运动碰到一起——碰得那么巧，以至于使有些批评家误以为是一种有机联系。他们认定，随着女性地位越来越高，小说也越写越好。完全错了。镜子不会因为反映了一系列历史事件而有所发展。只有在它上面重新镀上一层水银后——也就是说，要使它具有新的灵敏度——它才有所发展；同样，小说的成功也有赖于它自身的灵敏度，而不在于它所表现的题材有多成功。帝国衰亡、选举普及，但对那些在那个圆形房间里写作的人来说，最为重要的是他们对自己手里的那支笔的感觉如何。他们或许决定写一部关于法国革命或俄国革命的小说，但是，回忆、联想、激情会一涌而起，会遮掩他们的客观性，以至于写完后重读一遍时，会觉得好像是别人握着他们的笔写的，原来设定的主题变成了背景。毫无疑问，那个"别人"就是他们的自我，但不是那个活跃于时空、生活在乔治四世或乔治五世时代的自己。有史以来，作家写作时或多或少都有同样的感觉。他们都会进入一种同共的状态，就是可称为"灵感"的那种状态。就那种状态而言，我们或许可以说，历史是发展的，艺术是静止的。

历史是发展的，艺术是静止的，是一句笼统的格言，实际上这几乎就是一句口号，虽然我们不得不接受它，但也绝不能不承认它的粗浅。它只含有部分真理。

它一开始就禁止我们考虑人类心灵是否一代一代有所变化；譬如，伊丽莎白时代幽默地描写小店铺和小酒馆的托马斯·德龙尼①，是不是从本质上说不同于和他有同样才能的现代后继者尼尔·莱昂斯或佩特·里奇？事实上，我认为没什么不同；作为个人虽然不同，但在本质上并不因为他生活在四百年前就有所不同。四千年、一万四千年或许会使我们犹豫一下，四百年在人类生活中根本算不了什么，不至于会

---

① 托马斯·德龙尼：16世纪英国歌谣和散文故事作家，其散文故事是英国小说的原始形式。

有任何可观察到的变化①。所以，我们的口号没有实际上的障碍。我们可以毫不羞愧地高呼它。

如果我们转向传统的发展，看看我们因为不能对此有所审察而受到的损失，那情况更为严重。英国小说中，除了流派、影响和时尚，还有技巧，而且是一代一代有所变化的。譬如，嘲笑人物的技巧戏弄不同于揶揄；伊丽莎白时代的幽默作家摆弄嘲笑对象的方式，不同于现代作家，是用另一些手法引人发笑的。再譬如，幻想的技巧：虽然弗吉尼亚·伍尔夫在意图和整体效果方面和斯特恩很相似，但在具体写法方面并不相同；她虽属于同一传统，但属于这一传统的后期。再譬如，对话的技巧：在前面所举的实例中，我没能举出一对作家写的对话为例，虽然我很想这么做，但由于数百年来"他说"和"她说"的变化之多令人眼花缭乱，所以，即使对话人物可能是以相似方式构思的，但在引文中却显示不出他们的相似性。是啊，我们无法对各种问题都那样予以深究；我们就算能毫无遗憾地摒弃主题发展和人类发展，也必须承认我们能力不够。文学传统是介于文学和历史之间的边界地带，自有学识渊博的批评家会在那里花费大量时间，由此增强其判断力。我们不能到那里去，因为我们读书读得还不够多。我们不得不姑且把它归入历史，由此和它一刀两断。我们不得不和年代断绝所有关系。

---

① 这里的变化，是指人类心灵的变化。

为了使大家放心，我不妨在此引用本讲座的前任主讲 T. S. 艾略特①先生的一段话。在《圣林》的序言中，艾略特先生说到了批评家的职责：

> 批评家的部分职责是维护传统——当然是优良传统。他的部分职责是稳定地看待文学，而且完整地看待它；同时，这也是显而易见的：不能把文学看作时代的圣物，而要把它看作是超时代的……

第一种职责我们没有能力履行，第二种职责我们必须尽力履行。我们既没有能力检验传统，也没有能力维护传统。但我们可以把小说家看作是坐在同一个房间里的，这样——就凭我们的无知——强迫他们摆脱时间与空间的限制。我想这是值得一试的，否则的话，我也就不会贸然到这里来开讲座了。

那么，我们怎样来攻打这块叫作小说的泥淖之地呢？那些具有一定长度的散文体虚构作品，其长度是那么不确定，没有任何精确标准。原理和体系或许适用于其他艺术形式，但在此却是无用的——或者说，用了也没用，结果还是要有人来重新检验。谁来检验？是啊，恐怕是人心了，因为只有人心才能做这种人对人的检验工作，才能公正地不为小说粗

---

① T. S. 艾略特：20 世纪美国出生的英国诗人，著有《荒原》等。

糙的形式所迷惑。最后对一部小说作出检测的将是我们的感觉，就像我们凭感觉检测我们的朋友和其他所有无法定义的东西。凭感觉对有些人来说比凭年代更可怕——因为感觉会躲在后面说"哦，我就是喜欢那样""哦，那样对我没有吸引力"，但我完全可以保证，凭感觉说话不会太响或者太急。小说具有强烈的、紧迫的人性特征，这是不可避免的；小说浸泡在人性中；总会兴奋过头或颓废无度，就是在文学批评中也不能幸免。我们或许可以厌恶人性，但如果驱除掉人性或者净化掉人性，小说就枯萎了；所剩无几，一连串词语而已。

我以"面面观"（Aspects）为题，是因为这一说法不太严谨，有点含糊，因而可以给我们最大的自由；也就是说，我们可以用不同的方式看待小说，小说家也可以用不同的方式看待自己的作品。所谓"面面观"，就是要探讨小说的七个方面，即：故事、人物、情节、幻想、启示、图形和节奏。

第二章 故 事

我们都会同意小说的基本面是讲故事,但我们表示同意的语气会有所不同,而我们用怎样的语气表示同意,将决定我们最后的结论。

我们来听听下面三种语气。如果你问某个人:"什么是小说?"他会平静地回答说:"哦——我不知道——这问题问得好像有点可笑——小说就是小说——哦,我不知道——这么说吧,我想小说好像是讲故事。"这个人态度温和、含含糊糊,也许他此时正在驾驶公共汽车,没工夫关心文学问题。另一个人——我设想他正在打高尔夫球——则会态度粗鲁、气势汹汹。他会回答说:"什么是小说?还用问吗,当然是讲故事,如果不讲故事,我早就扔了它。我喜欢听故事。没错,我这个人没品位,但我就是喜欢听故事。去你妈的艺术,去你妈的文学,去你妈的音乐,我只要一个好听的故事。注意,我喜欢听像故事的故事,我老婆也是。"第三个人,他用一种无可奈何、勉勉强强的语气说:"是啊——亲爱的,是啊——小说就是讲故事。"我尊重而且赞赏第一个人。我讨厌而且惧怕第二个人。第三个人,就是我自己。是啊——亲爱的,是啊——小说就是讲故事。那是小说的基本面,没有它,小说是不可能存在的。那是所有小说共有的关键要素,虽然我希望它不是,而是其他什么东西——韵律,或者真理——而不是这种低级、原始的东西。

因为,我们越是审视故事(注意,像故事的故事),越是把故事和故事所支撑的那些美妙的派生含义区分开来,我们就越会觉得故事本身是不值得称道的。它就像一根脊椎骨——或者说,就像一条蛔虫,头和尾很难辨认①。它太古老了,可以追溯到新石器时代,甚至旧石器时代。尼安德特人②就听讲故事了,这或许可以根据头盖骨的形状来推断。远古时代的听众是张大嘴巴、围在篝火旁打着哈欠的听众,他们因为拼命猎杀猛犸象和长毛犀牛而筋疲力尽,唯有一点悬念才可使他们保持清醒。后来怎样?那个小说家叽里咕噜往下讲,一旦那些听众猜到了后来会怎样,他们不是睡着,就是把他杀了。我们只要想想后来山鲁佐德③要做的事,就可看出这有多么危险。山鲁佐德能免遭厄运,就是因为她懂得怎样使用悬念这一武器——唯有文学手段才能制服暴君和野蛮人。她虽是个了不起的小说家——叙

---

① 意为讲故事从哪里开始、到哪里结束往往是任意的。
② 尼安德特人:旧石器时代生活于欧洲、北非、西亚和中亚的原始人种。
③ 山鲁佐德:《一千零一夜》里的故事叙述者,她因不断讲故事吸引残暴的国王而免遭杀害。

事精确、评判公允、情节巧妙、寓意清新、人物生动，还熟知中东三大名城①——但她要想在她那个暴君丈夫手中保全性命，却不能依靠这些才能。这些才能仅仅是附带的。她能活下去的主要手段就是每次当她看到太阳升起时就突然停下来，不说下去了，从而使国王保持好奇心而不打哈欠。"此时山鲁佐德见曙光已露，便有意闭上了嘴。"这句无趣的短语，就是《一千零一夜》的脊椎骨；就是这条蛔虫，把一千零一夜的故事连在一起，从而保全了一位聪明绝顶的王妃②的性命。

我们和山鲁佐德的丈夫一样，也都想知道后来怎样。这是普遍性的，所以小说的脊椎骨只能是故事。有些人除此之外什么都不想知道——他们心中什么都没有，只有原始的好奇心；所以，对他们来说，其他方面的文学评判都是荒唐的。现在，可以对故事下定义了。故事就是按时序对事件所作的叙述——早饭之后是晚饭，星期一之后是星期二，死了之后是腐烂，如此等等。作为故事，它唯一的功效是：能使听故事的人想知道后来怎样。反过来说，它唯一的失效是：不能使听故事的人想知道后来怎样。这是两个仅有的判断，依此即可断定某故事是不是故事。故事属于最低级、最简单的文学体制。然而它又是最高级的要素，是所有被称作小说的那种非常复杂的文学机制所共有的。

---

① 中东三大名城：即耶路撒冷、大马士革和巴格达。
② 一位聪明绝顶的王妃：即山鲁佐德。

如果我们把故事从它所贯穿的那几个较高级的方面①分离出来，像夹虫子一样用镊子把它夹起来——那是一条扭动着的、无头无尾的、赤裸裸的时间之虫——其模样其实并不可爱，倒有点令人厌烦。但是，我们却可以从中得知许多事情。先来看看它和日常生活的关系。

日常生活同样充满时间感。我们会想一件事情发生在另一件事情之前或者之后，不仅我们脑子里经常这样想，我们的大多数语言与行为也都是以此为前提的。我们的大多数语言与行为是这样，但不是全部；因为生活中还有一些东西是与时间无关的，有的东西或许可以称作"价值"，有的东西不是用几分钟或几小时来衡量，而是用强度来衡量的；所以，当我们回想过去时，往事并不是平坦地伸展的，而是高低不平的，有几个高峰特别显眼；当我们展望未来时，未来时而是一堵墙，时而是一朵云，时而是一缕阳光，但绝不会是一张年度表。无论是回忆，还是前瞻，都对时间之父没有多大兴趣；所有做梦的人、搞艺术的和谈恋爱的人，都部分摆脱了时间之父的暴政②；他可以杀死他们③，但却不能引起他们的注意，就是到了世界末日，钟楼上的钟全都敲响时，他们或许仍然眼望着另一条路。所以，日常生活不管

---

① 那几个较高级的方面：即本书后面所探讨的人物、情节、幻想、预言、模式等。
② 意即这些人耽于幻想，而幻想不受时空限制。
③ 意即他们的时间会过完，会死。

多么实在，实际上是由两种生活——时间中的生活和价值观中的生活①——组成的，而且我们的行为也反映出一种双重取向。"我见到她只有五分钟，但是很值得。"这句话里就有两种取向。故事所讲述的是时间中的生活。但整部小说——如果是部好小说——所讲述的还要包括价值观中的生活，所用的方法就是后面几讲要探讨的。小说和日常生活一样，也具有双重取向。不过，在小说中，时间取向是必须的：没有一部小说没有这一取向。至于在日常生活中，这一取向倒并不一定是必须的：我们当然不能确定，但有些人的神秘体验似乎表明，这一取向不是必须的，也就是说，我们所认为的星期一之后是星期二——或者死了之后是腐烂——在他们看来，根本就是错的②。就是你们或者我，也有可能在日常生活中否定时间的存在而行为荒唐，甚至丧失理智而被我们的同胞送到他们称为疯人院的那个地方去。但小说家是绝对不能在小说中否定时间存在的：他必须抓住那条故事线索，不管那条线索多么细，他都必须抓住；他必须抓住那条无头无尾的蛔虫，否则的话，他就是行为荒唐，就是丧失理智。

关于时间，我尽力不把它哲理化③，因为（专家使我们相信）这对门外汉来说是一种极其危险的嗜好，比把空间哲

---

① 原文是 the life in time and the life by values。
② 意即神秘主义者无视现实生活中的时间顺序（先与后）。
③ 哲理化：意为抽象地谈论。

理化还要致命；有些很有名的哲学家就曾因为处理不当而出丑。我只是想说，此时此刻，就在我演讲的时候，我有没有听到时钟的滴答声，我有没有丧失时间感；至于在小说中，那里总是有时钟的。不过，作者可能不喜欢时钟。艾米莉·勃朗特在《呼啸山庄》中想把时钟藏起来①。斯特恩在《项狄传》中把时钟翻了个身②。马塞尔·普鲁斯特更为巧妙，他把时钟的指针拨来拨去，以致他的主人公在同一时间里既和情妇一起用餐又和保姆一起在公园里玩球③。这几种计策都是可行的，但没有一种违反我们的论点，即：小说的基础是故事，而故事就是按时序对事件的叙述。（顺便说一下，故事不等于情节。故事或许可以形成一个基础，情节则是一种较为高级的文学机制，这在后面一讲中加以定义和探讨。）

谁会讲故事给我们听？当然是瓦尔特·司各特④爵士。

对司各特这位小说家，我们会有剧烈的意见分歧。就我个人来说，我并不器重他，对他持久的名声更觉得难以理解。他生前就享有名声——那倒不难理解。那是有重要的历史原因的，如果我们的讲座是按年代讲的话，是应该探讨一下的。但是，如果我们把他从时间长河中钓出来，放到那个

---

① 意为《呼啸山庄》并未按时间顺序叙事。
② 意为《项狄传》是倒叙的。
③ 意为马塞尔·普鲁斯特的《追忆似水年华》主要是主人公的回忆，他往往在做一件事的同时想着另一件事。
④ 瓦尔特·司各特：19世纪英国小说家，以《威弗利》《艾凡赫》等历史小说闻名于世。

圆形房间里和其他小说家一起写作,他的形象就不怎么引人注目了。他在人看来不仅思想平庸,而且文笔笨拙。他不会构思。他既没有艺术家的超脱,又没有激情,而一个不具有这两种创作特性的作家,又怎么能深深打动我们呢?艺术家的超脱——这要求也许有点过分。但激情——这肯定是够低的要求了吧,而想想司各特辛辛苦苦堆起来的群山、用铁锹挖出来的峡谷和有意设计好的修道院废墟,那一切多么缺乏激情,多么需要激情,可就是没有激情!如果他有激情,他就成了伟大作家——即使文笔笨拙或者有点做作,也是无所谓的。但是他只有温和的心灵和绅士的感情,以及一种知性上的对乡村的偏爱,而凭这些是不足以写出伟大小说来的。至于他有忠实的品格——那比没有还要不好,因为那纯粹是道德上和商业上的忠实。他以此满足了自己最大的需要,就连做梦也没有想到,世上还有另一种忠贞不渝①。

他的出名有两个原因。第一,有许多老一辈的人在年轻时听过他本人的朗读;他是和幸福而动情的回忆、和苏格兰的节日气氛或日常起居混在一起的②。他们喜欢他,其实就像我出于同样原因一直喜欢《瑞士的鲁滨孙一家》③。关于

---

① 另一种忠贞不渝:意为对艺术的执着追求。
② 司各特是苏格兰人,其小说也大多与苏格兰历史、苏格兰风俗有关。
③ 《瑞士的鲁滨孙一家》:19世纪瑞士民俗学家、作家约翰·鲁道夫·魏斯根据其父亲的草稿整理和续写的一部小说,曾风靡一时。小说写一对传教士夫妇和四个儿子因船只失事漂流到东印度群岛的一个无人小岛上,一家人在岛上创建幸福生活。

《瑞士的鲁滨孙一家》，我现在就来给你们讲一讲，而且会讲得很激动，因为那是童年时代的感情。我就是大脑完全腐朽了，也不会对这部了不起作品有半点厌烦。我会回想起，在那幻想中的海滩，在那里"我们的船被骇人的风浪所毁"，出现四个半人半神的小英雄，名字叫弗里兹、欧内斯特、杰克和小弗朗兹，还有他们的父亲、他们的母亲，还有一块垫子，里面神奇地装着在热带生活十年所需的所有用品。那是我永恒的夏天——那就是《瑞士的鲁滨孙一家》对我的意义所在，而瓦尔特·司各特爵士对你们中的有些人来说，不也是这样吗？他不就是唤醒了欢乐童年的记忆吗？除此还有什么？如果我们的大脑还未腐朽，如果我们还想对小说有所理解，难道不应该把这种东西统统扔掉吗？

第二，司各特的名声还有一个真正的基础。他会讲故事。他有那种使读者保持悬念、挑动读者好奇心的先天才能。让我们来简述一下《古董商》——不是分析，分析是错误方式，而是简述。由此我们可以看到故事的层层展开，可以单纯研究其中的技巧。

《古董商》

第一章

那是十八世纪行将结束时的一个夏天的早上，天气晴朗，有个年轻人，外貌斯文，正要到苏格兰东北部去，买了一张来往于爱丁堡和女王渡口的公共马车的车票,而就如我们的北方读者所熟悉的,从女王渡口这个地名便可得知,那里还有穿越福斯湾的渡船。

这是《古董商》的第一句,并不精彩,只是告诉我们时间、地点和一个年轻人——这是为讲故事而设置的布景。我们稍稍有了点兴趣,想知道那个年轻人后来会怎样。他叫洛威尔,但他会怎样,还是个谜。他是男主人公,否则司各特就不会说他外貌斯文,而且他也一定会使女主人公得到幸福。他遇到了古董商乔纳森·欧德巴克。他们都上了马车,马车走得并不快,他们就在车上认识了,欧德巴克还邀请洛威尔到他家里去做客。在欧德巴克的家附近,他们遇到了艾迪·奥基尔特里——小说中的又一个人物。司各特在引入新的人物时做得很好。他让他们自然而然地出现,而且都带有某种预示的意味。艾迪·奥基尔特里预示着好事情。他是个乞丐——但不是一般的乞丐,而是一个既浪漫又守信的流浪汉,他会不会有助于揭开我们在洛威尔身上刚看到那个谜?至于其他人物的引入,有亚瑟·沃德尔爵士(古老家族,糟糕的管理者);有他的女儿伊莎贝拉(高傲的),男主人公无望地爱着她;还有欧德巴克的妹妹格丽泽尔小姐。格丽泽尔小姐的引入同样具有预示的意味。实际上,她只是个打诨插科的次要人物——没有其他作用,而你们的故事叙述者[①]引

---

① 你们的故事叙述者:指司各特。

入了许多这样的人物。他不必时时都要致力于有因必有果。只要他适当地保持在他的艺术范围内,就是说一些与故事无关的事情也是可以的。听故事的人总以为这些事情会有发展,然而听故事的人往往是昏头昏脑的、困倦的、健忘的。讲故事的人和编剧情的人则不然,枝枝蔓蔓对他反而有用。格丽泽尔小姐就是这样一束枝蔓,而在一部声称简洁而悲情的小说《兰默摩尔的新娘》① 中,我觉得可以找到更大的枝蔓。司各特在那本书里郑重其事地引入了那个掌玺大臣,而且没完没了地暗示他的性格缺陷会导致悲剧的发生,而实际上,即使没有这个人物,悲剧也几乎会一模一样地发生——因为关键因素是埃德加、露西、阿什顿夫人和巴克洛。哦,回头来讲《古董商》,那之后有一场晚宴,欧德巴克和亚瑟爵士争吵起来,亚瑟爵士一怒之下带着女儿走了。他们走回家要穿过沙滩。潮水涨上来。亚瑟爵士和伊莎贝拉被困在其中,而且正好遇到艾迪·奥基尔特里。这是故事中的第一个危急时刻,故事叙述者(他不失为故事叙述者)是这样处理的:

> 他们这样交谈着,停歇在他们能够到达的那块礁石的最高处;因为再继续往前走看来只能是惨遭厄运了。然而,在这里,他们也是等着那狂暴的海水慢慢地但确

---

① 《兰默摩尔的新娘》:瓦尔特·司各特的另一部小说。

定无疑地涌上来，情形就如早期教会的殉教者被异教的暴君置于野兽的撕咬之下，不得不看着受过刺激的野兽怒不可遏，等着开栅的命令下来，让野兽把他们撕成碎片。

然而就是这可怕的停歇给了伊莎贝拉时间来集聚一颗生来倔强而勇敢的心灵所拥有的力量，在这危难之际振作起来。"难道要我们毫不抗争，"她说，"就放弃生命吗？不管多么可怕，难道就没有路可以使我们攀上悬崖，或者至少可以爬到高出潮水的地方，在那儿坚持到天亮，或者坚持到有人来救吗？他们肯定知道我们的处境，会召集全村的人来救我们的。"

女主人公这么说，她的语气其实会使读者扫兴。但我们想知道的是后来怎样。那些礁石是纸板糊的①，就像我喜爱的《瑞士的鲁滨孙一家》里的一样；那暴风雨是司各特信手招来的②，他同时还胡乱地说到早期基督徒和其他什么事情；反正都是不真实的，整个事件也毫无危机感，而且一点激情也没有，平淡无奇，但我们就是想知道后来怎样。

原来——是洛威尔救了他们。是啊，这是我们应该想到的；那么，后来又怎样？

又是一束枝蔓。洛威尔被古董商安置在一个闹鬼的房间

---

① 纸板糊的：即任意虚构的。
② 信手招来的：亦即任意虚构的。

里睡觉,他梦见或者真看见了房主人的祖先,还对他说:"Kunst macht Gunsto."这话他当时听不懂,因为他对德语一窍不通,后来他才知道这话的意思是"技巧胜于喜爱":他必须要用手段捕获伊莎贝拉的心。这就是说,超自然事物对这个故事毫无帮助。虽然那是与绣帷和暴风雨一起引入的,效果却至多只能说一般。但读者并不知道。当他听到"Kunst macht Gunst"时,他的注意力一度集中……随后他的注意力又分散到其他事物上,而时间却照例过去了。

圣鲁斯教堂废墟里的野餐。引入杜斯特斯威维尔,一个邪恶的外国人,他伙同亚瑟爵士一起挖掘宝藏,而他的迷信被人嘲笑,因为不是真正的苏格兰边区的迷信。来了赫克托·麦克因泰尔,古董商的外甥,他怀疑洛威尔是个冒名顶替的人。两人决斗;洛威尔以为自己杀了对手,便和突然出现的艾迪·奥基尔特里一起逃跑了。他们躲进圣鲁斯教堂废墟,发现杜斯特斯威维尔正在那儿寻宝而且欺骗了亚瑟爵士。洛威尔上了一只小船走了——不见了,被忘了;但我们不用为他担心,他会再次出现。第二次在圣鲁斯教堂废墟寻宝。亚瑟爵士发现了一个满是白银的地窖。第三次寻宝。杜斯特斯威维尔被人痛打一顿,回过神来后看到人们在为年老的格伦纳兰伯爵夫人举行葬礼,因为那个家族信奉罗马天主教,她要半夜里秘密地葬在那里。

在这个故事中,格伦纳兰家族是很重要的,但他们的引入却是那么随意!使他们和杜斯特斯威维尔搭上关系的写法，也毫无艺术可言。杜斯特斯威维尔的那双眼睛正好在司各特手边，他也就用这双眼睛来窥视了。至此，读者一直是那么温顺地忍受着一连串插曲，现在正像原始的洞穴人那样打着哈欠。于是，对格伦纳兰家族的兴趣开始起作用，圣鲁斯教堂废墟被关闭，我们进入的也许可称为"前故事"①，这儿有两个新人物插入，而且既粗野又阴沉地谈论着罪恶的往事。他们的名字是：埃尔丝佩丝·马克尔班科特，一个渔妇兼女巫；格伦纳兰勋爵，已故伯爵夫人的儿子。他们的交谈又被其他一些事情打断——被艾迪·奥基尔特里的被捕、受审和释放打断，被另一个新人物的溺水而亡打断，被赫克托·麦克因泰尔在舅舅家里康复的趣事打断。不过，最要紧的还是格伦纳兰勋爵多年前违背他母亲的意愿，娶了一个叫伊芙林娜·内维尔的女士，后来又得知，她是他的异母妹妹。他震惊万分，未等她生下孩子就离她而去。埃尔丝佩丝原是他母亲的女仆，现在她正对他解释说，伊芙林娜和他没有血缘关系，她已死于分娩——当时埃尔丝佩丝和另一个女仆在场——但孩子却不知去向。后来，格伦纳兰勋爵就去咨询古董商，因为他兼任治安法官，知晓当时的事情，而且还曾爱过伊芙林娜。后来怎样？后来，亚瑟·沃德尔的家产被出售，因为杜斯特斯威维尔毁了他。后来呢？后来，据报道说法军将要登陆。后来呢？后来，洛威尔骑马到那里去指挥

---

① 前故事：pre-story，即"故事之前"，未正式形成故事的叙事形式。

英军。他此时自称内维尔少校。但就是这个内维尔少校也不是他的真名,原来他不是别人,就是格伦纳兰勋爵失踪的儿子,也就是格伦纳兰勋爵的法定爵位继承人。这样,部分通过埃尔丝佩丝·马克尔班科特;部分通过那个和她一起在场的女仆——格伦纳兰勋爵在国外遇到她时,她已是修女;部分通过一个已经过世的舅舅;部分通过艾迪·奥基尔特里,真相终于大白。其实,故事到此完全有理由结束了,但司各特对理由不感兴趣;他连解释也不解释,把所有理由统统扔到一边;他唯一要做的就是要使一件事情接着另一件事情发生。就是要——后来呢?后来,伊莎贝拉·沃德尔深受感动而和男主人公结了婚。后来呢?没有了,这就是故事的最后结局。我们千万不要过多地问"后来呢"。因为时间顺序若被逼得多出哪怕一秒钟,它也会把我们引到另一个国度里去①。

在《古董商》这本书里,时间中的生活是由小说家本能地予以展现的,这必然导致情感减弱、见解浅薄,特别是导致愚蠢地用结婚作为结局。其实,时间也是可以有意识地予以展现的,我们在另一本截然不同的书(一本令人难忘的书)即阿诺德·本涅特②的《老妇人的故事》中就能找到这样的例子。在《老妇人的故事》中,时间是真正的主人公。

---

① 此句的意思是,一部小说里的故事是既定的,若故事有所增加,那就是另一部小说了。

② 阿诺德·本涅特:与作者同时代的英国小说家。

它俨然就如造物主——实际上,唯有克里奇娄先生逃脱它的掌控,而这一不寻常的例外只能使它显得更有威力。索菲亚和康斯坦丝,从我们看到她们顽皮地穿上母亲的衣裙那一刻起,就成了时间的孩子;她们命中注定的衰老是以一种文学中罕见的完整性表现出来的。她们是女孩,后来索菲亚出走并结了婚,后来她们的母亲死了,后来康斯坦丝也结了婚,后来她的丈夫死了,后来索菲亚的丈夫也死了,后来索菲亚死了,后来康斯坦丝也死了,只剩下她们那只患风湿病的老狗,一拐一拐地去看看盆里还有没有吃的东西。我们的时间中的日常生活就是慢慢变老,老到像索菲亚和康斯坦丝那样血管被堵住,所以这个像是故事的故事讲得那么真实有力,一点没有胡说,其结局当然不可能是别的,只能是坟墓。这是个不讨人喜欢的结局。然而一部伟大的小说不能只有"当然",还要有其他东西,《老妇人的故事》固然写得很有力,真诚、悲伤,但还算不上伟大。

那么,《战争与和平》呢?那肯定很伟大,它同样强调时间的作用和一代人的兴衰。和本涅特一样,托尔斯泰也有勇气向我们展示人们怎样变老——尼古拉和娜塔莎的部分衰老,确实比康斯坦丝和索菲亚的完全衰老更加可悲①:除了青春已逝,我们还要丧失更多东西,但人却还活着。那么,

---

① 这里的"部分衰老"是指托尔斯泰仅写到尼古拉和娜塔莎过了中年后变得庸庸碌碌,"完全衰老"则是指本涅特写康斯坦丝和索菲亚一直写到她们死亡。

为什么《战争与和平》并不令人压抑？也许是因为它不仅在时间中展开，同时也在空间中展开，而感受空间，除非空间大得使我们害怕，否则总是令人振奋的，而且振奋之后还会有一种音乐般的效果。我们只要翻开《战争与和平》读一会儿，那粗大的琴弦就开始发出声响，而我们又无法确切地说出是什么拨响那琴弦的。这声响不是从故事中发出来的，尽管托尔斯泰和司各特一样关注后来怎样，而且和本涅特一样真诚。这声响也不是来自情节和人物。它们来自广阔的俄罗斯大地，情节和人物就分布在这大地之上；它们来自所有的桥梁和冰冻的河流、森林、道路、花园、田野，就是这些东西合在一起，使我们读到它们之后有一种宏大而响亮的感觉。许多小说家有地域感——譬如五镇、老雾都①，等等。但极少有小说家具有空间感，而具有空间感恰是托尔斯泰的一大天赋才能。《战争与和平》的主角是空间，而不是时间。

总之一句话，故事是由语音组成的②。小说家作品中的这一面③要求大声读出来，不像多数散文作品那样是用眼睛看的，而是要用耳朵听的；实际上，它和演讲有许多相似之处。它并没有曲调或韵律。因此，似乎有点奇怪，应该用眼睛看就可以了；眼睛有善变的心灵为后盾，轻而易举就能感知一段具有审学价值的文字或对话中的意思，而且以此为

---

① 五镇：福楼拜《包法利夫人》中的地名。老雾都：多次出现在司各特小说中的地名。
② 意为故事是要用嘴讲的。
③ 小说家作品中的这一面：即指故事。

乐——是的,眼睛甚至还能快速扫视一段文字,速度比我们背诵出来还快,就如有些人能快速读乐谱,速度比在钢琴上弹出来还快。但是,眼睛却不能同样快地感知语音。《古董商》开头那一句,并没有语音之美,但如果不是大声读出来,我们就会有所错失。我们的心灵固然能和司各特无声地沟通,但并不充分。故事除了讲述一件接着一件的事情,还有某种附加意味,因为它还连带着语音。

这种附加意味不会太多。它不会带给我们重要信息,譬如作者的个性如何。作者的个性——如果有的话——是通过比较正式的途径传递出来的,譬如人物、情节或者作者对生活的议论,等等。故事就其特殊功能而言,它所能做到的,仅仅是把我们从阅读者变为聆听者,让我们聆听"某种"语音,聆听某个人就像原始部落里讲故事的人那样蹲在山洞里讲述一件又一件事情,一直讲到那些坐在残骨剩肉之间的听众一个个昏昏欲睡。故事是一种原始的东西,从这里可以追溯到文学的源头;在不知阅读为何物的时代,是听故事满足了人的原始需求。正因为如此,所以我们才会那么无理性地对待自己喜欢的故事,才会那么粗暴地对待喜欢其他故事的人。譬如,我喜欢《瑞士的鲁滨孙一家》,只要有人嘲笑我,我就火冒三丈,而我现在又希望你们中的有些人对司各特火冒三丈!你们明白我的意思。喜欢不同的故事往往使人互不宽容。故事本身并无实质性的东西可言,又不能有助于我们对小说其他方面的理解。所以,我们还要想做点什么的话,最好还是走出这个山洞。

不过，我们暂时还不会出去，还要在这里考察一下，另一种生活——即价值观中的生活——是怎样从各个方面影响小说的，因为它时时都有可能进入小说，为小说提供人物、情节、幻想、宇宙观以及除"后来呢……后来呢"之外的一切东西，从而实实在在地改变小说，这是我们现在特别要加以探讨的。既然很明显，时间中的生活是低级的和粗劣的，那么问题自然就来了：既然神秘主义者甚至宣称可以把时间从自己的经验中清除，那么小说家能不能把时间中的生活从自己作品中清除而代之以那种灿烂辉煌的替换物①呢？

哦，已经有小说家——格特鲁德·斯坦因②——尝试过了，而且她的失败富有教益。格特鲁德·斯坦因比艾米莉·勃朗特、斯特恩或普鲁斯特走得更远，她砸碎了时钟并把碎片撒在像是俄塞里斯③遗留的世界里。她这么做并非出于任性，而是出于一个高尚的动机：她想把小说从时间暴政中解放出来，并在小说中仅仅表现价值观中的生活④。她失败了，因为小说一旦完全脱离时间，就什么都无法表现，而且就在她的后期作品中，我们还可以看到她一步步走向失败的足迹。她要把故事这一层面——也就是按年代编排的顺序——

---

① 那种灿烂辉煌的替换物：即指价值观中的生活。
② 格特鲁德·斯坦因：20世纪初和作者同时代的美国女作家。
③ 俄塞里斯：古埃及神话中的主神之一，统治亡故之人，并使万物自阴间复生，类似于中国的阎罗王。
④ 在小说中仅仅表现价值观中的生活：意即小说中完全没有故事。

全部清除，我对她真是佩服之至。因为她要这么做，就要把句子的先后秩序也清除。但就是这样，还是不行，还要把词语的先后秩序也清除，甚至要把词语中字母或发音的先后秩序也都清除。所以，她走到了悬崖上。不过，像她这样一种实验倒是一点不可笑。这样尝试一下总比改写"威弗利小说"① 有意思得多。只是这种实验注定要失败。因为去掉时间先后秩序不可能不把本来各就其位的一切一起去掉；本来想表现价值观的小说就会变得不可理解，也就毫无价值可言。

正因为如此，所以我要你们和我一起用适当的语气再说一遍我开始的时候说过的那句话。不要说得像那个公共汽车司机那样态度温和而含含糊糊，因为你们没有那个权利②。也不要说得像那个打高尔夫球的人那样态度粗鲁而气势汹汹，因为你们比他懂得更多。要说得略带忧伤，那就对了："是啊——亲爱的，是啊——小说就是讲故事。"

---

① "威弗利小说"：司各特历史小说的总称。"改写'威弗利小说'"意为仿效司各特的小说。
② 公共汽车司机可以含含糊糊，"你们"是剑桥大学的学生，不能含含糊糊。

第三章 人 物[①]

讨论了故事这小说最简单、最基本的一面之后，我们便可以转向一个较为有趣的话题了，那就是角色。我们不必再问"后来怎样"了，而只要问"他（或者她）怎么样"；小说家将要诉之于我们的理智与想象力，而不再仅仅诉之于我们的好奇心。一个新的重点，即价值重点，进入了他的话语。

由于故事中的角色通常是人，把小说的这一面称为"人物"看来并不勉强。其他动物也有被引入的，但成功的很有限，因为我们对它们的心理知之甚少。或许，将来可能会有所改变，就像小说家笔下的野蛮人早已有所改变。隔在吉卜林[②]

[①] 原文是 People，一般不译作"人物"。"人物"在英语中一般称作 character，该词又有"性格""特征"的意思。本书作者大概是为了强调肉体上的"人"，故而用了 people 一词，如简单译作"人"或"人们"，在汉语中似乎很古怪，甚至会误解，因为汉语从来都把文学作品中的角色称为"人物"而从不称其为"人"或"人们"，故而还是勉强译作"人物"。这和作者的意思不仅仅有出入，甚至是相背离的，因为他是故意不用 character（人物）一词——对此，英语读者自能领会其用意；汉语读者却只见"人物"一词，浑然不知其中有何区别。特此说明，翻译终究是翻译，聊胜于无。

[②] 吉卜林：20 世纪英国诗人、小说家，在其小说中有一些是动物故事，而且大多是狼群的故事。

的狼群和它们两百年后出现在文学中的后裔之间的鸿沟,也许和隔在礼拜五①与巴图阿拉②之间的鸿沟是相对应的,那时我们看到的动物将不再是象征物,不再是伪装的小矮人,不再是会走的四脚桌子,不再是会飞的彩色纸风筝。科学在这过程中或许会提供新的主题,从而使小说得以拓展。不过,这种助力现在还没有得到,因而在此之前我们或许可以说,故事中的角色不是真人,就是假装的人。

由于小说家自己也是人,因而在他和他所要表现的主题之间有一种亲和力,这在其他许多艺术形式中是没有的。历史学家也和人有关系,但就如我们将会看到的,并不怎么亲密。画家和雕塑家不一定要和人有关系;也就是说,除非他们有意,否则他们不一定要表现人,诗人更加不一定,而音乐家如果不借助于说明书,就是要想表现人也不可能。小说家则和他的许多艺术同行有别,他是用许多词语组合粗略地描述他自己③(粗略地,精细的还有待将来),他给予人物姓名与性别,赋予他们合适的姿态,还要用引号来表示他们在说话,也许还要使他们的行为保持前后一致。这些词语组合就是他的各种人物④。这些人物不是那么冷冰冰地出现在他

---

① 礼拜五:18 世纪英国小说家笛福的《鲁滨孙漂流记》中鲁滨孙所救的一个土著野蛮人,因那天是礼拜五,故鲁滨孙以此为他取名。
② 巴图阿拉:20 世纪第一位获龚古尔奖的法国小说家勒内·马伦的《巴图阿拉》中的野蛮人。
③ 他自己:意为人。
④ 意为小说家笔下的人物并非真有其人,而是用语词创造出来的。

的头脑中的，很可能是在精神错乱般的兴奋状态中创造出来的；然而，他们的性格却受制于他对其他人和对他自己的推测，同时又受制于作品的其他方面。这最后一点——人物与小说其他方面的关系——就是后面几讲要探讨的主题。现在我们主要关注的是人物与现实生活的关系。小说中的人物和小说家或者你们，或者我，或者维多利亚女王，有何区别？

当然是有所区别的。如果某部小说中的某个人物和维多利亚女王一模一样——不是一般的一样，而是绝对一样——那这个人物其实就是维多利亚女王，而这部小说，或者说和这个人物有关的一切，就成了一部传记。传记是历史，是以事实为基础的。小说则是以事实+X或者-X为基础的，这个未知数总会影响事实的效果，有时甚至会将其完全改变。

历史学家叙述人们的行为，而对人们的性格他只能从他们的行为中推知。他和小说家一样，极其关注人的性格，但他只能在人的性格浮现在表面时才能得知它的存在。如果维多利亚女王没有说"我们不快活"，坐在她旁边的人就不会知道她不快活，她的厌倦也就永远不会公之于众①。她可能皱过眉头，这样他们就会从中推知她的心情——眼神和表情也是历史事实。但是，如果她始终毫无表示——谁会知道什么？隐秘生活——严格地说——是隐秘的。隐秘生活若有显露迹象就不再是隐秘生活，就进入行为领域了。小说家的职

---

① 公之于众：意为写入史书。

责就是把隐秘生活从其源头上揭示出来：告诉我们比可知的更多的关于维多利亚女王的事情，由此而创造出一个人物，这个人物不是历史上的维多利亚女王。

关于这一点，那位笔名叫阿兰①的既有趣又敏锐的法国批评家有过一些稍显奇特但颇有裨益的评论。他涉水有点过深②，但没有我觉得我自己那么深，也许我们俩在一起可以爬上岸。阿兰曾逐一考察各种形式的审美活动，考察到小说时他断定人人有两面，分别属于历史和小说。在一个人身上所能观察到的——也就是说，他的行为和根据他的行为推知的精神状态——是属于历史范畴的。但是一个人还有他的罗曼史或者说浪漫的一面，包括"纯粹的激情，也就是说，梦想、欢乐、悲伤和碍于礼义或羞耻而难以启齿的自我亲密交谈③"；把人性的这一面表现出来，就是小说的主要功能之一。

> 小说所虚构的与其说是故事，不如说是方式，一种把思想变为行动的方式，这在日常生活中是绝对没有的……历史，连同它所强调的外在原因，是受必然性观念支配的，然而在小说中却没有必然性；在那儿，一切都以人性为基础，处于支配地位的是情感，它决定了这

---

① 阿兰：20世纪法国哲学家埃米尔-奥古斯特·夏蒂埃的笔名。
② 涉水过深：意为出格。
③ 自我亲密交谈：self-communing，心理学术语，意即沉思。

样一种存在：那里的一切都是随意的，甚至激情与犯罪，甚至苦难，都是如此。①

这也许只是用一种迂回的方式把每个英国学生都知道的事情再说一遍：历史学家是记录，小说家必须创造。不过，这仍是一种有益的迂回，因为它说出了日常生活中的人和小说中的人之间的本质区别。在日常生活中，我们绝无可能相互完全理解，既不可能完全了解他人，也不可能完全反省自己。我们只是相互有所认识，依据的是表面信息，而依据这些表面信息已经足以进行社会交往，甚至建立亲密关系。然而，小说中的人却能被读者彻底理解，只要小说家愿意；他们的内心世界可以像他们的外在活动一样暴露无遗。所以，他们比历史人物、甚至比我们自己的朋友似乎更容易了解；我们被告知了关于他们的一切，能告知的都告知了；即便他们是不完美的或者是不真实的，反正他们都不保守秘密，而我们的朋友不仅而且必须相互保守秘密，这是生活在这个星球上的一个必要条件。

现在让我们比较幼稚地重复一下这个问题。你们和我都是人。我们要是来看看我们自己生活中的那些重要事情——不是和个人前途有关的事情，而是和我们活着做人有关的那些事情——是不是更好？这样，我们就可以比较明确地说下

---

① 意译自《美的艺术体系》（Systeme des Beaux Arts）320—321页。感谢安德烈·莫洛亚的推荐，我读了这部激动人心的论集。——作者原注

去了。

人生有五件重要事情：生、吃、睡、爱、死。有人或许会增加几件——譬如呼吸——但这五件是最为显见的。让我们简单地问一下自己，这五件事在我们的生活中起怎样的作用，在小说中又是怎样的。小说家往往是精确地再现这五件事呢，还是夸大、轻视、忽略它们？小说中的人物和我们一样有名有姓，那么小说中所呈现的人物经历，和我们的生活经历是不是一样？

先来说两件最怪异的事情：生与死。说这两件事怪异是因为它们既是经历又不是经历。我们是听别人所说才知道这两件事的。我们都经历过出生，但我们谁都没有出生时的记忆。死亡甚至在人刚一出生时就来了，但是，同样，我们不知道它是怎么回事。我们最后的经历和我们最初的经历一样，都是推测出来的。我们活在两片黑暗之间。有些人不真实地告诉我们出生和死亡是怎样的：譬如，母亲说到婴儿出生，那是母亲的视角；还有医生、教士说到生与死，也都是他们的视角。这些都是从旁人的角度看到的，而那两种可以让我们知晓的人——婴儿和死人——却又做不到，因为他们的表达器官和我们的接收器官是不协调的。

所以，让我们这样想：人们是以一种业已忘记的经历开始生活而以一种可以相信又无法理解的经历结束生活的。这就是小说家打算把他们作为人物引入书中的一种生物；当然，还有一些似乎和他们相像的生物。小说家是可以记住和理解任何事物的,只要这对他有用。他还可以知道所有人的隐秘生活。刚出生的人,不是也被弄来当人物了吗?人物被送往墓地,他不是紧随其后吗?关于这两种怪异的经历,他会说些什么,或者会使人有何感受?

再来说吃,添料过程,维持个体的生命。这个过程在出生前就已经开始,之后由母亲予以继续,最后由个体自身接替,日复一日地把各种东西放进脸上的一个洞里,既不觉得惊讶,也不感到厌烦。食物是已知和已忘①之间的连接物;它的一头和我们无记忆的出生连接,另一头延续到我们今天的早餐。吃和睡一样——很多方面很相像——不仅能恢复体力,还有审美的一面,它能品尝出好坏。那么,这种两面性的东西,在小说中是怎么回事?

再后面是睡。我们平均大约有三分之一的时间并非用于社会活动或文化活动,甚至不是在通常所说的独居中度过的。我们会进入一个我们知之甚少的世界,而当我们离开之后,我们似乎会觉得,它部分是一片空白,部分像是现实世界的滑稽模仿,部分像是神示天启。我们醒来时会说"我没有梦见什么"或者"我梦见了一把梯子"或者"我梦见了天堂"。我并不想讨论睡眠和做梦的本质——只是想指出,睡眠和做梦占据了人类大量的时间,我们所说的"历史",只记录了三分之二的人类生命周期并加以理论化而已。那么,

---

① 已知和已忘:意为有记忆和无记忆,前者指幼儿开始有记忆之后的时期,后者指无记忆的婴儿期。参见下句。

小说是否也持同样的态度？

最后，爱。我使用这个众所周知的词，用的是它最宽泛、最混沌的含义。首先让我来枯燥而简短地说说性爱。一个人出生后过了若干年，就会像其他动物一样发生某些变化，这些变化通常是导致和另一个人结合，并生育出更多的人。我们的种族由此而延续。性爱出现于青春期之前，一直持续到生育力丧失；其实它是终生都有的，只是在结偶年龄，它对社会的影响更为明显。性爱之外还有其他情感，也助推年轻人成熟，即在精神上有所提升，譬如爱好、友谊、爱国主义、神秘主义——不过，当我们试图确认性爱和其他情感之间的关系时，我们一定会激烈争论起来，激烈程度不亚于关于瓦尔特·司各特的争论，或许还会更加激烈。让我仅把各种观点罗列出来。有人说性爱是基础，在其之上才有其他下面这些爱，即爱朋友、爱上帝、爱国家。另有人说，性爱和这些爱虽有关系，但也仅此而已，并不是它们的根源。还有人说，性爱和这些爱根本没有关系。我的看法很简单，我们可以把所有这些情感都称为爱，并把它们视为人必须有的第五种重要经历。当人们爱的时候，他们是想得到某种东西。他们也想给予某种东西，因而这种双重目的使爱变得比吃和睡要复杂得多。它是自私的，同时又是利他的，而且不管哪一面都不会专注到使另一面完全消退。爱需要多少时间？这个问题好像问得很可笑，但它却和我们现在所探讨的问题关系密切。睡需要二十四小时中的八小时左右，吃大约是两小时多一点。我们再花两小时来爱？这样的应允当然很慷慨。然而爱却往往是夹杂在其他活动中的——还有打盹和饥饿，也是这样。爱还可能引出各种次要活动，譬如，一个男人对家人的爱可能会使他把大量时间用在证券交易所里①，或者他对上帝的爱会使他把大量时间用在教堂里。但是，说他每天用两个多小时和他所钟爱的对象交流感情，就可能不大有人会相信了。然而正是这种感情交流，这种既想获得又想给予的欲望，这种慷慨与苛求的混合，使爱的经历和上述四种经历截然不同。

以上所说便是做人——或者说，做人的一部分。小说家也这样做人，只是他手里拿着笔，沉浸在一种不妨称为"灵感"的不寻常状态中，致力于创造人物。人物也许总会和小说中的其他东西纠缠在一起；这是经常发生的（亨利·詹姆斯的作品就是极好的例子），所以人物的面目理所当然就要相应地有所改变。不过，我们现在考虑的是比较简单的情况，即小说家主要关注的是人，为此他不惜牺牲许多有用的东西——故事、情节、形式，偶尔还有美。

那么，在何种意义上，小说中的各民族不同于地球上的各民族？对此没有人能予以概括，因为两者没有科学意义上的共同性；譬如，小说中的人没有腺体，而地球上的人都是有腺体的。但是，不管怎么说，它们的经历还是倾向于和地

---

① 意即想为家人多挣点钱。

球人保持一致的。

最初，它们来到世界上，和地球人相比，更像是不知从哪儿寄来的包裹。一个婴儿出现在一部小说中，通常都像是寄来的一个包裹。它是被邮寄"过来"的；接着，有个年长的人物去领取这个包裹并向读者展示。这之后，它通常就被放进冷藏柜里了，要到它会说话或者有点什么作用时才会出来。

关于这一点，以及其他方面小说人物和人间实况之间的种种差异，有好的和坏的两种理由；不过，这些我们过一会儿再说，现在只要注意，小说王国里的人口增长①是被随随便便地对待的。从斯特恩到詹姆斯·乔伊斯，没有一个作家想要如实描写有关婴儿出生的事实，甚至没有一个作家想要虚构有关婴儿出生的事实，而且，除了用一种姑妈似的欣喜方式看待婴儿，没有一个作家想要真正探知婴儿心理，进而发掘其中一定具有的文学价值。也许，这是难以做到的。我们等一会儿再作定论。

那么，死呢？另一方面，小说家对待死亡却要重视得多，方式也多种多样，可见小说家觉得还是死亡比较合乎心意。他之所以这样觉得，是因为他可以用死亡来干净利落地结束一部小说；还有一个不太明显的原因是，他在按时间顺序讲述②时发现，从已知事物讲到一片昏暗③要比从一片昏暗

---

① 意即关于婴儿出生。
② 按时间顺序讲述：即讲故事。
③ 一片昏暗：意即死亡。

的出生讲到已知事物来得容易。他的人物，随着时间过去而死了；他了解他们，他既要如实描写他们，又要发挥自己的想象力——这样的结合是最有力的。举个小小的死亡例子——《巴塞特的最后纪事》① 中普罗迪太太的死。一切都写得很有分寸，但效果却令人惊恐，因为特罗洛普让普罗迪太太在教区的好几条小路上走来走去，用她的步态，用她发出的噼啪声，使我们熟悉她，甚至厌烦她；我们熟悉了她的性格和诡计，熟悉了她的"主教，想想众生的灵魂吧"；然后，她在床边上心脏病发作，走到很远很远的地方去了——这就是普罗迪太太的结局。几乎没有什么东西是小说家不能从"正常死亡"中借取的；几乎没有什么东西是他不可以有效地予以虚构的。那扇通往昏暗的门对他敞开着，只要他有想象力，他甚至可以伴随他的人物一起走进去——只是，不要把那些关于"死后生活"的神神道道的东西带回来。

吃——我们列出的第三件事——又怎样？小说中的吃主要是社交的。食物把人物聚在一起，但人物很少是在生理上需要食物，也很少享受食物，而且从不消化食物，除非对此有特殊要求。他们像我们在生活中一样，相互撕咬，但我们对早餐与午餐的那种恒常不变的贪馋却没有反映在他们身上。就是在诗歌中也较多写到吃——至少在吃的审美方面。无论是弥尔顿，还是济慈，都比乔治·梅瑞狄斯更亲近饕餮

---

① 《巴塞特的最后纪事》：19世纪英国小说家特罗洛普的著名系列小说中的一部。

之乐。

睡。在小说中也很草率。没人想表现昏睡或真正的梦境。梦要么是逻辑化的,要么就是用往事和未来之事的小碎块做成的镶嵌画。梦是带着一种目的而被引入的,这一目的不是要表现人物的全部生活,而只想表现他的部分生活,即清醒时的生活。人物从来没有被看作是一种三分之一时间是在黑暗中度过的生物。这是历史学家的有限的白昼视野,是小说家在其他地方竭力避免的。那他为什么不去了解或再现睡眠呢?要知道,他是有权虚构的,而且我们知道他何时在真正地虚构,因为他的激情会使我们漂浮起来而无视不可能的事物。然而,他既没再现睡眠,也没有虚构睡眠。睡眠不过是一片混沌而已。

爱。你们都知道爱在小说中堆积得有多么巨大,你们或许还会同意我的看法:爱对小说已经有害,已经使小说变得单调乏味。为什么这种特殊经历——尤其是它的性形式——会这么不加节制地被到处移植?如果你们模模糊糊地想到一部小说,你们想到的总是一个爱的故事——一个男人和一个女人要结合,而且大多是成功的。如果你们模模糊糊地想到自己的生活,或者想到一群人的生活,你们得到的却是一个非常不同而且要复杂得多的印象。

为什么爱会被过分彰显,甚至在优秀的严肃小说中也是如此,看来有两个原因。

首先是,当小说家设想好人物并开始塑造人物时,"爱"

的各个方面便在他心目中变得很重要，因而不用他有意为之，他也会使他的人物对爱过分敏感——过分的意思是，他们在现实生活中是不会这样为了爱而费尽心机的。人物之间总是神经过敏——这即使在像菲尔丁那样被称作豪爽的作家笔下，也显而易见——而在生活中，除非有人闲得无聊，否则是不会这样的。激情，一时冲动——是有的，但不会这样时时刻刻地警觉，这样没完没了地纠缠，这样无休无止地追求。我相信这些都是小说家创作时的自身精神状态的反映，这是导致爱在小说中占尽优势的部分原因。

第二个原因。按理说这和我们将要探讨的另一个问题①有关，但在此提一下也无妨。和死一样，爱对小说家来说是很有用的，因为爱可以使他轻松地结束一部小说。他可以把爱写成是永恒的，读者对此也很容易接受，因为与爱有关的幻觉之一就是爱能忠贞不渝。其实从未有过——将来也不会有。全部历史、我们的全部经验都教导我们，没有哪种个人关系是持久不变的，而是像构成个人关系的人自身一样是不稳定的，人们必须像走钢丝一样保持平衡，才能使爱延续，而爱的延续即意味着它已不再是个人关系而变成了一种社会习俗，其着重点已经从爱变成了婚姻。所有这些我们都知道，然而我们却不愿意用我们苦涩的知识去对待未来；未来将和以往那么不同；完美的人将会出现，或者说，我们现在

---

① 即第六章"幻想"。

看到的人将会变得完美。将来不会再有变化，不必再那么紧张。我们将永远永远地幸福，要不就是永远永远地不幸。任何一种强烈的情感都会带有对永恒的幻想，而小说家抓住的就是这一点。他们总是用男女主人公结婚来结束小说，我们对此不能反对，因为是我们把自己的幻想借给了他们。

以上我们把那两个具有亲缘关系的物种——即 Homo Sapiens 和 Homo Fictus①——作了比较，现在必须总结一下。Homo Fictus 比他的表亲更加令人困惑。他是由成百个互不相同的小说家用头脑创作出来的，他们所用的创作方法又相互冲突，所以谁也无法加以概括。不过，关于他还是有点话可说的。他总是突然之间就生出来了，他可以一直处于临死状态而不死，他几乎可以不吃不睡，他从不疲倦地忙于个人关系。此外——最重要的——我们对他的了解可以胜过我们对任何一个同类的了解，因为他的创造者和讲述者是同一个人。要是不怕夸张的话，我们或许可以这样宣称："如果上帝来讲宇宙的故事，那么宇宙也可虚构。"因为这是同理的。

说过这些高深的理论之后，让我们拿个简单一点的人物来分析一下。就拿摩尔·弗兰德斯②来说吧。她在那本用她的名字命名的书中无处不在，或者说她在书里是孑然独立的，就像公园里的一棵树，所以我们可以从各个方面去观察

---

① Homo Sapiens：拉丁文，原意为"智人"，此处代指生活中的人。Homo Fictus：拉丁文，此语为作者所造，意为"虚构之人"，即指小说中的人。
② 摩尔·弗兰德斯：18世纪英国小说家笛福同名小说中的女主人公。

她而不受其他竞争物的干扰。笛福是在讲一个故事，就像司各特一样，我们会发现他用非常相似的方式留有一条条不知结果的线索，以备后面有机会将其继续：譬如摩尔早年所生的那几个孩子就是一例。不过，笛福和司各特之间的相似性不能过分强调。笛福感兴趣的是他的女主人公，这部小说的形式也很自然地出自她的性格①。她被一对兄弟中的弟弟诱奸而又和他的哥哥结了婚，她在年轻快乐的青春年代就嫁过好几个丈夫；这并非卖淫，在她正派而热情的内心深处，她对此其实是深恶痛绝的。她和笛福笔下的大多数底层人物很相像，他们不仅相互体谅，还很讲义气，不惜为此而冒险。他们的好心肠总是炙热得胜过作者的理性评判，其原因显然和作者在新门监狱的一些不寻常的经历有关②。我们不知道那是什么，也许他自己事后也不清楚，因为他是个忙忙碌碌的报刊撰稿人和一心一意的政治参与人。但他在监狱里肯定遇到过什么事，而且受其模糊而强烈的刺激才有摩尔·弗兰德斯和罗克珊娜③的诞生。摩尔·弗兰德斯是个肉体型的人物，健壮的四肢既善于上床，也善于扒窃。她并不靠容貌引人注目，而是以她的身高和体重、她的鼻息和胃口以及她所做的许多不同寻常的事情来打动我们的。她早年以嫁人为业：就算没有嫁过四次，至少也嫁过三次，其中有一个丈夫

---

① 《摩尔·弗兰德斯》的形式是女主人公自述其身世。
② 笛福早年经商破产，后又因政治罪名入狱，甚至戴枷示众，经历坎坷至极。
③ 罗克珊娜：笛福同名小说中的女主人公。

后来发现竟是她的哥哥。她和他们全都过得很快活，他们对她很好，她对他们也很好。请听我念，下面讲的是她的布商丈夫带她去作了一次愉快的旅游：

"嗨，亲爱的，"一天他对我说，"我们去乡下住上一个礼拜散散心怎么样？"

"好，亲爱的，"我说，"到哪儿去？"

"到哪儿去都成，"他说，"不过，我想在那一个星期里我们要扮成贵族的样子。我们到牛津去吧。"

"可怎么去呢？"我说，"我又不会骑马，坐马车去，路又太远了。"

"太远？"他说，"坐着六匹马的大马车，去哪儿都不会太远。我要带你出去，你就能像个公爵夫人一样阔气地旅行。"

"哈哈，"我说，"亲爱的，这真是恶作剧。不过，只要你愿意，我是不在乎的。"

于是定了一个日子，我们雇了一辆漂亮的马车，六匹马，一个马夫，一个帮手，两个仆人，穿着顶讲究的制服；还有一个骑马的跟班，和一个帽子上插着羽毛的侍童，也是骑马的。仆人们都叫我丈夫"爵爷"，旅馆的掌柜自然也是这般称呼，我就成了伯爵夫人了。

这样，我们旅行到牛津去，真是玩得很高兴。说句公道话，世界上没有哪个乞丐比我丈夫更懂得怎样摆爵爷的架子。我们看遍了牛津所有的名胜古迹，还和两三位大学里的学究谈天，说我们有个侄子现在要爵爷照应，想把他送到牛津来读书，打算请他们做师父。我们还和另外几个穷学者开玩笑，答应将来起码叫他们到爵爷家里来做家庭牧师，让他们戴上正式的教士披巾。在牛津住了几天，在花费方面真像个贵族，我们又到北安普敦去逛，总共逛了十二天才回家，大约用掉了九十四英镑。

与此情景相对照的是她的兰开夏郡丈夫，她深深地爱他。他是个拦路抢劫的强盗，他们两人都装得富有，相互诱骗对方误入婚姻陷阱。举行婚礼后，他们两人又相互揭穿对方的伪装，这时笛福如果按常规来写，那他就会让他们相互指责，就像《我们共同的朋友》里的兰姆尔先生和兰姆尔太太那样。但是，他却一反常规地让女主人公表现得既幽默又明智。

"说真的，"我对他说，"当时我看出你很快就会得到我；而现在我很为难，我没有到那种地步，让你一眼看出我会那么轻易就原谅你，会把你要的所有花招统统忘记，还会对你百依百顺。但是，亲爱的，"我说，"我们现在还能做什么？我们两个都完了，连怎么活下去都没有着落，还来谈什么原谅不原谅？"

我们打算做好几件事情,但是一点本钱都没有,就什么事情都没法做。他最后求我不要再谈这件事了,因为,他说,我会使他心碎的;所以我们就谈了一点别的事情,直到最后他和我做过丈夫之事后,我们便睡着了。

这样讲述日常生活,比狄更斯更真实,读来也更令人愉快。夫妇俩面对的是事实,不是作者的道德理论,而且这两个明白事理、心底不坏的无赖并没有闹得不可开交。后来,她不再以嫁人为业而以扒窃为生;她知道这样改行更加糟糕,自己的处境自然会是一片昏暗。但是她仍像以往一样既镇定又有趣。当她抢劫一个上完舞蹈课回家的小女孩的金项链时,她的反应是那么合情合理!她做这件事情是在通往位于史密斯菲尔德区的圣巴塞洛缪教堂的一条小巷里(你们今天仍可以到那个地方去看看——笛福出没于伦敦各处),而且还有想杀了那小女孩的一时冲动。她没有杀,那冲动很微弱,但她意识到那小女孩也太冒险,进而她又对那小女孩的父母感到无比愤怒,因为他们"竟然让这只可怜巴巴的小羊羔独自回家,这回就是给他们一点教训,让他们下回照顾好它"。现代心理学家若致力于表述这一心理,将会何等笨拙、何等做作!然而笛福只是信笔写来,譬如在另一段中也是如此,那里讲到摩尔·弗兰德斯欺骗了一个男人,后来又高高兴兴地告诉了他,结果是她无法对他的感激不尽漠然处之,就再也不想欺骗他了。她的所作所为使我们有点震惊——不是理想破灭时的震撼，而是对一个那么活生生的人感到惊奇。我们会对着她笑，但既不是苦笑，也不是嘲笑。她既不是伪君子，也不是傻子。

在小说行近结束时，她在一家布料店里被两个从柜台后面出来的年轻女士抓获："我本想对她们说几句好话，但根本不是地方：那两个女人比两条喷火的毒龙还要凶猛。"——她们叫来了警察，她被逮捕并被判处死刑，后改为流放到弗吉尼亚①。不幸之云消散得奇快。流放途中非常愉快，因为有一个最初教她偷盗的老女人对她很好。此外（还要好），她的兰开夏郡丈夫也正巧和她一起流放。他们在弗吉尼亚上岸后，她很苦恼，因为她发现她的哥哥丈夫也在那儿。她隐瞒了此事，他死了，那个兰开夏郡丈夫仅仅抱怨说她不该隐瞒此事；他没有指责她别的什么，因为他和她依然相爱。小说就这样结束了，很圆满，而且很坚定，就像女主人公一开始说的那句开场词所用的语调："……我们决定在对以往邪恶生活的真心忏悔中度过我们的余生。"

她的忏悔是真心的，只有浅薄的法官才会指控她是伪君子。像她这种人通常不能区分做坏事和被抓住②——她偶尔会有所区分，但这两件事基本上是混在一起的，这就是为什么她的看法会那么零零碎碎，那么自然而然，即认为"活着

---

① 弗吉尼亚：即今美国弗吉尼亚州，当初是英国的海外流放地。
② 意即这种人认为只要不被抓住就不是做坏事。

就是这样",地狱就是新门监狱。如果我们非要逼迫她或者她的创造者笛福,说:"来,说实话。你相信永生吗?"他们会说(按他们现代后裔的说法):"我当然相信永生——你把我当作什么了?"——这样一种信仰供认,比干脆否认还要彻底地把永生拒之门外。

所以,《摩尔·弗兰德斯》将为我们提供这样一种小说范例,其中一个人物就是一切,并给予这个人物最自由的表现。笛福似乎有意设置一段以那个哥哥丈夫作为中心的情节,但这个人物却写得完全是敷衍了事,而她的那个合法丈夫(就是那个带她到牛津去旅游的人)简直就消失得无影无踪了。什么都无关紧要,除了女主人公;她就像矗立在一片空地上的一棵树,而且,要说她无论从哪个角度看似乎都是绝对真实的,我们必须问问自己,如果在日常生活中遇到她,我们是否会把她认出来。因为那是我们正在讨论的要点:生活中的人和小说中的人之间的区别。奇怪的是,就是像摩尔·弗兰德斯这样一个被我们认为是自然的而非概念化的人物,她的每一个细节都和日常生活相符,我们还是不会在日常生活中发现和她完全一样的人。假如我现在突然改变演讲人的腔调,用平常口吻对你们说:"当心——我在听众当中看到了摩尔·弗兰德斯——当心,这位先生"——你们中的哪一位,请说姓名——"她就在你旁边,会偷你的怀表。"——你们马上就会知道我是错的,知道我不但违背了或然率——这倒不算要紧——还混淆了日常生活和小说之间的界限。如果我说："当心，听众当中有个像摩尔·弗兰德斯的人。"你们可能不相信我，但不会怪我，说我无知无识，因为我只是违背了或然率。说摩尔·弗兰德斯今天下午就在剑桥或英国的什么地方，或者说她到过英国的什么地方，都是白痴。为什么？

这个特殊的问题只要到下星期①就能得到回答，那时我们将讨论比较复杂的小说，那里的人物需要和小说的其他方面相适应。那时我们将有可能得到某种常见的答案，某种在各种文学手册中也能找到的答案，某种总是要求在考卷上写出来的美学答案，其意思是：小说是艺术作品，遵循其自身规则，而不是日常生活中的那些规则，小说中的人物要按照这样的规律生活才是真实的。那时我们会说到，爱米丽娅或者爱玛②是不可能来听本次讲座的，因为她们仅存在于以她们的名字命名的小说中，仅存在于菲尔丁或简·奥斯丁的世界里。艺术中的沐浴者③把她们和我们分开。她们是真实的并不是因为她们和我们相像（尽管她们也可能和我们相像），而是因为她们是可信的。

这是个很好的回答，由此可以得出某些有力的结论。但是，对于像《摩尔·弗兰德斯》这样一种主人公就是一切、主人公可以想做什么就做什么的小说，这样的回答并不令人

---

① 下星期：即下一讲（讲座每星期一次）。
② 爱米丽娅：18世纪英国小说家菲尔丁同名小说中的女主人公。爱玛：19世纪英国小说家简·奥斯丁同名小说中的女主人公。
③ 艺术中的沐浴者：即指艺术家。

满意。我们需要一种较少美学成分和较多心理学成分的答案。为什么她不可能出现在这里？把她和我们分开是什么？我们的答案其实已经隐含在前面那段引自阿兰的引文中了：她不可能出现在这里是因为她属于一个可以看见隐秘生活的世界，一个不是也不可能是我们的世界，一个讲述者和创造者是同一人的世界。既然这样，关于小说人物何时才是真实的，我们便可以得到一个定义了：当小说家对某人物有透彻的了解时，该人物就是真实的。小说家也许并不选择把他所了解的一切都告诉我们——许多事情，甚至那种我们称为显而易见的事情，都可能被他隐瞒。但是，他会使我们觉得该人物虽然没有予以说明，却是可以理解的；由此，我们便有了某种日常生活中不可能有的真实感。

因为个人交往——如果我们看其自身而非其社会属性的话——看来是鬼影幢幢的。除了敷衍客套，我们不能相互理解；我们不能显露自己，甚至在我们想显露时也不能；我们所谓的亲密交往不过是权宜之计；推心置腹是一种幻想。但是，在小说中，我们不仅可以透彻地了解人，如果不是仅仅为娱乐而读书的话，我们还可以在这里为生活中的昏暗找到某种补偿。就这方面而言，小说比历史更真实，因为它不受事实的限制，而我们人人凭自己的经验都知道事实之外还有别的东西，这东西虽然小说家自己也没有准确地把握，是啊——但他尽力了。他可以把还是婴儿的人物投递到世界上来，他可以使他们不睡觉或者不吃饭而继续生活，他可以使他们相爱,而且只有爱没有其他,因为他对他们似乎无所不知,因为他们是他创造的。这就是为什么摩尔·弗兰德斯不可能出现在这里的原因,这就是为什么爱米丽娅和爱玛不可能出现在这里的一个原因。她们是别人可以看到她们的隐秘生活的人;我们是别人看不到我们的隐秘生活的人。

这就是为什么小说即使写一些邪恶之人也能给我们以安慰的原因:小说中的人都是容易理解因而容易操纵的人,他们给了我们自以为有智慧、有力量的幻觉。

第四章 人物(续)

现在,我们从移植转向适应①。我们已经讨论了能不能把人从生活中取出来放进小说,还反过来讨论了他们能不能从小说中走出来坐在这个房间里。得到的回答是否定的,而且还引出一个更加重要的问题:在日常生活中,我们能相互理解吗?我们今天的论题更具有学术性。我们要关注人物和小说的其他方面的关系,如情节、寓意、相关人物、环境,等等。人物要服从创作者的其他需要。

这之后我们将不会再指望人物在总体上和日常生活相一致,而只能是相对应。当我们说简·奥斯丁的某个人物——譬如贝茨小姐②——"那么像生活"时,我们是说她的每一点都和生活中的某一点相一致,但是从总体上说她只是和我们在茶会上遇到的某个唠唠叨叨的老处女相对应。贝茨小姐和海伯里③的关系千丝万缕。我们不可能把她扯出来而不带上她的母

---

① 移植:意为小说中的人物是如何从生活中移植过来的。适应:意为人物在小说中是如何和其他方面相适应的。
② 贝茨小姐:简·奥斯丁小说《爱玛》中的人物。
③ 海伯里:《爱玛》中的地名。

亲，带上简·菲尔费克斯和弗兰克·邱吉尔，还有整座包克斯山；然而我们却有可能——至少可以尝试一下——把摩尔·弗兰德斯扯出来。简·奥斯丁的小说比笛福的小说复杂得多，因为其中的人物都是相互依存的，还有复杂的情节。《爱玛》中的情节并不引人注目，而且贝茨小姐的作用也很小。尽管如此，情节还是有的，贝茨小姐是和主要人物联系在一起的，所以就如一块紧密编织的布料，其中任何东西都不能改动。贝茨小姐和爱玛都像是一片灌木丛中的两株灌木——不是像摩尔·弗兰德斯那样是一棵独立的树——而要想使灌木丛变稀疏的人都知道，如果把这两株灌木移到别处，它们会显得多么古怪，而且其余的那些灌木也会显得多么凌乱。在大多数小说中，人物是不能自顾自分散的。他们必须相互纠缠在一起。

现在，我们可以看到，小说家有许多混杂的材料需要处理。有故事，以及它的"后来呢……后来呢……"的时间顺序；还有奇闻逸事，他不仅可以用来讲故事，还可以讲一个非常好听的故事，但是，不，他宁愿讲他关于人的故事；他关注时间中的生活，也关注价值观中的生活。人物招之即来，但又难以驾驭。因为他们在许多方面和我们这样的人相对应，所以他们也竭力想过自己的生活，以致经常会和小说的主要意图相背离。他们会"逃离"，会"失控"；他们是创造物里的创造物[①]，经常和前者是不和谐的；如若给他们完

---

① 创造物里的创造物：意即小说（创造物）中的人物（创造物）。

全自由，他们会把小说踢碎，而若对他们管制太严，他们又会死气沉沉，使小说因为内部腐烂而完蛋。

这些考验也是剧作家要经受的，而且他还要应对另外一套材料——男演员和女演员，他们有时看来很服从所要扮演的角色，有时很服从整个剧本，但在大多数情况下他们是这两者的仇敌。他们造成的影响是不可估量的，这么一来我真不知道还有什么艺术作品可言。好在我们讨论的是一种较低级的艺术形式，不必为此担忧——不过，顺便说一下，难道舞台上的演出就一定比书房里的阅读更好？难道让一群自以为是、神经兮兮的男女来演一下就一定能加深我们对莎士比亚和契诃夫①的理解？

不，小说家也有够多的难题，我们今天就来考察一下小说家解决难题的两种手法——两种出自本能的手法，因为小说家的工作方式和我们考察他的作品时所用的方式是不太一样的。第一种手法是采用不同种类的人物。第二种手法和叙事角度有关。

一

我们可以把人物分为扁平的和圆形的。扁平人物在十七世纪被称作"幽默人物"，有时也被称为类型人物，或者漫

---

① 契诃夫：19世纪俄国小说家，还是重要的剧作家，尤其在20世纪初，其剧作曾风靡一时。

画人物。这种人物就其最单纯的形式而言，是围绕着某一种观念或者某一种品质而塑造的；如果他们身上出现不止一种要素，那我们就开始有一条趋向圆形的弧线了。真正的扁平人物可以用这样一句话来表明——"我绝不会抛弃米考伯先生。"这是米考伯太太——她说她不会抛弃米考伯先生①；她没有抛弃他，于是才有她。或者这样一句话："哪怕用诡计，我也一定要隐瞒我的主人家有多穷困。"这是《兰默摩尔的新娘》②中的凯莱布·巴尔德斯通。他说的不是实话，但这句话完整地表现了他；他除此之外什么都没有，没有快乐，没有那些必然会使大多数忠仆纠结在心的个人欲望和个人痛苦。他不论做什么，不论去哪里，不论说什么谎或者打碎什么盘子，就是为了隐瞒他的主人家有多穷困。这不是他的固定观念，因为在他身上根本没有什么观念可以固定。他就是个观念，而他过的这种生活则是从这个观念的边缘、从这个观念和出现在小说中的其他东西碰撞时发出的火花中散射出来的。或者以普鲁斯特为例。普鲁斯特的小说中有为数众多的扁平人物，譬如帕尔玛公爵夫人，或者勒格朗丹③，都可以分别用一句话来表明。公爵夫人的那句话是："我必须特别谨慎要待人友善。"她除了特别谨慎什么都没有，而其他那些比她复杂得多的人物很容易看穿她的友善，因为那只是

---

① 米考伯夫妇是狄更斯小说《大卫·科波菲尔》中的两个喜剧性人物。
② 《兰默摩尔的新娘》：19世纪英国小说家司各特的历史小说。
③ 帕尔玛公爵夫人：普鲁斯特《追忆似水年华》第三部中的一个次要人物。勒格朗丹：《追忆似水年华》第一部和第三部中的一个人物。

谨慎的副产品。

扁平人物最大的一个优点是他们不论何时出现都容易被辨认出来——是被读者的情感之眼辨认出来,不是视觉之眼,它只是注意到某个名字出现而已。在俄罗斯小说中,虽然扁平人物出现得那么少,但他们仍有极大帮助。他们不仅便于作者全力描写,还会对他非常有用,因为他们不需要多作介绍,既不会跑开,也不用加以发展,更不用为他们设置特定的氛围——就如一些固定尺寸的亮铮铮的小盘子,可以像筹码一样在空桌面上甚或在两个星球之间推来推去,非常令人满意。

第二个优点是他们容易被读者记住。他们留在读者心中而不会有变化,因为他们不为环境所改变;他们穿越各种环境,始终有一种令人愉悦的性质,而当创造出他们的作品或许也已经湮没之际,人们仍会记住他们。譬如,《埃文·哈林顿》① 中的伯爵夫人就是个小小的例子。我们来比较一下我们对这个人物的记忆和我们对蓓基·夏泼②的记忆。我们已不记得这位伯爵夫人做过什么事情或者有过什么经历。但清楚地记得她的那副模样和她所奉行的那个信条,即:"我们以亲爱的爸爸为荣,但我们必须隐瞒我们对他的怀念。"她所有的滑稽可笑都源于此。她是个扁平人物。蓓基·夏泼则是圆形的。她也一样追求名利,但却没法用一句话来概

---

① 《埃文·哈林顿》:19世纪英国小说家梅瑞狄斯的一部不太重要的小说。
② 蓓基·夏泼:19世纪英国小说家萨克雷的著名小说《名利场》中的女主人公,文学史上有名的典型人物。

括，我们是连同一些重要场面一起记住她的，因为她不仅出现在这些场面中，而且是由这些场面烘托出来的——也就是说，我们并不是那么轻易就记住她的，因为她时好时坏，而且像生活中的人一样有性格侧面。我们所有人，甚至不再天真的人，都渴望永恒，而天真的永恒正是艺术作品的主要诉求。我们都要求作品能持久，能成为庇护所，要求作品中的人物永远不变，扁平人物往往就是借此为自己辩护的。

同样不变的是批评家总是双眼紧盯着日常生活——就如我们上星期也是这样[①]——他们对这样表现人性几乎全都难以容忍。他们争辩说，既然维多利亚女王是不可能用一句话来概括的，那么米考伯太太为什么就能呢？我们的一位重要作家，诺曼·道格拉斯先生，就属于这种批评家，我将引用他的一段话来表明，他气势汹汹地提出了反对扁平人物的意见。这段话出现在他致 D. H. 劳伦斯的一封公开信中，当时他正和 D. H. 劳伦斯论战：两个骁勇善战的斗士相互攻击，其激烈程度使我们其余一些人觉得自己像是一群在楼台上观战的女士。他指责 D. H. 劳伦斯在一部为他们的一个共同朋友写的传记里使用"小说家笔法"歪曲了事实真相，接着他对"小说家笔法"作了这样的定义：

> 我想说，这是一种失败，一种在真实表现普通人性

[①] 上星期讲的是小说人物和现实生活的关系。参见前章"人物"。

的深奥与复杂时的失败，即出于文学的目的仅选择一个男人或一个女人的两三个特点，通常是他们性格中最显眼因而最"有用"的成分，其他一概不予理会。凡是和这几个精选出来的特点不相符的东西都被去掉了；而且必须去掉，否则人物描写就无法成立。诸如此类就是材料；和这些材料不相容的任何东西都要统统舍弃。所以，小说家笔法说起来时常道理十足，其实基于一个错误的前提；它只取它想要的而不顾其他。它所选的那几个方面就其自身来说或许是对的，但实在太少了；作者所说的或许是真的，但绝对不是全部真相。这就是小说家笔法。它歪曲了事实真相。

是啊，由此看来用小说家笔法来写传记确实很糟糕，因为没有一个人是简简单单的。但是，用它来写小说还是可以的：一部小说终究比较复杂，时常既需要圆形人物，又需要扁平人物，而两者撞在一起的结果，要比道格拉斯先生所说的更为确切地与生活相对应。狄更斯就是极好的例子。狄更斯的人物几乎全是扁平的（匹普[①]和大卫·科波菲尔试图成为圆形，但又那么战战兢兢，以至于他们似乎更像是两个气泡而不是实心球）。几乎每个人物都能用一句话来概括，但又如此奇妙地令人感觉到人性的深度。也许是狄更斯的巨大

[①] 匹普：狄更斯小说《远大前程》中的主人公。

活力使他的人物有所震动，故而他们借助于他的活力而显得各有各的活力。这是一种魔术手法；不论何时，我们只要去看看匹克威克先生①的边沿，就会发现他并不比一张唱片更厚。但我们从来不从边上看他。匹克威克先生真是太机灵、太老练了。他总有那种沉甸甸的意味，他被人塞进女子学校的衣橱时仿佛就像福斯塔夫在温莎被人装进洗衣筐里时一样重②。狄更斯的部分天才就在于他对类型人物和漫画人物③的运用，这些人物一出现我们就能一眼认出来，但产生的效果不是机械的④，而是并不肤浅的人性展示。不喜欢狄更斯的人有一个绝佳的理由。他本该写得很糟糕。而事实上，他却是我们的一个大作家，他用类型人物取得的巨大成功表明，扁平人物的潜力也许比那些苛刻的批评家所承认的要大得多。

或者以 H. G. 威尔斯为例。除了吉普斯⑤和《托诺-邦盖》中的那个姑妈可能是例外，威尔斯的所有人物都像照片一样扁平。但是那张照片被那么有力地摇晃着，以致我们忘了它令人眼花缭乱是表面的，只要把那张照片撕破或者卷起来，它就消失了。威尔斯的人物确实不能用一句话来概括；

---

① 匹克威克先生：狄更斯小说《匹克威克外传》中的主人公。
② 福斯塔夫：莎士比亚戏剧中多次出现的圆形人物。此句意为：匹克威克虽是扁平人物，但他给人的感觉就像圆形人物福斯塔夫一样有分量。
③ 类型人物和漫画人物：即扁平人物。
④ 机械的：意为反复出现。
⑤ 吉普斯：H. G. 威尔斯同名小说中的主人公。

他非常重视观察,他没有创造类型人物。但不管怎样,他的人物很少是靠自身力量动起来的。他们被作者的那双熟练而有力的手摇晃着,致使读者误以为他们很有深度。像威尔斯和狄更斯这种并不纯真的好小说家,都非常善于转送活力①。

在他们小说中,生动的部分带动了不生动的部分,从而使人物活跃起来,说话头头是道。他们和纯真的小说家完全不同,后者直接处理所有材料,似乎把他富有创造力的手指伸进了每一个句子和每一个词语。在这一方面,理查生②、笛福、简·奥斯丁就特别纯真;他们的作品也许并不伟大,但他们的手总是放在上面的;就是在按门铃和门铃响的瞬间,他们的人物也在他们的直接掌控之下。

由此我们必须承认,扁平人物就其自身来说不像圆形人物那样成效卓著,而且扁平人物只有作为喜剧人物时才是最好的。严肃的或者悲剧性的扁平人物总会令人厌烦。他每次出现都喊着"报仇!"或者"我的心在为人类而流血!"或者其他什么信条,我们的心却沉下去了。有一部出自一位颇受欢迎的当代作家之手的传奇小说是围绕着一个苏塞克斯农夫写的,那个农夫总说着:"我要种一点荆豆。"有这样的农夫,有这样的荆豆;他说他要种荆豆,他种了荆豆,但这和说"我绝不会抛弃米考伯先生"不一样,因为他的坚定不移

---

① 意即用作者的渲染力使人物显得生动。
② 理查生:塞缪尔·理查生,18世纪英国小说家,著有《克拉丽莎》《帕米拉》等。

会使我们厌烦，结果也就不想关心他到底有没有种荆豆了。如果他的信条是被斟酌过的，而且和人之常情有关，我们就不会那么厌烦，那信条也不再代表那个人而成了那个人的一种痴迷；也就是说，他就会从一个扁平的农夫变成一个圆形的农夫。不论时间长短，唯有圆形人物才适合担当悲剧角色，才能激起我们各种各样的情感反应，除了幽默感和分寸感。

现在，让我们抛开这些二维人物①，而且，在转向圆形人物途中，让我们到曼斯菲尔德庄园②去看看贝特兰夫人，她正抱着她的哈巴狗坐在沙发上。哈巴狗是扁平的，就如小说中的大多数动物一样。它就像是用纸板剪出来的③，有一次被写到闯进了玫瑰花坛，但也仅此一次，而在小说的大部分篇幅中，它的女主人似乎也是用同样简单的材料剪出来的，就像她的狗一样。贝特兰夫人的信条是"我心肠好，但就是不能劳累"，而且她实施了这一信条。但是结局却很悲惨。她的两个女儿招来了麻烦——奥斯丁小姐的世界里最严重的麻烦，比拿破仑战争还要严重。朱丽亚私奔；玛利亚婚姻不幸，和情人一起出走了。贝特兰夫人的反应如何？下面的词句说到她的反应，说得意味深长：

> 贝特兰夫人并不深思，但在托马斯爵士指点下，她

---

① 二维人物：即扁平人物。
② 曼斯菲尔德庄园：简·奥斯丁同名小说中的地名。
③ 意即扁平的。

还是恰当考虑了所有重点；所以，她明白发生了什么事情，看到了它的严重性，而且并不寻思积虑，也不和芬妮商量，想掩饰罪孽和丑行。

这些有力的字句曾使我很担心，因为我以为简·奥斯丁的道德感正在失控。她自己或许可以指控罪孽和丑行，而且也确实是这么做的，她及时使爱德蒙和芬妮心里产生各种可能有的焦虑，但她有权去干扰平静、安逸的贝特兰夫人吗？这不是就像在哈巴狗身上装上三个脑袋并派它去守卫地狱的大门①吗？这位夫人难道不应该继续坐在沙发上说着"朱丽亚和玛利亚的事情真是可怕，叫人伤心透了，可是芬妮到哪里去了？我又漏织了一针"吗？

我曾这样以为是我误解了简·奥斯丁的创作方式——就像司各特一样出于误解而恭维她是在一小块象牙上画画。她是个纤细画家，但她从来不是二维的。她的人物都是圆形的，或者是可以圆的。就是贝茨小姐也有头脑，就是伊丽莎白·艾略特②也有心思，认识到这一点，贝特兰夫人的道德热情也就不再使我们困惑了；那只小圆盘突然膨胀起来，变成了一个小圆球。当小说结束时，贝特兰夫人又回复到扁平，这是事实；她给人的主要印象可以用她的信条来概括。但是，那并非简·奥斯丁有意为之，所以，这个人物再度出

---

① 据希腊罗马神话，地狱门口由三头猛犬刻耳柏洛斯守卫。
② 伊丽莎白·艾略特：简·奥斯丁小说《劝导》中的人物。

现仍会有新鲜感。简·奥斯丁的人物每次出现总能给我们一点新的乐趣，就如狄更斯的人物正相反，仅仅给人一次次重复的乐趣，这是为什么？简·奥斯丁的人物都能那么好地组合在一次谈话中，而且好像并不有意要让这个人物引出那个人物，从不做作，这又是为什么？这个问题可以从几方面回答：可以说简·奥斯丁和狄更斯不同，是个真正的艺术家，她从不求之于夸张手法，等等。但最好的回答是，她的人物虽然比狄更斯的小，但却是高度组合的。他们全都有圆形功能，就是她的情节对他们有更多要求，他们依然可以胜任。假设路易莎·穆斯格罗夫在科布码头上摔断了脖子①。这样，写她的死当然会是柔弱而女人样的——因为奥斯丁小姐完全没有能力写激烈动作——但是，等尸体一运走，其他人却会有适当的反应，他们会使人看到他们性格的另一面。这样一来，《劝导》作为一部小说虽然已被删改，但我们对温特沃斯上校和安妮却会有更多了解。所有简·奥斯丁的人物都为一种更为广阔的生活、一种在她设计的小说里不大可能有的生活而准备的，这就是为什么他们能那么轻松如意地对付现有生活的原因所在。

我们回头再来看贝特兰夫人和那段关键词句。看看它是怎样微妙地从她的信条变换到一个信条不起作用的领域的。"贝特兰夫人并不深思。"正是，就如她的信条。"但在托马

---

① 路易莎·穆斯格罗夫：简·奥斯丁小说《劝导》中的人物，在小说中她只是在码头上略受了点伤。

斯爵士指点下,她还是恰当考虑了所有重点。"托马斯爵士的指点——这是信条的一部分——虽然一如既往,但它却把这位夫人推向了一个原本和她不相干、她也不愿关心的道德领域。"所以,她明白发生了什么事情,看到了它的严重性。"这是道德的最强音——非常强烈,但却是谨慎引入的。然后呢,是一个极为巧妙的渐弱音,具有否定意味。她"并不寻思积虑,也不和芬妮商量,想掩饰罪孽和丑行"。信条再次出现,因为作为一种准则,她总是尽量减轻烦恼,总是找芬妮商量她该怎么做,而芬妮在过去十年间也确实没有做过其他任何事情。虽然这是个否定句,但仍这样提醒我们,她的惯常状态再次呈现。总之在这段简短的词句中她先是被充气而变成圆形人物,继而又被放气而回复成扁平人物。简·奥斯丁多么能写!她寥寥数语就扩展了贝特兰夫人,同时又增强了玛利亚和朱丽亚私奔的可信性。我说"可信性"是因为私奔属于激烈动作,而我已经指出过,简·奥斯丁在这种地方是柔弱而女人样的。除了她早年求学时写的小说,她从不表现激烈场面。各种激烈事件都不得不置于"后台"——路易莎的意外受伤和玛丽安·达什伍德[①]的咽喉糜烂是两个最接近激烈事件的例外——因此,所有关于对私奔的议论都必须真诚而可信,否则我们就会怀疑是否真有其事。贝特兰夫人帮助我们相信她的两个女儿出走了,而且必

[①] 玛丽安·达什伍德:简·奥斯丁小说《理智与情感》中的人物。

须出走，否则芬妮就成不了理想人物。这是一小点、一小句而已，但它却表明一个伟大的小说家能多么微妙地把扁平人物调整为圆形人物。

在她的所有作品中，我们能看到这样的人物，表面上是简单而扁平的，从不需要多作解释，然而又从不失其深度——譬如，亨利·蒂尔尼、伍德豪斯先生、夏洛蒂·卢卡斯①。她也许会给她的人物贴上"理智""情感""傲慢""偏见"等标签，但他们并不局限于这些品性。

至于圆形人物本身，其实前面已经通过暗示下了定义，不需要再多说了。我需要做的仅仅是给出一些在我看来是圆形的小说人物作为实例，从而使定义进一步得到验证。

《战争与和平》中的所有主要人物、陀思妥耶夫斯基的所有人物、普鲁斯特的有些人物（譬如那个老仆人、盖尔芒特公爵夫人、夏吕斯先生和圣-卢②）、包法利夫人（她和摩尔·弗兰德斯一样，有一整部以她的名字命名的小说，因而她既可以彰显，又可以不被发觉地隐藏）、萨克雷的有些人物（譬如蓓基·夏泼和碧爱崔丽克斯③）、菲尔丁的有些人物（譬如亚当斯牧师④、汤姆·琼斯），还有夏洛蒂·勃朗特的

---

① 亨利·蒂尔尼：简·奥斯丁小说《诺桑觉寺》中的人物。伍德豪斯先生：简·奥斯丁小说《爱玛》中的人物。夏洛蒂·卢卡斯：简·奥斯丁小说《傲慢与偏见》中的人物。
② 那个老仆人、盖尔芒特公爵夫人、夏吕斯先生和圣-卢：均是普鲁斯特小说《追忆似水年华》中的人物。
③ 碧爱崔丽克斯：萨克雷小说《亨利·艾斯芒德的历史》的女主人公。
④ 亚当斯牧师：菲尔丁小说《约瑟夫·安德鲁斯》中的主要人物。

有些人物（特别是露西·斯诺①），都是圆形人物（还有很多——这儿不必罗列）。验证圆形人物即看他是否能以一种可信的方式使人感到意外。如果从不使人感到意外，就是扁平人物。如果是不可信的，就是伪装成圆形的扁平人物。圆形人物的生活——当然是一部小说内的生活——是难以预料的。小说家有时单独使用这种人物，但更多是和另一种人物组合使用，以此完成他的协调工作，使作品中的人和作品的其他方面和谐一致。

二

现在，来看第二种手法：讲故事采用的角度。对有些批评家来说，这是基本手法。

> 就小说技巧而言，在整个复杂的方法问题中，（珀西·卢伯克②先生说），我认为最重要的是角度问题——即关系到讲故事的人能否把故事继续讲下去的问题。

他在《小说的技巧》一书中富有智慧和见识地考察了各种角度。他说，小说家既可以作为一个不偏不倚或者偏心十

---

① 露西·斯诺：夏洛蒂·勃朗特小说《维莱特》中的女主人公。
② 珀西·卢伯克：20世纪初英国小说理论家。

足的旁观者，从外部讲述人物；也可以自认为无所不知，从内部讲述他们；还可以站在其中一人的立场上，佯装对其他人的动机浑然不知；或者，采用某种中介人的姿态。

追随他的那些人想为小说美学设定一个稳固的基础，一个我一刻也不能同意的基础。这是个草率的考察，因为在我看来，解决整个复杂的方法问题不是把它分解为几个公式，而是要关注作者挑动读者使其信以为真的能力，一种卢伯克先生承认而且赞赏的能力，只是他把它放在问题的边缘而非中心位置。我将把它重重地放在中心位置。看看狄更斯在《荒凉山庄》中是怎样挑动我们的。《荒凉山庄》第一章是无所不知的。狄更斯把我们带到大法官的法庭上而且快速介绍了那里所有的人。在第二章里，他是偏袒地无所不知。我们仍旧用他的目光在看，但不知出于什么原因，他的目光开始变得暗淡：他可以把累斯特·德洛克爵士介绍给我们，同时只介绍德洛克夫人的部分而不是全部，一点也不介绍图金霍恩先生。在第三章里，他甚至更加可受谴责：他直接越过戏剧方式①而附在一位年轻女士——即埃斯特·萨默森——身上说话。"我刚开始写我的这部分时困难重重，因为我知道我并不聪明。"埃斯特传话说，而且只要她被允许握着笔，她就用这种笔调持续不断地、理所当然地继续写下去。她的作者在任何时候都可能把笔从她那里夺过来，洋洋洒洒地写

---

① 戏剧方式：此处意即旁观者角度。

他自己要写的东西,让她坐在天知道的什么地方,忙着我们不关心的什么事情。按理说,《荒凉山庄》是支离破碎的,但狄更斯挑动了我们,以至于我们并不在乎角度的混乱。

批评家比读者更容易提出非议。他们热衷于抬高小说的地位,又不太容易看出那些对小说来说是特有的问题,不太容易把小说和戏剧区分开来;他们觉得在小说成为一门独立的艺术之前是应该有其自身的技术难题的;而由于角度问题确实是小说特有的,他们还有点过分强调这个问题。就我来说,我认为这个问题没有人物的适当混合那么重要——那是剧作家也要面对的一个问题。小说家必须挑动我们;那才是至关重要的。让我们来看看转换角度的另外两个实例。

法国著名作家安德烈·纪德出版过一部名为《伪币制造者》的小说,关于这部小说我们在下星期将予以详说:这虽是一部极具现代性的小说,但有一个方面却和《荒凉山庄》是相同的,即:逻辑上全都支离破碎。作者时而无所不知:他解释每一件事情,他站在后面,"判定每一个人物"[①];时而他的无所不知又是片面的;还有,他既是戏剧性的,同时又通过一个人物的日记来讲述故事。同样是不讲角度,但在狄更斯那里是无意识的,在纪德那里却是有意为之;他不厌其烦地故意跳来跳去。小说家若对自己的方法太感兴趣,那么除了兴趣就不会有什么了;他放弃了人物塑造,命令我们

---

① 原文为法文。

去帮助他分析自己的心理，结果是令人热情大减。《伪币制造者》就是最近出版的一部对自己更感兴趣的作品；不是那种充满活力的作品；把它当作一种编织物我们固然会非常佩服它，但是实在没法毫无保留地称赞它。

作为第二个实例，我们要再次来看看《战争与和平》。这儿的结果是活力大增：我们被挑动到了俄罗斯各地——这里那里，这时那时，有无所不知角度，有半无所不知角度，还有戏剧化角度——最后，我们全都接受了。卢伯克先生不会接受，确实不会：他虽然也觉得这部作品很了不起，但这部作品如果只用一个角度的话，他会觉得更加了不起；他觉得托尔斯泰没有发挥全部才能。我觉得写作的游戏规则并不在于角度。只要有效，小说家可以转换角度，它在狄更斯和托尔斯泰那里就是有效的。实际上，这种扩展和收缩感知范围的能力（转换角度就是它的一种征兆），这种暂停认知的权利——我觉得还体现了小说的一大优势，因为这和我们在生活中的感知是相对应的。我们有时会比别人愚蠢一点；我们有时会了解别人的想法，但并不总能这样，因为我们的头脑会疲倦；这种时断时续从长远来看会使我们的经历变得多样和多彩。所以，有不少小说家，尤其是英国小说家，在小说中就这样对待他们的人物：表现他们时既紧凑又松弛①。我不明白为什么他们要受到指责。

---

① 紧凑：即指同一角度。松弛：即指转换角度。

如果他们这么做时被我们当场察觉,那他们必须受到指责。这是理所当然的,而且会引出另一个问题:作者可以把他关于人物的设计通盘告诉读者吗?答案其实在前面已有所暗示:最好不要。因为这很危险,通常会使读者热情大减,心不在焉,甚至会觉得滑稽可笑,好像受到友好邀请到后台去看看那些木偶是怎样挂起来的。"木偶 A 看上去不错吧——她一直是我最喜欢的。""请考虑一下,木偶 B 为什么要那么做——也许是他内心要比表面丰富得多——是的,看——他有一颗金子般的心——连这个都给你们看过了,我就把他放回去吧——我不想让人再注意到他。""还有木偶 C——他这个人总是神秘兮兮的。"亲近感是有了,但代价是幻觉与庄重感的丧失。这就像是拉一个人去喝酒,好叫他不批评你的意见。这就是对受人尊敬的菲尔丁和萨克雷来说,也是毁灭性的,这是酒吧间里的亲密聊天,对以往的小说来说没有比这更有害了。不过,把关于小说背景的设计通盘告诉读者却是另一回事。这没有危险,小说家仍可以和人物拉开距离[①],就如哈代和康拉德所做的那样,而且仍可以使他所设想的生活环境具有普遍意义。有害的是把关于人物的设计直接告诉读者,因为这会使读者离开人物去注意小说家的想法。而在这种时候,从小说家的想法中是没什么东西可发

[①] 小说家和人物拉开距离:意即小说家不可把他设计人物的意图直接告诉读者,而是要通过人物间接地使读者领悟他的意图。

现的,因为它根本不在创作状态①:就是"过来,我们聊聊"这句话使它冷却了。

我们对人物的讨论到此必须结束了。等后面讨论情节时,我们也许还会有所补充。

---

① 不在创作状态:意即没有用人物去面对读者。

第五章　情　节

亚里士多德说:"性格给予我们品质,而我们是幸福的还是相反,则在于行为——即我们怎么做。"① 我们早已断定亚里士多德是错的,所以我们现在必须面对不同意他的后果。"人的幸福与不幸,"亚里士多德说,"全都取决于行为。"② 我们比他知道得多。我们相信幸福与不幸存在于我们每个人在私下里的隐秘生活③,而小说家(在他的人物身上)所进入的就是这种生活。我们这里说的秘密生活是指那种完全没有外在迹象的生活,即一般认为的,不会因为偶尔一句话或一声叹息而被泄露的生活。偶尔一句话或一声叹息就是迹象,既可能是做讲座的迹象,也可能是想杀人的迹象;反

---

①　引自亚里士多德《诗学》第六章。中译亚里士多德《诗学》(罗念生译,中国戏剧出版社,1986)的译文是:"剧中人物的品质是由他们的'性格'决定的,而他们的幸福与不幸,则取决于他们的行动。"
②　同上,引自亚里士多德《诗学》第六章。中译亚里士多德《诗学》的译文是:"幸福与不幸系于行动。"
③　隐秘生活:即内心世界。现代心理学揭示,幸福感与不幸感并不取决于人的外部行为,而是取决于人的内心感受,因为同样的行为对不同的人来说会有不同甚至相反的感受。

正,这种生活一旦泄露就不隐秘了,就进入了行为领域。

不过,我们没有理由责备亚里士多德。他从未读过小说①,更不用说现代小说了——他读的是《奥德修纪》,不是《尤利西斯》②——他生性不喜欢隐秘事物,实际上他把人的心灵看得就像洗澡盆一样,不管里面有什么东西,最终都是可以拿出来看的;再说他写上面那句话,是针对戏剧的,那无疑是对的。在戏剧中,所有人的幸福与不幸必须取决于行为。否则的话,幸福与不幸的存在都无法为人知晓,这就是戏剧与小说的巨大区别。

小说的特别之处就是作者既可以谈论他的人物,也可以透视他们,还可以让我们听到他们的自言自语。他进入人物的思想,甚至还可以进一步深入而窥探他们的潜意识。人说到自己不会完全说真话——甚至对自己也是这样;他隐秘感觉到的幸福与不幸,其原因连他自己也说不清楚,因为一旦他把它们提升到讲得清楚的层次时,它们就失去了原来的性质。对此,小说家有个真正的方便之处。他可以把潜意识直截了当地表现为动作(剧作家也可以这么做);他还可以用与此相关的独白加以表现。他支配整个隐秘生活,而且要保证自己的特权不被剥夺。"作者怎么知道这个?"时而有人说。"他的立足点在哪里?他不连贯,他从有限角度转为全

---

① 一般认为,小说(novel)产生于18世纪。
② 《奥德修纪》:荷马史诗之一。《尤利西斯》:英国现代小说家詹姆斯·乔伊斯所著意识流小说,尤利西斯即奥德修斯,这部小说的人物和结构都有意模仿《奥德修纪》。

知角度，现在又慢慢地在转回来。"诸如此类的问题都具有太多法庭审判的意味。然而读者所关心的只是角度转变和隐秘生活是否可信，是否真的 πιθανσν①，这是亚里士多德最喜欢的词，而随着这个词在他耳边回响，他便退休了。

但是，他却给我们留下了难题，因为随着人性的展现，到底是什么东西变成了情节？在大部分文学作品中有两个要素，即我们刚刚讨论过的人物和笼而统之所称的艺术。关于艺术，我们也谈到过了，只不过是一种非常低级的形式——故事，即一定长度的时间绦虫。现在，我们要来讨论比较高级的一面——情节；因为就情节而言，譬如在戏剧中，人物或多或少是服从情节需要的，但在小说中则不然，人物众多，虚幻而难以驾驭，就像冰山一样四分之三隐藏在水下。这表明，把亚里士多德的三段论用于这些难以应付的人物，想以此清晰地说明他们之间矛盾的产生、激化和解决过程是徒劳的。少数几个或许适用，那是因为本该是一个剧本的被写成了一部小说。但是普遍没有反应。他们要求分开坐而且各有所思或者有什么事，因而情节（我把它视为某种上级官员）对他们缺乏公共精神感到担忧："这样不行，"它似乎在说，"个人主义确实是最可贵的品质；实际上我的职位也是以众多个人为基础的；我从来就无条件地承认。但不管怎么说，还是有某些限制的，而那些限制现在正在被打破。那些

---

① Πιθανσν：（希腊文）可信。

人物各有所思绝不能太久,他们绝不能浪费时间,在自己心里的那座楼梯上跑上跑下,他们必须有所贡献,否则更高利益就会受到损害。"那句话听来多么熟悉——"对情节有所贡献"!这是戏剧人物所做的贡献,而且是必需的;那么,小说人物有没有必要呢?

让我们对情节作一定义。我们已经把故事定义为按时序对事件所作的叙述。情节也是对事件的叙述,只是重点放在因果关系上。"国王死了,后来王后也死了"是故事。"国王死了,后来王后因为伤心过度也死了"是情节。时序虽被保留,但因果关系把它掩盖了。或者说:"王后死了,谁也不知道什么原因,直到后来才发现是因为国王死后她伤心过度。"这是个有点神奇的情节,一种得到高度发展的形式。它取消了时序,它最大限度地有别于故事。想一想王后的死。如果是个故事,我们会说:"后来呢?"如果是个情节,我们会问:"为什么?"这就是小说的这两个面之间的根本区别。对打着哈欠的洞穴人,或者对暴虐的苏丹①,或者对他们的现代后裔电影观众,是不能讲情节的。他们只能用"后来呢——后来呢——"来保持清醒。他们只有好奇心。但情节需要的是智力和记忆力。

好奇是人类的一种最低级本能。在日常生活中你会注意到,当人们好奇地寻问时总是毫无记性而且往往愚蠢到极

---

① 苏丹:阿拉伯国王的称呼。此处指《一千零一夜》里那个喜欢听故事的国王。

点。一个刚认识你就问你有几个兄弟姐妹的人肯定不是一个有情有义的人,因为不到一年后你再碰到他时他很可能还会问你有几个兄弟姐妹,他的嘴还会张得老大,眼睛还会瞪得像要暴出来似的。和这样的人交朋友是很难的,而两个这样好奇的人要交朋友是绝对不可能的。仅仅因为好奇不会使我们得到什么,也不会使我们深入小说——至多看看故事而已。如果想要掌握情节,我们必须要有智力和记忆力才行。

先说智力。和只有好奇心、只想知道后来怎样的读者不同,有智力的读者用心对待情节。他从两个角度看一段情节:单独看,和把它跟前面读到的东西联系在一起看。他也许没有理解这段情节,但他并不指望自己一看就懂。一部结构严密的小说(如《利己主义者》),其中的事物往往具有交叉对应的性质,一般读者要到最后才有一定高度,才有可能适当地看待这些事物。情节中的这种令人惊奇或者令人觉得神奇的因素——时常也被颇为空洞地称为侦探因素——具有极大的重要性。它是由于取消了时序才出现的;一个神奇事物就是一个时间中的一个口袋①,现在它赤裸裸地出现在像"王后为什么会死?"这句话中,还比较隐蔽地出现在令人似懂非懂的举止和言语中,其真正含义只有读下去才能明白。神奇是情节的本质所在,如果没有智力,是难以欣赏的。对好奇心来说,这不过是又一个"后来怎样"。要欣赏神奇

---

① 意为时间中隐藏着神秘。

事物，部分心力要退后，要沉思，同时把另一部分心力发挥出来①。

这就是我们要说的第二个条件：记忆力。

记忆力和智力是密切相关的，因为我们非得记住才能理解。如果王后死了，我们把国王的死忘了，那我们永远也弄不清楚王后的死因。编出情节的人②希望我们有记性，我们希望他不要草草收场。情节中的每个动作或每个词语都应该是有用的；应该是简洁明快的；就是复杂情节也应该是有条有理的，不能漫无头绪。它可以是难懂的或者易懂的，可以而且应该具有神奇因素，但不应该误导读者。当它展开时，读者的记忆力便会盘旋在它上面（有了这种半暗半明的心力才会有智力的闪亮锋芒），若看到新的线索、新的因果关系，它便会不断加以重组和复审；所以最后感觉到的（如果这是个好的情节的话）却不仅仅是一些线索或者因果关系，而是某种具有审美价值的组合物，某种本可以由小说家直接交代、但直接交代不会有美感的东西。我们在这里遇到了美——这是我们开讲以来第一次：因为美从来不是小说家追求的目标，虽然他不达成美会导致失败。我稍后会把美神安排到适合她的地方。同时还要恭请她参与一段完整的情节。她在这里看上去有点受惊，不过她是应该看上去有点受惊的；这种表情和她的面孔最为相称，就如波提切利在画她从

---

① 部分心力：指注意力。另一部分心力：指记忆力。
② 编出情节的人：指小说家。

风与花之间、从波浪中诞生时①所知道的那样。看上去毫不受惊的美神，不慌不忙赫然登台的美神——这会使我们觉得她太像一名首席女高音。

不过，还是让我们回头来谈情节吧，我们将以乔治·梅瑞狄斯为例。

梅瑞狄斯的名声已不如二三十年前了，那时大半个世界和整个剑桥都为之震动。我记得我曾读到他的一行诗而多么深感压抑——"我们活着不为利剑便是木柴"②。我不想二选一，但我知道我不是利剑。后来好像也没有真的使我压抑，因为时到今日，梅瑞狄斯自己也颇像在水槽里沉浮，虽然时尚会转变而把他抬高一点，但随便怎样也不会再像一九〇〇年前后那样成为精神力量了。他的哲学经不起时间考验。他对感伤情调的那种猛烈抨击使现在这一代人感到厌烦，他们虽然和他目标一致，但装备要精良得多，而且往往怀疑使用老式装备的人自己就是感伤主义者。还有他对自然景物的描绘也不像哈代那样有持久的吸引力，他总是写萨里郡的景物，而且写得既空洞又花哨。他写不出《还乡》第一章，就如包克斯山不会出现在索尔兹伯里平原上③。他看不出什么

---

① 波提切利：意大利文艺复兴时期大画家。此处说到的是他的名作《维纳斯的诞生》。

② 此诗句原文是 "We breathe but to be sword or block."，引自梅瑞狄斯 "The Thrush in February" 一诗。

③ 《还乡》：哈代的小说，其第一章中的景物描写堪称经典。包克斯山：位于萨里郡，梅瑞狄斯后半生即定居于此郡。索尔兹伯里平原：位于威尔特郡南端，哈代小说常以此为背景。

是英格兰景物中真正具有悲剧意味和永久意味的东西,也看不出什么是生活中真正的悲剧。当他想显得严肃而高尚时,总会发出一种特别刺耳的弦外音,一种咄咄逼人的腔调。实际上,我觉得他在某一方面和丁尼生①很相像,就是没能心平气和地应对自己的内在情绪。他小说中的社会价值观大多是虚假的。裁缝不像裁缝,板球比赛不像板球比赛,甚至火车都不像是火车,乡镇人家好像是临时拆封的,几乎没有什么准备就匆匆上场,胡子上还沾着草屑。这确实很古怪,他的人物就是安置在这样的社会场景中的;其中的原因部分是他的幻想,这本没有错,但还有部分原因是他肆无忌惮地伪造,那就错了。正是由于伪造,正是由于说教,他的小说其实是不可接受的,现在说来就是虚假不实的;正是由于把伦敦周围的几个郡当作全世界,所以毫不足怪,梅瑞狄斯现在躺在水槽里。然而,他在一个方面却是个了不起的小说家。他是英国小说界迄今最好的情节设计师,任何谈论情节问题的人都必须对他表示敬意。

梅瑞狄斯的情节并不紧凑。我们无法像概括《远大前程》②那样用一句话来概括《哈利·里奇蒙》③的主要情节,尽管这两部小说讲的都是一个年轻人错失发财机会。梅瑞狄斯式的情节既不是悲剧艺术也不是喜剧艺术的殿堂,而是像

---

① 丁尼生:19世纪英国桂冠诗人。
② 《远大前程》:狄更斯的长篇小说。
③ 《哈利·里奇蒙》:梅瑞狄斯的长篇小说。

一连串精心建筑在林地山坡上的凉亭,他的人物由于各自的原因来到这些凉亭,并由此而呈现出他们各自的面貌。事情都出自他们的性格,其后又改变他们的性格。人物与事件被紧密地联系在一起,而他能做到这一点所凭借的就是这些情节设计。它们通常是轻松愉快的,有时很感人,但总是出人意料的。这种震惊,接着又觉得"哦,那很有道理",表明情节设计得很完美;人物若要真实,就应该表现得很平常,但情节却应该出人意料。《比彻姆的事业》①中的施雷普内尔医生遭鞭打就很出人意料。我们知道埃弗拉德·罗姆弗莱肯定不会喜欢施雷普内尔,肯定会厌恶和误解他的激进思想,而且会嫉恨他对比彻姆的影响;我们还看到他对罗萨蒙的误解不断加深,看到塞西尔·巴斯克莱特的阴谋诡计。就人物来说,梅瑞狄斯是在桌面上打他的牌,但一有意外发生,他就会给我们、也给人物一个怎样的震惊!一个老人出于最高尚的动机鞭打另一个老人——这件令人啼笑皆非的事情不仅反映了他们的那个世界,同时还改变了小说中所有的重要人物。但这不是《比彻姆的事业》的核心事件,实际上这部小说根本没有核心事件。这本质上是一种情节设计,是一扇门,通过这扇门使小说得以继续,得以用不同形式予以表现。小说行将结束时,比彻姆溺水而亡,施雷普内尔和罗姆弗莱在他的尸体前言归于好,这里有一种意图,想把情节提

---

① 《比彻姆的事业》:梅瑞狄斯的长篇小说。

升为亚里士多德式的对称形式,想把小说变为一个宽容与和解的殿堂。但梅瑞狄斯在这里失败了:《比彻姆的事业》终究只是一系列情节设计(就如设计到法国去旅游一样),只是出于人物和反映人物的情节设计而已。

现在来简短说明一下情节——即"王后死了,后来发现她死于伤心过度"这个公式中的神奇因素。我想举一实例,不是狄更斯(尽管《远大前程》提供了很好的一例),也不是柯南·道尔①(我的古板使我无法欣赏他的小说),而仍是梅瑞狄斯:从《利己主义者》的精彩情节中举一个有关隐秘情感的例子:它发生在人物利蒂希娅·戴尔身上。

一开始,我们就被告知利蒂希娅心里所想的一切。威洛比爵士两次抛弃她,她很悲伤,认命了。这之后,出于戏剧化原因,她的想法被隐瞒了,不让我们知道,这是很自然的发展,但是到了那关键的午夜一幕,她的想法再次出现,这时威洛比爵士向她求婚,因为他对克拉拉没有把握,而这时,利蒂希娅已变成另一个女人,她说"不"。梅瑞狄斯隐瞒了她的变化。如果让我们对此始终了解,就会有损他的高雅喜剧②。威洛比爵士非得遭受一系列打击,非得顾此失彼,结果发现每件事情都摇摇晃晃。如果我们事先就看到作者正在布置陷阱,我们就不会觉得有趣,事实上还会觉得无聊,

---

① 柯南·道尔:19世纪英国小说家,著有《福尔摩斯探案集》等。
② 高雅喜剧:high comedy,以优雅和机智为特点的喜剧,与以滑稽和搞笑为特点的低俗喜剧(low comedy)相对。

所以利蒂希娅的变得冷漠就被隐瞒了,不让我们知道。这是无数不是有损人物就是有损情节的实例之一,在这儿,梅瑞狄斯出于明确的理由让情节获胜。

作为一个错误获胜的实例,我想到的是夏洛蒂·勃朗特在《维莱特》中的一个过失——一个过失而已。她让露西·斯诺对读者隐瞒了她的发现,即约翰博士就是她早年的玩伴格雷厄姆。当知道真相时,我们确实得到了一次不错的情节震撼,但露西的性格却为此付出了太多代价。在此之前,她一直给人诚实的印象,而且可以说,她一直承担着一种把她知道的一切如实言讲的道德义务。她也有事情瞒着不讲,虽然只是小事一桩,并不会永久损害她的形象,但总有点令人难过。

有时情节获胜获得太彻底。人物不得不一次次地暂停其个性表现,甚至不可抗拒地被一扫而光,以至他们在我们心目中的真实性大为减弱。这方面的实例,我们可以在一个比梅瑞狄斯伟大得多、但作为小说家并不怎么成功的作家那里找到,那就是托马斯·哈代。在我看来,哈代本质上是个诗人,他在一个极高的高度上构思他的小说。它们要成为悲剧或悲喜剧,它们在呈现时要发出锤击声[①];换句话说,哈代叙述事件是以因果关系为重点的,基本构想的是情节,人物都要服从情节的需要。除了苔丝这个人物(她给人的感觉是

---

① 锤击声:喻命运之神的叩门声。

她能胜过天意),哈代的作品在这方面是不能令人满意的。他的人物都置身于各种各样的罗网,他们最后都被缚住了手脚,这里不断强调的就是命运,然而就所有这些命运的牺牲者来说,我们却从未看到我们在《安提戈涅》《蓓蕾妮丝》或《樱桃园》①中看到的那种活生生的行为。高悬于我们之上的命运,不是在我们身上起作用的命运——那就是威塞克斯小说②中显赫而令人难忘的东西。还有艾格顿荒原③,游苔莎·斐伊④还未站在那里。还有林地⑤,还没有林地居民。还有丘陵旁边的巴德茅斯·里吉斯⑥和那里的公主们,仍在睡梦中,但会在晨光中驱车穿过丘陵。哈代写《列王》⑦(他在那里采用了另一种文学样式)是完全成功的,在那里,可听见锤击声,人物尽管挣扎,但被因与果紧紧绑住,因为他们已经和情节完全联系在了一起。但是在哈代的小说中,虽然同样有庄严而可怕的机制⑧在起作用,但它却从未紧扣人性,在《无名的裘德》的不幸遭遇中,有些至关重要的问题都没

---

① 《安提戈涅》:古希腊悲剧家索福克勒斯的作品。《蓓蕾妮丝》:17世纪法国古典主义悲剧作家拉辛的作品。《樱桃园》:19世纪俄罗斯作家契诃夫的戏剧作品。
② 威塞克斯小说:哈代主要作品的总称,因都以虚构的"威塞克斯"为故事的发生地。
③ 艾格顿荒原:哈代小说《还乡》中虚构的地名。
④ 游苔莎·斐伊:《还乡》中的女主人公。
⑤ 指哈代小说《林地居民》中的林地。
⑥ 巴德茅斯·里吉斯:哈代多部小说(如《还乡》《在绿荫下》和《号兵长》等)中的一个海边小镇。
⑦ 《列王》:哈代的诗剧。
⑧ 庄严而可怕的机制:即悲剧机制。

有得到回答，有些甚至都没有提出来。换句话说，那些人物为了情节需要而付出了太大代价；他们除了还有点乡土气息，全部活力都被耗尽，变得枯萎而干瘪。在我看来，这是哈代所有小说的通病，即：他对因果关系的强调超出了这种文学样式所能承受的限度。作为诗人、预言家和观察者，他是乔治·梅瑞狄斯无法与之比拟的——相比之下，梅瑞狄斯只是个乡村歌手——但是梅瑞狄斯知道小说的限度，知道在哪里情节可以要求人物做出贡献，在哪里情节必须让人物发挥其自身作用。至于谁是谁非——哦，我看不出谁是谁非，只是因为哈代的作品是我非常熟悉的，梅瑞狄斯的作品就不能这么说：反正本讲座即使说到谁是谁非，也不是亚里士多德赞成的那种谁是谁非①。在小说中，人的幸福与不幸并不全都取决于行为方式，除了情节，小说还寻求其他表现手段，它绝对不是单一途径的。

在情节与人物进行的这场失利的争斗中，情节时常会卑劣地予以报复。几乎所有小说到最后都是疲乏无力的。这是因为情节需要有头有尾。为什么必须这样？为什么小说家不被允许想要停笔就停笔？是啊，他必须要有收场，而这时人物通常是要死的，所以我们对他们的最后印象就是他们的死。在这方面，《威克菲尔牧师传》②就是个典型的例子，小

---

① 亚里士多德赞成的那种谁是谁非：即指前文所引亚里士多德所说："人的幸福与不幸全都取决于行为方式。"在小说中，也就是情节（有因果关系的行为）是最重要的。
② 《威克菲尔牧师传》：18世纪英国作家哥尔斯密的自传体小说。

说前半部分那样机智和清新,把一家人都描绘出来,还把普里姆罗斯夫人描绘得像维纳斯,但到了后面却是那样呆板和低能。前面因其自身缘故而出现的事件和人物此时都不得不为小说收场作自我奉献。在结尾处连作者自己也觉得有点傻。"我写不下去了,"他说,"因为我没有好好想过,那些巧合虽然每天都有,但并不会使我们感到惊奇,除非有什么特别的事情。"哥尔斯密当然只是个轻量级小说家,但大多数小说都是在这里受挫的——只要由逻辑取代血肉①来发号施令,就会有这种灾难性搁浅。如果不用死亡和结婚,我真不知道一般小说家还能用什么来结束小说。死亡和结婚几乎是他用来联系人物和情节的唯一纽带,而读者也作好了准备在这里和他相会,如果它们后来在小说中出现,就像书呆子似的看待它们;作家啊,可怜的家伙,总得允许他有个收场吧,他和其他人一样也要谋生,所以并不惊讶什么都听不到,只听见敲锤子、拧螺丝的声音。

概括地说,这是小说的先天缺陷:总是草草收场。其中原因有二:第一是小说家精力不济,他和所有劳力者一样有这种危险;第二就是我们已经开始讨论的那个难题:人物渐渐失去控制,渐渐有了自己的基础而且倾向于以此构筑未来。此时,小说家为了能使小说如期完工,就不得不自行其是了。他装得好像那些人物一直是由他控制的。他继续提到

---

① 逻辑取代血肉:意为情节(因果关系)取代人物。

他们的名字，继续使用双引号①。但是那些人物却已经走了或者死了。

所以说，情节就是小说中合乎逻辑和理性的一面；它需要有神奇感，但神奇的东西到后来总要被揭穿的；读者或许可以在虚幻世界里游荡，但小说家却是毫无疑惑的。他很胜任，他居于他的作品之上，在这儿投下一束光，在那儿抛下一顶无形的帽子，而且（作为情节编造者的他）不断和作为人物制造者的自己协商，以求达到最佳效果。他预先规划好了他的作品；或者说，不管怎样也是居于他的作品之上的，他对因与果的兴趣使他有一种预定论的意味。

现在，我们必须问自己，对于小说来说，这样构想出来的东西有没有可能就是最好的。我们终究要问，为什么小说要有规划？它不可以自然产生吗？为什么小说要像戏剧一样需要收场？它不可以不收场吗？小说家总是居于作品之上控制着作品，为什么他不可以投入作品之中随机寻找一些他未曾预见的目标？情节很动人，也许还很美，但那不是从戏剧那里、从空间有限的舞台上借来的一种摆设物吗？为什么小说结构不可以不那么逻辑化而更符合小说自身的特征？

现代派作家说可以，下面我们就来看一看最近的一个实例：一次对我们所定义的情节的猛烈袭击，一种想用其他东西取代情节的积极尝试。

---

① 继续使用双引号：意为继续写人物对话。

我已经说到过这部小说：安德烈·纪德的《伪币制造者》。它的内容中含有两种方式。因为纪德把他在写这部小说时所写的日记夹在小说中一起出版了，而且没有理由说他为什么将来不可以把他重读这部小说和这些日记时的感想也夹在其中再出版一次，即在将来完成一种更为玄妙的综合，日记、小说和感想相互交织在一起。他对于这个大杂烩实际上比一个作者应有的认真还要认真，而且就是因为被认为是大杂烩，这部小说更加令人感兴趣，还受到了批评家的悉心研究。

首先，我们看到在《伪币制造者》中有一种我们正在探讨的那种合乎逻辑客观性的情节——或者说，有几组情节片段。主要片段讲的是一个叫奥列维的年轻人——一个有趣、动人和可爱的人物，他先是错失幸福，后来在小说精心设计的结局又重获幸福；还给人以幸福。这个情节片断，如果允许我用陈腐套话来说，可说是妙笔生辉、活力非凡，是俗套情节方面的成功之作。但它绝对不是这部小说的核心。其他逻辑片段①也不是——譬如写到奥列维的弟弟、中学生乔治，他不仅使用伪币，还是导致一个同学自杀的推手。（关于这一片断，纪德在他的日记中向我们交代了它的来源：他是根据一个想在书摊上偷书而被他抓住的男孩构思乔治形象的，还有根据在鲁昂被抓的那个制造伪币的团伙，以及发生在克

---

① 逻辑片段：即情节片段。

莱蒙费朗的未成年人自杀事件,等等。)无论是奥列维、乔治,还是另一个弟弟文桑和他们的朋友裴奈尔,都不是这部小说的核心。那么,我们通过爱德华来接近核心。爱德华是个小说家。他和纪德的关系就像克里索德和威尔斯①的关系。大概就是这样,我只能这么说。他和纪德一样,也在写日记,和纪德一样,他也在写一部叫《伪币制造者》的小说,而且和克里索德一样,他也被否认是作者本人。爱德华的日记是全部印出的。它开始于情节片段之前,在它们之间继续,形式上是纪德这部小说的主干。但爱德华不仅仅是个记录者。他还是一个人物;实际上就是他救了奥列维又被奥列维所救;我们离开这两个人物时他们都很幸福。

不过,这仍然不是核心。最接近核心的是一场关于小说艺术的讨论。爱德华在他的秘书裴奈尔和几个朋友面前大发议论。他说生活的真实和小说的真实不是同一回事,然后他又说,他要写一部同时具有这两种真实的小说。

"那么主题是什么?"莎弗洛尼斯卡问。

"没有主题,"爱德华厉声说,"我的小说没有主题。当然,这听上去很愚蠢。让我们这么说吧,如果你们愿意听,它不会有'一个'主题……不会是自然主义流

---

① 克里索德:英国小说家 H. G. 威尔斯的小说《威廉·克里索德的世界》中的主人公。

派①惯常所说的'生活的一个切片'。这个流派的错误就在于总是在同一方向,总是纵向的,在时间方向上切取切片。为什么不上上下下一起切?或者横向切?至于我,我根本就不想切。你们懂我的意思。我要把所有东西都放进我的小说,而不是这里那里地截取素材。我已经考虑了一年,没有什么东西是我不可以放进去的:我所看到的、我所知道的、我从其他人的生活和我自己的生活中所学到的,都可以放进去。"

"可怜的人啊,你会把读者闷死的。"萝拉大声说,忍不住笑了出来。

"绝对不会。为了达到效果,我要用一个小说家作为中心人物,小说的主题就是现实给予他的东西和他要给予的东西之间的矛盾冲突。"

"那你已经规划好了这本书吗?"莎弗洛尼斯卡问,她尽力保持冷静。

"当然没有。"

"'当然'什么意思?"

"因为对这样一本书,任何规划都是不适用的。如果我事先想好细节,它整体上就会出错。我是等着现实来指示我怎么做的。"

"但是我原以为你是想摆脱现实的。"

---

① 在法国,现实主义通常被称作自然主义。

"书里的那个小说家是想摆脱,但我要坚持把他拉回来。说实话,这就是我的主题:事实上的现实和理想中的现实之间的矛盾冲突。"

"那你就告诉我们这本书的题目吧。"萝拉无可奈何地说。

"好啊。裴奈尔,告诉他们。"

"《伪币制造者》。"裴奈尔说,"那你现在能不能告诉我们这些伪币制造者是些什么人?"

"我还一点没有想过呢。"裴奈尔和萝拉听了面面相觑,接着又看了看莎弗洛尼斯卡。然后是一声长叹。

实际上,关于金钱、货币贬值、通货膨胀和伪币制造等等的想法渐渐地侵入了爱德华的小说——就如关于服装的种种理论侵入卡莱尔的《旧衣新裁》,甚至取代了人物的作用。"这儿谁曾使用过伪币吗?"过了一会儿他问,"想一想,一枚十法郎的硬币,金的,假的。它实际上只值两个苏,但在它被发现之前,它始终会有十法郎的价值。假如我从这个想法开始,怎么样?"

"但是为什么要从一个想法开始呢?"裴奈尔脱口而出,这时他已有点恼火。"为什么不从一个事实开始?你只要恰当引入事实,想法就会随之而来。如果让我来写你的《伪币制造者》,我就会从一枚伪币开始,就是你刚才说的那枚十法郎伪币，它就在这里！"

说着，裴奈尔从口袋里掏出一枚十法郎硬币，往桌子一扔。

"听，"他说，"声音没什么两样。这是我今天早上从杂货店老板那里得到的。它不止只值两个苏，因为外面镀了金，但实际上它是玻璃做的。到时候它就会变得透明。不——不要擦它——你会毁了我的这枚伪币。"

爱德华已经把那枚伪币拿在手里，正仔细地查看着。

"那么杂货店老板又怎么会有这枚伪币的呢？"

"他自己也不知道。他把它找给我只是开个玩笑，随后就明说了，他是个规矩人。他把它算着五法郎给了我。我想，你正在写《伪币制造者》，总该知道伪币是什么样子，所以就拿来给你看看。现在你看过了，还给我吧。见你对现实不感兴趣，我很遗憾。"

"不，"爱德华说，"我对现实是感兴趣的，但现实把我排挤在外。"

"真遗憾。"裴奈尔说。

上面这段引文就是这部小说的核心。其中含有关于生活真实与艺术真实相对立的古老命题，而且形象地用一枚真正的伪币来加以说明。这里的新意是要把这两种真实结合起来，也就是要作家把自己和素材混在一起，而且要混而又混；不要再试图控制，而要希望被控制，被带走。至于情节——情节就是锅里的汤料。要切碎，要煮透。要像尼采所说的"外形大溃烂"。所有预先准备的东西都是虚假的。

有位著名的批评家①很赞同纪德——那位老夫人据说被她的几个侄女斥之为不讲逻辑。她一度曾不能理解什么是逻辑，而当她弄懂逻辑的真实性质后，她与其说是愤怒，不如说是鄙视。"逻辑！天哪！什么垃圾！"她宣称，"在我不知道我是怎么说的之前我怎么说得出我是怎么想的？"她的几个侄女都是有教养的年轻女性，她们认为她是迂腐，其实她比她们还要时尚。

那些了解当今法国情况的人说，现在这一代人都遵循纪德和那位老夫人的教诲，毅然投身于混乱，而实际上又很羡慕那些因为所做尝试很少成功而只好脚踏实地的英国小说家。听恭维话总令人高兴，但这句很特别的恭维话却有点说反话的意思。说来就像你想生个蛋，别人说你生了个椭圆形——你听了至多是惊讶而不舒服。反之，如果是你自己想生个椭圆形，结果会怎样，我就无法想象了——也许是母鸡之死。这似乎就是纪德的危险处境——他就是想生个椭圆形②；他没有很好地想过，如果他要写的是潜意识小说，想把潜意识那么幸运、那么耐心地解释，那他就会在某个错误

---

① 有位著名的批评家：即斯泰因夫人，格特鲁德·斯泰因（1874—1946），出生于美国而旅居巴黎的"先锋派"女作家。
② 因为椭圆形只是个抽象概念，并不实际存在。鸡蛋确实是椭圆形的，但并不存在可以离开鸡蛋的椭圆形。这里的意思是，纪德要想表现离开现实的现实性，这其实是不可能的。

阶段引入神秘主义。不过，那是他的事情。作为批评家，他是最令人刺激的，而他称为《伪币制造者》的那一大堆杂乱无章的词语，只有那些在不知道自己是怎么说的之前说不出自己是怎么想的人或者那些不是厌烦了情节暴政、就是厌烦了人物暴政的读者才会欣赏。

我们眼前显然还有一些东西要看，还有未考察过的其他几个方面。说什么东西是有意识的潜意识，我们或许会有所迟疑，然而后面要讲到一种既含糊又普遍的东西①却是与潜意识有关的。诗歌、宗教、激情——我们还没有说到它们的作用，而我们是评论者——评论者而已——就必须要说到它们的作用，要分析彩虹②。我们是在我们母亲的坟墓上窥探和采集样本③。

因此，我们必须尝试清点彩虹的经线和纬线，必须把注意力转向下一个题目——幻想。

---

① 既含糊又普遍的东西：即指幻想。
② 分析彩虹：意为把虚幻的东西分门别类。
③ 此句套用华兹华斯《一位诗人的墓志铭》一诗中的诗句 "One that would peep and botanise/Upon his mother's grave?"（原本是说医生："他会窥探和采集样本/在他母亲的坟墓上。"）作者套用此语是因为后面一章要讲的是幻想——幻想与潜意识有关，而潜意识，根据弗洛伊德心理学，大多源自恋母情结。

第六章 幻 想

一个系列讲座,如果不仅仅是一组说明的话,就必须有一个观念贯穿其中。它还必须有一个主题,那个观念还要贯穿于那个主题。说这么浅显的道理似乎有点愚蠢,但任何一个要想做讲座的人都会认识到这是一件真正的难事。一个系列讲座,就像其他语言组合一样,会营造出一种气氛。它有自身的组成部分——有一个主讲人,还有一群听众或者可以作为听众的人——它有固定的间隔时间,它有海报预告,还有财务方面的事情,虽然这最后一项是巧妙地加以保密的。这么一来,它就以特殊的方式有了它自己的生命力,它和贯穿于它的观念往往会朝向某一面而主题却偷偷地朝向了另一面。

贯穿于我们这个讲座的观念至此还是相当清楚的,那就是小说中有两种势力:人的势力和各种各样物的势力,小说家要做的就是协调这两种势力,满足它们各自的要求。这是相当清楚的,但它是不是贯穿在所有小说中呢?也许,我们的对象,也就是我们读过的所有小说,已经偷偷离开了我们,而我们还在高谈阔论,就像谈论一只已经高飞的鸟投下的影子①。鸟没错——它高高飞翔,持续而彰显。影子也没错——它掠过大路和花园。但是这两样东西的相像之处少而又少,它们也不像鸟落地时那样相互交接。文学评论,特别是评论性的讲座,很容易把人引入歧途。不管它意图多么崇高,它的方法多么完美,它的主旨却会从它下面溜走,不知不觉地溜走了;对此,主讲人和听众也许要到有了这样的发现才会觉醒:他们在一本正经地讨论,但讨论的东西和他们读过的任何东西其实都毫不相干。

使纪德担忧的就是这件事,或者说,这是使他担忧的事情之一,因为他有一种焦躁不安的想法。当我们试图把真实从一个领域移植到另一个领域时,不论是从生活中移植到小说中,还是从小说中移植到讲座中,真实出了问题:它出错了,不是突然出错,这样或许还能被觉察到,而是慢慢地出错。前面从《伪币制造者》中所引的那一大段引文,也许可把鸟召回到它的影子旁边。但是这之后,就不可能再用老一套的方式了。小说中除了时间、人物、逻辑和它们的衍生物,甚至命运,还有更多东西。我说"更多东西",意思既不是指在这些东西之外还有什么东西,也不是指在这些东西之内还包括了什么东西。我是说有一种东西就像一束光线一样穿越这些东西,它有时和它们关系密切,会不厌其烦地把它们所有的问题都显现出来,但有时只是从它们上面或者它

---

① 鸟和影子分别比喻小说本身和对小说的评论。

们之间一扫而过,好像它们并不存在。这束光线,我们将给予它两种称呼——幻想和启示。

我们至此所讨论过的小说,其中都讲述一个故事,都有若干人物,都有情节或者情节片段,因而我们可以采用适合于菲尔丁和阿诺德·本内特的那种方式来对待它们。但是,当我说到《项狄传》和《白鲸》①这两个书名时,我们显然就要停下来考虑一下了。那只鸟和它的影子离得太远了。必须找到一个新的公式;这样才能用一句话来同时说明《项狄传》和《白鲸》。要把这两部小说放在一起说,多么不可能!它们就像南北两极一样远远分离。是的。然而就像南北两极一样,它们却有一个共同连接点,这是赤道周围的地区所没有的,那就是地轴②。斯特恩和麦尔维尔这两部小说的本质所在,就属于小说中的这新的一面——幻想-启示之轴。乔治·梅瑞狄斯也与此有关:他或多或少有点耽于幻想。夏洛蒂·勃朗特也是如此:她有时像个女性启示者。但这不是他们的本质所在。把这除去,《哈利·里奇蒙德》或《谢利》③仍不失为一部小说。但若从斯特恩或麦尔维尔的小说中除去,若从皮科克或马克斯·比尔博姆④、弗吉尼亚·伍尔夫

---

① 《项狄传》:18世纪英国小说家斯特恩的长篇小说。《白鲸》:19世纪美国小说家麦尔维尔的长篇小说。

② 地轴:即连接南北两极的地球中心轴。

③ 《哈利·里奇蒙德》:梅瑞狄斯的长篇小说。《谢利》:夏洛蒂·勃朗特的长篇小说。

④ 皮科克:19世纪英国小说家、诗人。马克斯·比尔博姆:20世纪英国作家、漫画家。

或沃尔特·德拉梅尔①、威廉·贝克福德②或詹姆斯·乔伊斯、D. H. 劳伦斯或斯威夫特③等人的小说中除去，那就什么都没有了。

我们要用最简便的办法对小说的各个方面下定义，总要考虑到它对读者会有何种要求。故事要求读者有好奇心，人物要求读者懂得人之常情和价值观念，情节要求读者有智力和记忆力。那么，幻想对我们有什么要求呢？它要求我们作出一点额外的努力。它要求我们作出一种调整，一种不同于一般艺术作品所要求的调整，一种额外的调整。其他小说家说"这儿的事情很可能会在你们的生活中发生"，幻想小说家则说："这儿的事情是不可能发生的。我必须要求你们，第一要整个儿地先接受我的小说，第二才接受小说中的某些事情。"许多读者接受了第一个要求，但却拒绝第二个要求。"我知道一本书里说的不是真的，"他们说，"但我希望它是合乎自然的，而这些天使啦、侏儒啦、鬼魂啦，还有愚蠢的推迟孩子出生啦——不，这太过分。"他们要么连第一个要求也不再接受而停止阅读，要么就是冷冰冰地坚持读下去，他们看着作者折腾而不明白这到底是什么意思。

毫无疑问，从文学批评的角度看，上面这种方式是不恰当的。我们都知道一部艺术作品是一个独立自主体，等等，

---

① 沃尔特·德拉梅尔：20世纪英国小说家、诗人。
② 威廉·贝克福德：18世纪与19世纪之际英国哥特式小说家。
③ 斯威夫特：18世纪英国政论家、作家，著有《格列佛游记》等。

等等；它有自身的法则，这些法则不是日常生活中的法则，任何适合其自身的东西就是真实的，所以，为什么会对天使产生疑问，无非是问：它是否适合这本书？为什么把一个天使置于和一个股票经纪人不同的基础上？既然是在虚构世界，一个幽灵和一张抵押债券又有什么区别？我知道这问得有道理，但我内心拒绝承认。小说的基调一般都是平实无华的，因而当幻想被引入时就产生了一种不寻常的后果；有些读者觉得很有劲，有些读者觉得很没劲；由于这种写法或者这种题材很怪异，这就需要读者额外地加以调整——就像要参观展览会里的附设展区，除了要付入场费还要额外付六便士。有些读者很乐意付，他们就是要看附设展区才到展览会上来的，而我也就是对这些读者才有话可说。其他读者很不乐意付，他们应该受到真心诚意的尊重，因为不喜欢文学中的幻想并不等于不喜欢文学。这甚至都不能说是缺乏想象力，只是不乐意接受对他们的想象力提出的某些要求而已。阿斯奎斯①先生（如果传闻属实的话）就拒不接受《淑女变狐狸》②对他提出的要求。他说，如果那只狐狸又变回了那位淑女，他就不会反对了，但像现在这样，使他有一种不舒服、不满意的感觉。这种感觉既不表明一位杰出的政治家没有鉴赏力，也不表明一部有趣的小说没有吸引力。它仅仅表明，阿斯奎斯先生虽是一位真正的文学爱好者，但不愿付额

---

① 阿斯奎斯：1908—1916 英国自由党内阁首相。
② 《淑女变狐狸》：20 世纪英国小说家加尼特的幻想小说。

外的六便士——或者不如说，他是愿意付的，只是到最后想把它要回来。所以说，幻想要求我们额外付出。

接下来我们要区分一下幻想和启示。

两者同样相信神灵，但它们相信的神灵却有所不同。它们都具有神话意味，这是它们和小说其他方面的一大区别。召唤神灵又成为可能，现在就让我们以幻想的名义召唤所有那些栖居在不怎么高的空中、不怎么深的水中和不怎么大的山中的神灵，召唤所有的法翁①、德律阿得斯②和记忆失误，召唤所有的语音巧合，潘神③和碰巧，召唤所有那些坟墓这边的④中世纪的东西。但当我们说到启示时，我们就不会说召唤神灵，而是说某种超越我们能力的东西，有时甚至是超越我们能力的人类激情，它是印度、希腊、斯堪的纳维亚或犹太人的神祇，是所有坟墓那边的⑤中世纪的东西和晨之子路西法⑥。我们只要根据它们的神话就可以区分这两种小说。

因而，今天仍有不少小小的神灵出没于我们中间——我本想称它们为"小精灵"，如果这个词没有被转义为低能的话⑦。（你们相信小精灵吗？不，随便怎样都不相信。）在幻

---

① 法翁：古罗马神话中半人半羊的农牧神。
② 德律阿得斯：古希腊神话中的森林女神。
③ 潘：古希腊神话中半人半羊的畜牧神。
④ 坟墓这边的：即人间的。
⑤ 坟墓那边的：即阴间的。
⑥ 晨之子路西法：即堕落天使，指撒旦。
⑦ fairy 一词本意为"小精灵""仙女"，但在现代口语中经常用以指男同性恋者。

想小说中，或是恶作剧地，或是处心积虑地，日常生活事务会被撕扯得四分五裂，大地会被弄得微微倾斜，灯光会毫无理由、毫无征兆地照亮意想不到的东西，这虽不能说不是悲剧，但这悲剧本身却会具有一种幸运的意味，好像一个咒语就能使它不再是悲剧。幻想力渗入宇宙的每个角落，但并不影响那些统治宇宙的力量——作为空中之大脑的星辰，那不可改变的法则所拥有的部队①，仍未被触动——这种小说具有即兴的意味，这是它们富有魅力的奥秘所在。它们或许含有坚实的人物性格刻画，含有对人类行为和文明的深刻批判；但我们用光线所作的比喻②仍须保留，而且，如果要特别召唤一个神灵的话，那就让我们召唤赫耳墨斯③——他是信使，也是盗贼，还是灵魂的领路人，引导灵魂前往一个不太可怕的死后世界。

现在，你们料想我会说幻想小说要求我们接受超自然事物。我会说的，但很勉强，因为一说到它们的题材就会把这些小说带入批评家之手，而重要的是它们不应该有此遭遇。它们其实比大多数小说更真实，我们只有读过它们之后才会

---

① 此句原文是"The stars that are the brain of heaven, the army of unalterable law"，引自乔治·梅瑞狄斯的十四行诗《星光中的撒旦》十一至十四行："He reach'd a middle height, and at the stars, /Which are the brain of heaven, he look'd, and sank. /Around the ancient track march'd, rank on rank, / The army of unalterable law."。
② 用光线所作的比喻：见前文"有一种东西就像一束光线一样穿越这些东西"，即指幻想和启示。
③ 赫耳墨斯：古希腊神话中众神的使者，又是掌管疆界、道路、商业以及科学发明、辩才、幸运、灵巧之神，同时还是盗贼、赌徒的保护神。

知道它们写的是什么，它们显然都特别有个性——它们是展览会中的附设展区。所以，我还是想尽可能地保留余地，说它们要求我们接受的或许是超自然事物，或许不是。

探讨一下这种小说中最杰出的一部作品——《项狄传》——就能说明这一点。在项狄家族的生活中是没有超自然事物的，但有许多偶然事件暗示超自然事物离他们并不遥远。如果项狄先生卧室里的家具——他听到儿子出生的详情后绝望地退缩在自己的卧室里——就像《秀发遭劫记》[①] 中贝琳达的梳妆台一样活了起来，或者托比叔叔的那座吊桥可以通往小人国[②]，那不是真的很离奇了，是不是？这部小说的整个叙事过程都是鬼气森森的——人物做得越多，成功得越少；越是要少说，越是会多说；想得越激烈，做得越柔弱；事情似乎总是不祥地朝着过去溃退，而不是像在一般小说中那样朝向未来，还有那些无生命物体的难以控制，譬如斯娄泼医生的提包[③]，也是非常可疑的。显然，有个精灵隐藏在《项狄传》中，它的名字就叫"捣蛋鬼"，但有些读者却不愿承认它。这个捣蛋鬼几乎就要现身——斯特恩没有刻意把它的可怕面目完全隐藏起来；那是潜伏在这部杰作背后的神祇——那不可言说的捣蛋鬼所拥有的部队，那就像一颗滚烫的栗子一样的宇宙。无怪乎另一个超凡的捣蛋鬼——写

---

① 《秀发遭劫记》：18世纪英国诗人蒲伯的长篇叙事诗。
② 托比叔叔：《项狄传》中的人物，一个幻想家。小人国：18世纪英国作家斯威夫特的讽刺小说《格列佛游记》中虚构的一个国度。
③ 斯娄泼医生：《项狄传》中的人物。

于一七七六年的约翰生博士——会说:"离奇之作都不会长久:《项狄传》没有流传下来!"① 约翰生博士在文学评判方面并不总是很成功的,但这句怪话却说得令人心服口服。

好吧,那就把这当作我们对幻想所下的定义。它含有超自然事物,但不必表现出来。当然,时常有表现出来的,而分类如果有好处的话,我们可以把作家们用以表现幻想的手法列举出来——譬如,把精灵、鬼魂、天使、猿猴、怪物、侏儒、女巫引入日常生活;或者,把普通人引入无人之地、未来、过去、地球内部、四维空间;或者,潜入和分化个人的人格;或者,最后一种,使用滑稽模仿或者改头换面的手法。这些手法从来都不会过时;它们会很自然地为某种气质的作家所采用,而且会有新的用法;但需要关注的是,它们的数量其实非常有限;也就是说,这束光线只能以某些方式加以使用。

作为典型例子,我想选择最近出版的一部关于一个女巫的小说,即诺曼·麦特森②的《弗莱克的魔法》。这部小说在我看来写得不错,于是我就把它推荐给一个朋友,因为我很赏识他的判断力。他认为这部小说写得不好。新书就是那么容易遭人厌烦:我们读它们时从来不会像读经典作品时那样心平气和。《弗莱克的魔法》几乎没有什么新东西——幻想

---

① 这是反话,其实意为:谁说离奇之作不会长久,《项狄传》不是流传下来了吗?
② 诺曼·麦特森:20世纪美国作家,以女巫题材的小说而出名。

小说不可能有新东西；无非就是那种老而又老的指环许愿的故事，而那指环除了带来悲愁什么都不会有。弗莱克是个在巴黎学画的美国年轻人，有个年轻姑娘在一家小餐馆里给了他一个指环；她告诉他说，她是个女巫；他只要确定自己想要什么，就能得到什么。为了证明她的法力，她使停在大街上的一辆大客车慢慢升起，并在空中翻了个身。车里的乘客不但没有甩出来，还一个个在往外看，好像什么事都没有发生。客车司机此时站在人行道上，看得目瞪口呆，但当客车安然无恙地落回到地面后，他却若无其事地坐到他的位子上，像往常一样把车开走了。大客车是不会在空中慢慢翻转的——确实不会。所以，弗莱克接受了那个指环。他的性格虽然是简笔素描的，但很有个性，正是这种简洁明快的特点，使这部小说具有了吸引力。

它渐渐紧张地、有点令人震惊地展开。其方式是苏格拉底式①的。那年轻人一开始想要一样显赫的东西，譬如一辆劳斯莱斯轿车。但这么大的东西他放在哪里？那就要一个美丽的女士吧。但身份证怎么办？那就要钱？哦，这才对了——他没钱，简直像个乞丐。要一百万美元。他准备转动指环，实现这一愿望——等一等，要两百万好像更保险一点——要不就一千万——要不——钱要多得叫人发狂，而这同时他又想到他要活得长寿：要四十年后再死——不，五十年后——一百

---

① 苏格拉底式：即自问自答的方式（此说法来自柏拉图的《对话录》，其中苏格拉底提问，最后又由他自己回答）。

年后——可怕，可怕。其后又有一件事要解决。他一直想成为大画家。那好，他马上就行。但怎样的大画家呢？像乔托那样？还是像塞尚那样？当然不是；要像他自己这样；但他又不知道自己究竟是怎么，所以这一愿望同样不可能马上实现。

这时，有个可怕的老女人开始出没在他白天的生活和夜里的睡梦中。她含含糊糊地提到那个给他指环的年轻姑娘。她知道他的想法，凑在他耳边说："亲爱的孩子！希望幸福吧！"这时我们才知道，她是真正的女巫——那个年轻姑娘只是她用来勾搭弗莱克的一个普通人。她是最后一个女巫——非常孤独。其他女巫在十八世纪都自杀了——她们无法活到二加二等于四的牛顿世界；即便是爱因斯坦世界也不足以使她们得以重生①。她一心希望粉碎这个世界，她要那个年轻人用那个指环来获得幸福，是因为自从有了那个指环后还没有人提出过这样的愿望。

也许，弗莱克是发现自己处于这种困境的第一个现代人？因为在过去的世界里，人们很少确切知道自己想得到什么。他们只知道万能的上帝——他留着一把大胡子，坐在田野上方大约一英里高的空中的一把扶手椅

---

① 牛顿世界：意即机械论的科学时代，指19世纪。爱因斯坦世界：意即相对论的科学时代，指20世纪。爱因斯坦的相对论虽打破了牛顿机械论的局限，但仍是理性主义的，仍容不得非理性的巫术。

里——知道生活过得既快又慢，因为每天的生活都是在昏昏沉沉的辛苦劳作中度过的。

有史记载的以往时代，人们总希望有一座建在山上的城堡，能在那里终其一生。但是那座山不够高，从窗户里看出去，不能像在一个凉台上那样，看到过去的三千年。城堡里没有图文并茂、记述古人从世界各个角落的沙土中挖掘出来的奇珍异宝的典籍；只有对恶龙的一种半信半疑的感伤情绪，但又全然不知一度只有恶龙生活在世界上——人类的祖父和祖母就是恶龙；那里没有像思想一样在一堵白色的墙上闪闪烁烁的电影，没有留声机，没有用来获得惊人速度的机器；没有讲解第四维空间的图表，也没有像沃特维尔镇①和巴黎之间的那种生活对比。城堡里的光线昏暗摇曳，走廊里黑洞洞的，房间里阴沉沉的。外面那个小小的世界也是阴影密布，就是住在城堡里的人，他的心头也只有一层微光——下面全是阴影、恐惧、愚昧，自愿的愚昧。最要命的是，山上的城堡里连那种行将获得启示的屏息凝神都没有——这即使不在今天也肯定会在明天使人类力量倍增，从而再次改变世界。

古老的神魔故事都是来自穷乡僻壤的胡思乱想——所以，弗莱克想，至少是令人反感的。这些故事没有为

---

① 沃特维尔镇：美国明尼苏达州一小镇，以幽静闲适的生活而闻名。

他指点迷津。他的世界和它们的世界太多不同……

他不知道他是否漫不经心地放弃了祈求幸福的愿望?他对此似乎想不明白。他还不够聪明。在那些古老故事里从未有过祈求幸福的愿望!他不知道为什么。

他或许可以试试——看看究竟会怎样。这想法使他震颤。他跳下床,在红砖地上踱来踱去,同时搓着手……

"我要永远幸福,"他喃喃而语,谨慎地不去碰那个指环。"幸福……永远"——第一个词的两个音像是两块小而硬的卵石打在他的想象之钟上,听来很美妙,但第二个词却像是一声叹息。永远——重重一击,他心灰意懒了。这个词停留在他思想中,发出一阵忧郁的乐声,又渐渐消逝了。"幸福……永远"——不!!

作为一个真正的幻想家,诺曼·麦特森用适当的词语同时呈现了魔法的王国和常识的王国,而且他所创造的这种混合物是生动而鲜活的。至于故事的结局如何,我就不说了。你们猜也猜得出一个大概,但不管怎样,有创新精神的作品总有惊人之处,好的文学永远是某种愿望为核心的。

从这个有关超自然事物的简单例子转向一个比较复杂的例子——一部文笔极其优美华丽而又带有闹剧意味的小说:马克斯·比尔博姆[①]的《朱莱卡·多布森》。你们都知道多布

---

① 马克斯·比尔博姆:20世纪英国作家、漫画家。

森小姐——不是有私人关系①,否则你们就不会在这儿了。她是那种人见人爱的少女,牛津大学的学生在八人周②期间无不爱上了她,只有一人例外,他从窗口跳了下去。

一个绝妙的幻想主题,但一切都要靠如何处理。它是用一种把现实、机智、迷惑和神话混合在一起的手法处理的,其中最重要的是神话。马克斯·比尔博姆借用或者自创了好几种超自然工具——把朱莱卡仅交付于其中的一种当然是不行的;幻想会变得太笨重或者太单薄。然而我们却看到了汗流浃背的皇帝、黑色和粉色的珍珠、厉声尖叫的猫头鹰、缪斯克利俄③的干预、肖邦和乔治·桑④的阴魂、内莉·奥莫拉⑤的阴魂;真是一个接着一个,把葬礼也弄得美轮美奂。

> 经过广场,穿过大路;他们沿着格罗夫街前行。公爵抬头仰望默顿塔,ωc ονποτ' ανθc αλλα νον πανμσγατον⑥。奇怪啊,它今晚还矗立在这里,还是那么肃穆壮丽——还是越过屋顶和烟囱,凝视着玛格达伦塔,它的合法的新娘。经过不知多少个世纪后,它还会这样矗立,这样

---

① 因为多布森小姐只是小说中的一个人物。
② 八人周:Eights Week,即牛津与剑桥每年举行的划船比赛,一船八人,赛期一周,故称。
③ 缪斯克利俄:古希腊神话中九位缪斯女神之一,主管历史。
④ 肖邦和乔治·桑:19世纪波兰钢琴家和法国女作家,曾是同居情人,后又分离,其韵事一直被人谈论。
⑤ 内莉·奥莫拉:Nellie O'Mora,女巫、咒语的代名词。
⑥ 希腊语:最后一次,永远不再。

凝视。他悚然一惊。牛津城墙总使我们自惭形秽,而公爵却不愿把自己的末日视为小事。

是啊,所有矿物都可嘲笑我们。草木年年有枯荣,当与我们更有同感。紫丁香和金链花把通往基督教堂墓地的围栏小路点缀得多么美好,当公爵从它们旁边经过时,它们全都向他摆摆身、点点头。"永别了,永别了,阁下。"它们喃喃而语,"我们非常为您难过,真的非常难过。我们想都不敢想您会比我们先走。我们都把您的死看作一场大悲剧。永别了!我们或许在另一个世界还能相见——是的,如果动物王国的成员也有不朽的灵魂,像我们一样。"

公爵不太精通它们的语言;不过,当他在这些低吟絮语的花卉之间经过时,他至少能领会它们在向他致意,所以他时而朝右边,时而朝左边,微笑着表示一种含糊但彬彬有礼的答谢,给人以非常美好的印象。

像这样的段落,不是有一种严肃文学所没有的美感吗?它有趣而诱人,华丽但很深刻。对人性的批判不是像射箭而是像随风轻轻飘过。小说行将结束时,就有点乏力了——糟糕的结尾对小说来说经常是不可避免的——牛津大学的学生全都自杀,这事再怎么看好像也不应该会使人开心,还有诺克斯的跳窗简直令人厌恶。不过,这仍是一部了不起的作品——我们这个时代最协调、最完善的幻想小说,其中写到朱莱卡卧室里的那个充满不祥预兆的场景,可谓无懈可击。

接着她屏住呼吸、心跳加剧,站在那里盯着镜子里的那个女人看,却没有看到她自己;接着她突然转身,快步走向那张小小的桌子,那上面放着两本书。她伸手拿起那本《布拉德肖》①。

我们看到有谁拿起《布拉德肖》来查看,总要过问一下。"小姐会允许我来帮她找她要找的东西吗?"梅丽桑德问。

"别多嘴。"朱莱卡说。不管谁来过问我们和《布拉德肖》有关的事情,我们一开始总是很反感。

最终,我们又总会接受别人的过问。"看看能不能从这儿直接去剑桥,"朱莱卡说,一边把《布拉德肖》递了过去,"要是不能,那——那就看看怎么走法。"

我们又从不信任别人的过问。而那个过问的人呢,到时候也真没什么用。朱莱卡气鼓鼓地坐下,满脸不信任地看着她的女仆漫无头绪地乱翻。

"算了!"她突然说,"我有更好的办法。你一早到火车站去。去找站长。给我预订一列专车。说,要十点钟开。"

----

① 《布拉德肖》:全名《布拉德肖火车时刻表》(*Bradshaw's Railway Guide*),即全英火车时刻表,因由乔治·布拉德肖出版公司于1839年出版,故称。

说着她站起身来，举起双臂伸了个懒腰。她双唇一张打了个哈欠，闭上时微微一笑。她用双手把披在肩上的长发向后一捋，打了个蓬松的发髻。她非常轻快地躺到床上，非常迅速地睡着了。

看来，朱莱卡是理应来到这个地方①的。但她好像没有到达，对此我们只能猜测是因为神灵的过问而使她的专列没能发车，或者，更有可能，一直就停在布莱彻里的侧线轨道上。

我在前面列举的手法中提到过"滑稽模仿"或者"改头换面"，现在就来探讨一下。这里有位幻想小说家，他在某部早期作品中采用了神话方式，而且出于他自己的目的把它当作一个框架或者某种来源。这样一个中途失败的范例，就是《约瑟夫·安德鲁斯》。菲尔丁一开始就是把《帕美拉》当作一个可笑的神话②。他认为虚构一个帕美拉的哥哥，一个心地单纯的男仆，他像帕美拉抗拒 B 先生一样抗拒博比夫人的勾引，这一定很有趣；他还把博比夫人说成是 B 先生的姑妈。这样，他不仅可以嘲笑理查生，还可以附带表达他自己的人生观。然而，菲尔丁的人生观是那种只有通过塑造坚

---

① 这个地方：即剑桥。
② 《帕美拉》是理查生一部著名小说，讲述女仆帕美拉在女主人去世后如何抗拒少爷 B 先生勾引，最后赢得少爷的尊重，正式娶她为妻。菲尔丁的《约瑟夫·安德鲁斯》是对《帕美拉》的滑稽模仿，意在嘲讽帕美拉的所谓"美德"。

实的圆形人物才能表达出来的人生观,所以随着亚当斯牧师和斯里普斯洛普太太①的逐渐显现,幻想就结束了,我们看到的是一部独立的作品②。《约瑟夫·安德鲁斯》(当然有其文学史上的重要性)使我们感兴趣是因为它可当作一个开错头的范例。作者起初是想在理查生的世界里装傻子,结果却回到了他自己的那个严肃的世界——汤姆·琼斯和阿米莉亚③的世界。

滑稽模仿,或者说改头换面,对有些小说家来说,特别是对那些有许多东西要说而且富有文学才华、但却不善于通过一个个男人和女人来看世界的小说家来说——也就是说,对那些不善于创造人物的小说家来说,却是大有用处的。这些人是怎样开始写作的呢?一部现存的作品或者一种现存的文学惯例或许会启发他们——他们或许会在其中的某些节点上发现某种模式而以此作为开端,他们或许会反复琢磨其中的某些节点而获得写作动力。洛斯·迪金森的那部幻想小说《魔笛》看来就是这样写成的:其中的神话来自莫扎特的世界④。塔米诺、萨拉斯特罗和黑夜王后⑤就在它们的神奇王国

---

① 亚当斯牧师和斯里普斯洛普太太:《约瑟夫·安德鲁斯》中两个性格复杂的人物。
② 意即菲尔丁原本只是想写一部滑稽模仿《帕美拉》的作品,结果却写成了一部和《帕美拉》其实不相干的作品。
③ 汤姆·琼斯和阿米莉亚:菲尔丁小说《汤姆·琼斯》和《阿米莉亚》中的主人公。
④ 洛斯·迪金森:20世纪英国小说家,其《魔笛》的写作灵感来自莫扎特的歌剧《魔笛》(取材于德国诗人维兰特的《童话集》)。
⑤ 塔米诺、萨拉斯特罗和黑夜王后:均系莫扎特的歌剧《魔笛》中的人物。

中等待着作者有什么想法,一旦作者注入他的想法,它们就活动起来,一部优美的新作品就此产生。另一部幻想小说——詹姆斯·乔伊斯的《尤利西斯》——其实也是这样产生的,只是并不优美。这部引人注目的作品——也许是当今最有意思的文学实验——之所以能完成,就是因为乔伊斯把《奥德修纪》①的世界作为他的向导和取笑对象。

  我说的只是《尤利西斯》的一个方面;这部作品当然不仅仅是一部幻想小说——它是一次意图颠覆维多利亚风尚②、把全世界埋进泥土里的大胆尝试,一次意图在仁爱与纯洁的失败之处代以粗鄙与污秽的尝试,一种出自邪恶意图的人性简化。简化总是很诱人,总会使人离开(在《项狄传》的一片混乱中比较接近的)那种真实,所以《尤利西斯》对我们来说肯定用不到去讨论它是否具有某种道德含义——否则的话,连亨弗莱·沃德夫人③我们也要讨论了。我们关注这部小说是因为,乔伊斯是通过一个神话才得以创造出他所需的那个舞台和那些人物的。

  这部小说用四十万字所写的仅是一天里的事情,地点是都柏林④,主题是一次外出——那个现代男人⑤的一次外出,

---

 ① 《奥德修纪》:荷马史诗之一,主人公奥德修斯,古希腊神话中的人物,在古罗马神话中被称作尤利西斯。
 ② 维多利亚风尚:即大英帝国风尚,因其巅峰期在19世纪维多利亚女王执政时期,故称。
 ③ 亨弗莱·沃德夫人:19世纪英国女作家,作品很多,但全都平庸至极,后人常把她当作三流作家的典型。
 ④ 都柏林:爱尔兰首都。
 ⑤ 那个现代男人:指主人公利奥波德·布卢姆。

从早上到午夜，从床到各种污秽低贱的小事，到一个葬礼上，到报社、图书馆、酒馆、厕所、产科医院，到海滩边溜达，到妓院、咖啡摊，然后回到床上。这是一连串事情，因为它是挂靠在一位英雄穿越希腊诸海的那次外出①上的，就像一只蝙蝠挂在一个屋檐上。

这里的尤利西斯就是利奥波德·布卢姆先生——一个改宗的犹太人②——贪吃、好色、胆小、卑微、懒散、浅薄、随和，最糟糕是他还总要装得很有志向。他试图通过肉体探知生活。这里的珀涅罗珀③就是玛里恩④·布卢姆太太，一个胖鼓鼓的泼妇，从不挑剔她的追求者⑤。第三个人物是年轻的斯蒂芬·代达罗斯⑥，布卢姆把他认作精神上的儿子，对应于尤利西斯认出特勒马科斯是他的亲生儿子。斯蒂芬试图通过思考探知生活——我们曾在《青年艺术家画像》⑦中遇到过他，现在他又被放进了这部污秽和颓废的史诗中。他和布卢姆在夜城相遇（这"夜城"部分对应于《奥德修纪》中的喀耳刻妖宫，部分对应于奥德修斯深入冥府），而且在城

---

① 一位英雄穿越希腊诸海的那次外出：即指《奥德修纪》所述奥德修斯十年海上漂泊。
② 改宗的犹太人：即改信基督教的犹太人。
③ 珀涅罗珀：《奥德修纪》中的女主人公，奥德修斯的妻子。
④ 玛里恩：昵称莫莉。
⑤ 莫莉是珀涅罗珀的滑稽模仿，在《奥德修纪》中，奥德修斯十年未归，珀涅罗珀拒绝了所有的求婚人。
⑥ 代达罗斯：此姓取自古希腊神话。古希腊神话中的代达罗斯是个为国王修建迷宫的建筑师，斯蒂芬·代达罗斯也是这一神话人物的滑稽模仿。
⑦ 《青年艺术家画像》：詹姆斯·乔伊斯的早期作品，其中的主人公即斯蒂芬·代达罗斯。

中神奇而肮脏的小巷中建立了脆弱而真挚的友谊。这里是小说的关键之处，在此处——实际上各处都有——滋生和麇集了许多较小的神话，就像在一条毒蛇的鳞片间蠕动的寄生虫。天地之间充满乌烟瘴气，人格消融，性别互换，直到整个世界——包括可怜的、寻欢作乐的布卢姆先生在内——全都卷入一场无欢的狂欢。

这部小说是不是很成功？不，不完全成功。文学中的愤世嫉俗从来不会完全成功，无论是尤维纳尔①，还是斯威夫特，还是乔伊斯，都一样；因为字里行间总会有某种和单纯的愤激之情不相容的东西。夜城相遇一场写得并不成功，不过是一种幻想堆积，一种怪异的记忆组合。只是在这方面得到了可以得到的满足，而在整部小说中我们所看到的都是类似的实验——其目的就是要把一切事物都里外翻转、上下颠倒，从而贬低一切事物，特别是文明与艺术。有些热心人或许会认为《尤利西斯》应该放到后面去讲，应该归在启示名下，我理解这种意见。但我宁愿在今天把它和《项狄传》《弗莱克的魔法》《朱莱卡·多布森》以及《魔笛》放在一起讲，因为乔伊斯的狂怒和其他几个作家比较愉悦、比较平静的心情一样，本质上是幻想，缺乏我们下次就会听到的那种特点②。

我们必须进一步对神话的这一特点加以更为全面的探讨。

---

① 尤维纳尔：古罗马讽刺诗人。
② 那种特点：即指启示。

第七章 启　示

我们在此涉及的不是狭义上的、意为预示未来的启示，我们也不太会涉及意为伸张正义的启示。我们今天感兴趣的——或者说我们必须予以思考的，因为仅仅说感兴趣现在已不太合适——是小说家说话时的一种语调，一种我们在幻想的长笛和萨克斯管合奏①中已有所听闻的语调。他的主题是全人类，或者关于全人类的什么事情，但他肯定不是想"说说"关于全人类的任何事情；他是想唱出来，而且奇怪的歌声②在小说大厅里响起时一定会使我们大为震惊。这歌声是不是和伴奏的常识③很协调？我们会问自己，而且会无奈地回答说"不太协调"：这个歌手④总是没有为他的表演找对地方，那里的桌子和椅子⑤都是破的，而由这个歌手唱出来的小说经常给人乱七八糟的感觉，就像一个地震后的或者

---

① 幻想的长笛和萨克斯管合奏：即指前一章探讨的种种幻想。
② 歌声：喻启示。下同。
③ 伴奏的常识：伴随着启示（"歌声"）的常识（因为启示总要合乎常识）。
④ 这个歌手：喻启示小说家。
⑤ 桌子和椅子：喻小说家使用的素材。

一群孩子开过派对后的客厅。读过 D. H. 劳伦斯小说的人知道我是什么意思。

启示——在我们看来——是一种语调。这种语调也许适用于任何一种出没于人类的宗教信仰——基督教、佛教、二元教、恶魔教；或者说，它适用于把人心中的爱与恨强化到这样一种程度，以致一般人都不再能接受；但它提出了非常奇特的宇宙观——这和我们没有直接关系。和我们有关的是渗入小说家行文中的意味和意愿，所以在这一讲中，由于要讲的东西那么模糊不清，我们或许会更多地讲到风格方面的细微之处。我们将不得不关注小说家的心理状态，关注他所使用的词汇；我们将尽可能地忽略常识问题。尽可能地：因为所有小说中都有桌子和椅子，而且大多数小说读者首先注意的就是这些东西。在指控小说家伪造和歪曲之前，我们必须先了解他的观点。他根本就没有注意桌子和椅子，它们本来就在焦点之外。我们只是看到他没有聚焦什么——不是看到他聚焦了什么——于是就盲目地嘲笑他了。

我曾说，小说的各个层面要求读者具有不同的素质。现在，启示这一层面要求两种素质：谦逊和幽默感缺失。谦逊是一种我不太赞赏的素质。它在生活的许多方面都是一大过错，而且很容易变成懦弱或虚伪。但谦逊在这里正合适。没有它，我们就听不出启示者的语调，我们的眼睛就看不到他的光环，而只看到一个可笑的形象。至于幽默感——那在这里是不适宜的；那种有教养的人具有的可贵品质必须被丢在一边。有人就像《圣经》里说到那些学童一样，看到启示者就忍不住要笑——他剃光了脑袋真的很荒唐——但是，有人却可以忍住不笑，而且认识到嘲笑没有任何学术价值，只是图一时之快而已。

我们来区别一下启示者和非启示者。

曾有两个小说家，他们都是在基督教环境中长大的。他们都思考而且都有所突破，但他们虽没有继续留在教会，却又不想背离基督教精神，因为他们把它解释为一种仁爱精神。他们都认为罪恶是永远要受到惩罚的，因为惩罚是一种净化，但他们又不像古代希腊人或者现代印度人那样冷漠地看待这一过程，而是双眼流着泪水。他们觉得，怜悯他人是一种合乎逻辑的道德氛围，否则的话，道德就会变得粗鲁而失去意义。如果对有罪之人的惩戒没有附带天国的恩惠，那么惩戒还会有什么作用？那么，这附带的恩惠来自何处？并非来自某种机构①，而是来自惩戒过程中的氛围，来自爱与怜悯，（他们相信）这是上帝的属性。

这两个小说家多么相似！然而，他们一个是乔治·艾略特，另一个是陀思妥耶夫斯基。

有人会说，陀思妥耶夫斯基有洞察力。乔治·艾略特又何尝没有。要把他们分开——必须把他们分开——并不那么容易。不过，我只要从他们的作品中选两段来读一下，马上

---

① 某种机构：指教会机构。

就能清楚地看出他们之间的区别。这两段文字对分类的人来说会觉得很相像,但对听歌的人来说却是来自两个不同的世界。

我先读《亚当·比德》中的一段——五十年前这是非常著名的段落。海蒂因谋杀自己的私生子而被关进监狱,并被判处死刑。但她不愿认罪,态度僵硬而毫无悔意。卫理公会①教徒狄娜,前来探望她。

> 狄娜开始怀疑海蒂是否意识到坐在她身旁的人是谁。……但是她越来越感觉到圣灵的存在——不,仿佛她自己就是圣灵的一部分,她内心里搏动着的就是圣灵的怜悯,就是想拯救这个无助之人的愿望。最后她按捺不住想说话了,想知道海蒂对眼前的情况到底意识到了何种程度。
>
> "海蒂,"她轻声说,"你知道坐在你身边的是谁吗?"
>
> "知道,"海蒂缓慢地回答,"是狄娜。"……过了一会儿,她又说:"可你帮不了我。你没法叫他们做什么。下星期一他们会吊死我——今天是星期五。"……
>
> "可是,海蒂,在这牢房里除了我还有别人,还有某个人在你身旁。"
>
> 海蒂很害怕,喃喃地说:"谁?"

---

① 卫理公会:基督教新教一教派。

"某个人在你犯罪和遇到麻烦的时候一直和你在一起——他知道你的每一种想法——他看到你去了哪儿,在哪儿躺下又爬起来,还有所有你想隐瞒的那些事情,他也看到了。到星期一那天,我没法随你去——我没法拥抱你——死亡会把我们分开——但他现在和你在一起,知道一切,到那时还会和你在一起。无论我们是生是死——这没有什么区别——上帝永远与我们同在。"

"哦,狄娜,不会有人来帮我的是吗?他们肯定会吊死我的是吗?……我不会想,他们会不会让我活……帮我……我也没法像你那样想……我的心已经僵硬。"

狄娜一手搭住她,她的灵魂全都倾注在她的言语中:

"……万能的救世主,来吧!让死去的人听到你的声音,让盲目的人睁开眼睛:让她看见上帝就在她身边;让她为自己的罪、为自己背离上帝而颤抖吧!融化她僵硬的心,开启她紧闭的嘴,让她用整个灵魂哭喊:'在天之父啊,我有罪!'……"

"狄娜,"海蒂抽泣起来,伸出双臂抱住狄娜的脖子,"我愿意讲了……我愿意说出来……我不会再隐瞒了……是我做的,狄娜……我把他丢在树林里……那个孩子……他哭了……我听到他哭……就在那边……一整夜……因为他在哭,我回到那里。"

她停了一下,接着又突然用乞求的语气大声说:

"可我想他大概不会死的——或许有人会发现他。

我没有杀他——我自己没有杀他。我只是把他放在那儿,拿东西盖起来,但我后来回到那里时他不见了……我不知道自己是怎么想的,直到我看见孩子不见了。我把他放在那儿时,我是想有人会发现他的,会救他的;可我看见他不见了,那时我吓呆了,像块石头。我一直都没想动,我觉得一点力气也没有。我知道我不能走开,人人看见我都会知道孩子的事。我的心变得像块石头:我没有一点希望,也不想做点什么;就好像我要一辈子待在那儿,什么都不会变了。可是他们来了,把我带走了。"

海蒂沉默了,但她又颤抖起来,好像后面还有什么事情;狄娜等着,因为她心里有数,她开口前一定会流泪。最后,海蒂呜咽着突然说:

"狄娜,我现在全都说了,你说上帝会带走那哭声和树林里的那个地方吗?"

"让我们祈祷吧,可怜的罪人:让我们再次跪下,祈求上帝的慈悲。"

我没有公正对待这个场景,因为我不得不做了一点删节,而乔治·艾略特依靠的是大段铺陈——她不具备简洁明快的风格。这个场景写得真挚、朴实、动人,浸透着基督教精神。狄娜召唤的那位神①对这位女作家来说还是一种活生

---

① 指耶稣基督。

生的力量;他不是为了感动读者而被引入的;他是人类错误与苦难的天然伴随者①。

现在,把这个场景和下面引自《卡拉马佐夫兄弟》的一个场景加以比较(在这一场景中,米嘉被控犯有杀父罪;他有此动机,只是没有实施)。

> 他们开始对口供的笔录做最后一次修订。米嘉站起身来,从他的椅子边走到帷幕旁的屋角里,在一只铺着毛毯的大箱子上躺下来,立刻就睡着了。
>
> 他做了个奇怪的梦,一个和此时此地的情景毫不相干的梦。
>
> 他梦见自己正在他很久以前驻扎过的那个大草原上的什么地方乘车行驶。有个农民替他赶着一辆两匹马儿拉着的马车在雪片和雨珠中穿行。……前面不远是个村庄。他看得见黑色的茅舍。那儿一半的房子已经被烧毁,只剩下烧焦的梁柱还竖立在那儿。当他们驶进村子里去的时候,沿路排列着许多农妇——许许多多女人,整整一长排,都又瘦又弱。她们面色焦黄,尤其是最边上那个又高又瘦的女人。她长着一张长而瘦的脸,看上去有四十岁了,可也许只有二十岁,她的怀里抱着一个正在啼哭的婴儿。她的乳房看上去干瘪得连一滴奶水都

---

① 意为在乔治·艾略特的作品中耶稣基督从来就是以救世主的形象出现的。

挤不出来了。婴儿哭了又哭,伸出小小的赤裸着的手臂,小小的拳头冻得发青。

"她们为什么哭?她们为什么哭?"当他们的马车轻快地疾驶而过的时候,米嘉问。

"是那娃儿,"车夫答道,"那娃儿在哭。"

米嘉听到他用乡下土话说"娃儿",不由得一惊,他喜欢听乡下人把孩子叫作"娃儿"。这听上去更有哀怜之心。

"可他为什么要哭?"米嘉傻乎乎地接着问,"他的小胳膊为什么露在外面?为什么不把它裹起来?"……

"为什么,她们是穷苦人,房子烧了。她们没饭吃了。她们在讨饭,因为东西都烧光了。"

"不,不,"米嘉好像还是不明白,"你倒讲讲看,那些可怜的母亲为什么要站在那儿?她们为什么穷?那娃儿为什么穷?大草原为什么这么荒凉?她们为什么不拥抱,不亲吻?她们为什么不唱唱歌,开心开心?她们为什么愁眉苦脸?她们为什么不给娃儿喂奶?"

他觉得,尽管他的问题不合情理,又毫无意义,但是他却偏要问,而且一定要用这种方式问。他觉得心里有一种从未有过的哀怜之情,甚至想哭,想为那些人做点什么,想让那娃儿不再啼哭,想让那些憔悴而干瘪的母亲不再哭泣,想让人人都从那一刻起不再流泪,而且他想马上就做,立刻就做,不管有多少阻碍,也挡不住卡拉马佐夫家的执着……此时他的心在燃烧，他奋力向往光明，他渴望生活，渴望朝着新的、令人振奋的光明生活下去，而且要快，要快，现在，立刻！

"什么！去哪里？"他睁开眼睛，喜形于色地大声说，同时像从一阵昏迷中醒来似的从箱子上坐了起来。只见尼古拉·帕尔费诺维奇站在他面前，请他听人读那份笔录，然后签字。但是米嘉没有听见尼古拉·帕尔费诺维奇在说些什么，他觉得自己好像睡了有一个小时或者还不止。他突然一愣，发现刚才他头下有个枕头，而当时他困倦地躺下时，箱子上并没有枕头。

"是谁把枕头放在我头下的？是谁那么好心？"他惊喜而感激地大声问道，声音里好像还含着眼泪，好像领受了大恩大惠。没有人告诉他那个好心人是谁，也许是前来作证的农户中的一个，也许是尼古拉·帕尔费诺维奇的小秘书，好心地在他头下塞了个枕头，但他的整个灵魂都为此而震颤，为此而流泪。他走到桌前，说不管怎样的文件，他都会签字。

"先生们，我刚才做了个好梦。"他说，声音有点奇怪，脸上又有了神采，像是喜悦的神采。

现在，来看这两大段引文之间的区别：第一段引文的作者是个传教士；第二段引文的作者是个启示者。乔治·艾略特讲到上帝，但她从不改变焦点；上帝与桌子和椅子始终处于同一层面，结果是我们一点也没有感到全人类都需要怜悯与爱——只有在海蒂的牢房里才需要。在陀思妥耶夫斯基那里，人物和情景并不仅仅代表其自身；它们被赋予了无限性；虽然始终是个别人物和个别情景，但它们扩展而包含了无限性，同时又使无限性包含了它们；如用锡耶纳的圣凯瑟琳①的那句话来说就是：上帝在灵魂中，灵魂在上帝中，就如大海在鱼群中，鱼群在大海中。陀思妥耶夫斯基所写的每句话都暗示着这种扩展，而暗示就是他的作品的主要特征。他是普通意义上的伟大小说家——也就是说，他的人物都和日常生活相关联而且都生活在自身的环境中，他的故事情节始终使我们深感兴趣，等等——不仅如此，他还是个伟大的启示者；对此，我们就不能用普通标准来衡量了。

这就是海蒂和米嘉之间的鸿沟，虽然他们处于同样的道德世界和神话世界。海蒂就其自身来说，是恰如其分的。她是个可怜的姑娘，被带来承认自己有罪，由此而被带入一种较好的情绪状态。但米嘉就其自身来说并不恰如其分。他只是通过他所暗示的东西才变得真实，他的情绪并不完全处于某种状态。就其自身来说，他似乎是被扭曲而不成形的，似有似无的；我们开始对他的解释是，说他为一只枕头过分感激是因为他太容易激动——确实很像一个俄国人。直到我们看到他扩展，看到陀思妥耶夫斯基写到他时所聚焦的不是那

---

① 锡耶纳的圣凯瑟琳：14世纪罗马天主教圣女。

只木箱子，甚至不是梦境，而是一种可能和全人类有关的境况时，我们才能理解他。米嘉是——我们所有人。阿辽沙也是如此，斯麦尔佳科夫也是如此。他是启示的幻象，也是小说家的创造。他在这里还没有成为我们所有人；他在这里还是米嘉，就像海蒂是海蒂。通过爱与怜悯而达到的扩展、融化、统一是发生在一个只能被暗示出来的范围内的，这也许并不适宜用小说来表现。卡拉马佐夫兄弟的世界、梅希金的世界和拉斯柯尼科夫的世界，还有我们马上就要涉及的莫比·狄克的世界①——它不是一块面纱，不是一个寓言。它是普通的小说世界，只不过是倒退的②。我们在前面谈到过③的贝特兰夫人的幽默形象——贝特兰夫人抱着她的哈巴狗坐在沙发上——也许有助于我们理解这些比较深的问题。我们认为，贝特兰夫人是个扁平人物，当情节需要时可以扩展成圆形人物。米嘉是圆形人物，但他也可以扩展。他并不（神秘主义）暗藏着什么，他并不（象征主义）意味着什么，他仅仅是德米特里④·卡拉马佐夫而已，但在陀思妥耶夫斯基那里，仅仅是一个人也是和身后的其他所有人联系在一起

---

① 梅希金和拉斯柯尼科夫：分别是陀思妥耶夫斯基的小说《白痴》和《罪与罚》中的主人公。莫比·狄克：19世纪美国小说家麦尔维尔的小说《白鲸》（原著即名《莫比·狄克》）中的白鲸名。

② 倒退的：意为小说主题不是发展的，而是倒退到既定主题。按本书作者的看法，启示小说家是主题先行的，也就是先定下一个主题，然后用故事情节和人物来表现这一主题。由于先有主题，所以说整部小说是"倒退的"。参见下文。

③ 见第四章"人物（续）"。

④ 德米特里：米嘉的大名（米嘉是小名或昵称）。

的。因此，洪水会突然涌来——在我看来，就紧随着"先生们，我刚才做了个好梦"那句话。我也做了那个好梦吗？没有，陀思妥耶夫斯基的人物要求和我们分享的是某种比他们的经历更为深刻的东西。他们给我们一种只有部分肉体的感觉——觉得仿佛进入一个半透明的球体内，看见我们所经历的一切在我们上方的球体表面浮动，渺小、遥远，但仍是我们所经历的一切。我们仍是我们这些人，我们没有失去什么，只是"大海在鱼群中，鱼群在大海中"。

在此，我们接触到了本讲主题的极限。我们并不涉及启示者所作的启示，或者说（既然事物和方式是不可分开的）我们尽可能地不予涉及。我们注意的是启示者的语调，他的歌声。海蒂在监狱里也可能做了个好梦，这梦会是她真想做的，真使她满意，但它会突然中断。狄娜会说她很乐意听，海蒂会讲她梦见了什么，但和米嘉不同，她会有逻辑地把她的梦和她的危难处境联系在一起，乔治·艾略特则会动情地说几句关于好梦的好话，说好梦会神奇地有助于安抚痛苦的心灵。这两个场景、这两部小说、这两个作家看似相同而绝对不同……

现在，还有一点要提一下。就作为一个小说家而言，启示者有某些神奇的用处，有时甚至为了处理家具也要请他进客厅。他也许会拆散或者弄坏东西，但他也许会使所有东西熠熠生辉。启示者就如我说到幻想家时所说的一样，手里也有一束光线，这束光线时而会照到那些被常识之手触摸得满是污垢的东西上，使它们显得甚至比家里的东西还要洁净光亮。这种间歇性的现实主义①在陀思妥耶夫斯基和赫尔曼·麦尔维尔的所有较为重要的作品中都随处可见。陀思妥耶夫斯基会不厌其详地描述一次庭审或者一把楼梯。麦尔维尔会把鲸鱼制品详尽列表（他说："我总发现你们所说的平常东西是最难弄的。"）。D. H. 劳伦斯会描绘一块草地、一个花坪或者弗里曼特尔②的港口。有些显眼的小东西似乎时而会受到启示者的关切——他会坐下来安静而忙碌地摆弄这些东西，就像一个孩子摆弄两个洋娃娃。在这间歇期间他的感觉如何？是奋激的另一种表现呢，还是在休息？我们不得而知。毫无疑问这就像 A. E.③ 在做奶酪时的感觉，或者就像克洛岱尔④在搞外交时的感觉，但那是什么感觉？不管怎样，反正这赋予了这些小说以某种特征，一种艺术作品常引起争议的特征：外表粗糙。当我们读这些小说时，总觉得这里坑坑洼洼、那里疙疙瘩瘩，总是一会儿惊叹，一会儿皱眉；而当我们读完之后，那些坑坑洼洼和疙疙瘩瘩又全被忘记，只觉得它们就像月光一样柔和如水。

由此看来，启示小说似乎是有固定特征的。它要求读者谦逊和幽默感缺失。它是倒退的——虽然我们不能以陀思妥

---

① 间歇性的现实主义：intermittent realism，意即夹杂着启示的现实主义。
② 弗里曼特尔：澳大利亚港口城市，劳伦斯曾在那里居住过。
③ A. E.：19世纪与20世纪之际爱尔兰诗人乔治·威廉·拉塞尔的笔名，他写诗期间以经营奶酪工场谋生。
④ 克洛岱尔：20世纪法国诗人、剧作家，兼做外交官。

耶夫斯基为例就贸然得出结论说它总是倒退到爱与怜悯。它的现实主义是断续性的。它给我们一种像听到一首歌或者一种声音的感觉。它和幻想小说不同，因为它是面向一方的，而幻想小说是左顾右盼的。它的迷乱是偶然的，而幻想小说的迷乱是固有的——《项狄传》本该是一团混乱，《朱莱卡·多布森》本该是一连串神话变换。此外，启示者的"离谱"——可以想象——比幻想家更加彻底，他写作时处于一种更为疏远的情感状态。没有多少小说家属于这个层面。爱伦·坡太多偶然。霍桑太纠结于个人灵魂得救问题而不太自由。哲学家和了不起的诗人哈代，也许可以算一个，但哈代的小说都是观察，并没有发出声响①。这个作家本人确实是反身坐下了，但他的人物却没有倒退②。他让我们看到的是，他们把双臂伸向空中又放下了；他们也许和我们的苦难是对应的，但绝不可能加以扩展——我的意思是，裘德绝不可能像米嘉那样进一步说"先生们，我刚才做了个噩梦"，从而释放出我们的情感洪流。康拉德的情况有点相似。那个马洛的声音中含有太多经验而不是歌声③，它已被许许多多错误的和美好的回忆弄得沙哑，它的主人因看到过太多事情而看

---

① 发出声响：意为启示。
② 此句意为哈代本人是想有所启示的，但他的人物却没有回到已有主题（这里的"反身"意为背离，因为要启示就要背离现实）。
③ 马洛：康拉德多部小说中的人物，被视为作者的代言人。含有太多经验：意为太注重现实。不是歌声：意为不是启示。

第七章 启 示 | 143

不到因与果之外的东西了①。只要有一种哲学——就是像哈代和康拉德的那种诗意的和情感的哲学也一样——就会导致对人生和事物的思考。但启示者并不思考。他也不争论。这就是为什么我们把乔伊斯排除在外的原因。乔伊斯在许多方面都和启示很接近而且他（尤其在《一个青年艺术家的画像》中）还表现出一种把握人性邪恶的想象力。但是，他太工匠似的挖掘人性，太注重寻找这件工具或那件工具；虽然他内在很放松，他表现得还是太紧张；除非经过深思熟虑，他从不浑然发声；这是在讲，是讲，绝不是唱。

所以，虽然我相信这次讲座讲的是一个真正的小说层面，不是一个虚假层面，但我认为只有四个作家——陀思妥耶夫斯基、麦尔维尔、D. H. 劳伦斯和艾米莉·勃朗特——体现了这一层面。艾米莉·勃朗特留到最后讲，陀思妥耶夫斯基已经提及，麦尔维尔是我们要讲的核心，而麦尔维尔的核心是《白鲸》。

如果我们把《白鲸》当作一个夹杂着一些诗句的捕鲸故事或者捕鲸记录来读，这是一部很浅显的小说。但是，如果我们觉察到其中的歌声，它就变得很难懂而且非常重要了。偏狭而武断地说，《白鲸》的主题思想是这样的：与邪恶的抗争，或拖延得太久，或所用方式错误。那条白鲸就是邪

---

① 它的主人：即指马洛。此句意为太注重现实而没有理想（此处"因与果"代指世事、故事）。

恶，而亚哈船长对它的紧追不舍最终使他的骑士行侠变成了纯粹的报复。话虽这么说——如果我们愿意，可以把它看作一种象征——但这么说仍然把这部小说看作一个故事，并没有使我们有所深入——也许，还会使我们有所倒退，因为这么说很可能会误导我们，使我们心平气和地去看待那些事件，以致忽略了它们的粗犷表现和丰富内涵。我们或许可以接受这种抗争说法：所有的情节就是一场抗争，唯一的幸福就是和平。但是，谁与谁抗争？如果我们说是善与恶的抗争，或者说是两种不相容的恶之间的抗争，那我们就错了。《白鲸》的精髓，它的启示之歌，就像一股暗流贯穿在它的情节和寓意之中。它是言外之意。甚至到最后，那艘捕鲸船连同钉在桅杆上的那只天堂鸟一起沉没，那只空棺材从漩涡中浮起，把以实玛利①带回大陆——甚至到这时，我们仍无法听清歌词。重音是有的，还有停顿；但没有清晰可辨的尾声，确实没有倒退到全人类的爱与怜悯；没有"先生们，我刚才做了个好梦"。

从较早发生的两件事情——关于约拿的布道和以实玛利与魁魁格的友谊——可看出这部小说具有非比寻常的性质。

约拿的布道和基督教其实没有关系。他呼吁宽容或不图回报的忠诚。这个布道人"跪在船首的布道坛前，巨大的棕色双手交叉在胸前，抬起闭紧的双眼，怀着那么深沉的虔诚

---

① 以实玛利：《白鲸》中一次要人物，亚哈船长和其他主要人物最后与白鲸同归于尽的故事就是由他讲述的。

之心，仿佛他是跪在海底似的开始祷告"。最后他用比威胁更可怕的语气说到喜悦：

> 当这艘卑鄙狡诈的世界之船沉没时仍用坚强的双臂撑住自己的人，喜悦吧！以不折不扣的真理之名把所有罪恶、哪怕是从议员和法官的长袍下搜出来的罪恶全部消灭干净的人，喜悦吧！不理会法律或主人而只信奉救主耶稣为上帝、只忠于天国的人，喜悦吧——尽情喜悦！无论是海上的巨浪还是群氓的喧嚣都不能把他从这古老的龙骨①上摇落的人，喜悦吧！他将永远喜悦，永远欢愉，就是到他临终之际，他也会用最后一口气说——哦，我的在天之父！——用你的权杖指点我，让我知道——我现在死了，是进地狱还是得永生。我努力想属于你，超过属于这个世界，超过属于我自己。这还算不了什么：我把永恒归于你；因为一个人怎么会活得比他的上帝还要长久？

我相信这不是巧合，我们在小说行将结束、那场大灾祸来临之前看到的最后那艘船，就叫"喜悦号"；一艘不祥之船，它遇到了莫比·狄克而被它击得粉碎。不过，在这位启示者心里，这是怎么相联系的，我没法说，他也没法告诉

---

① 古老的龙骨：喻基督教信仰。

我们。

讲过布道这件事之后，以实玛利就和食人肉的野蛮人魁魁格结下了生死之交，这使得这部小说一时看起来像是一个歃血为盟的传奇故事。不过，麦尔维尔对人际关系没有多大兴趣，在一次既怪异又狂暴的出场后，魁魁格就几乎被忘记了。几乎——不是完全。在小说快要结束时他病倒了，为他做好的一口棺材后来没用，因为他没死而且康复了。就是这口棺材，最后像一只救生船，把以实玛利从大漩涡里救了出来。这同样不是巧合，而是一种不成形的模糊联系，是在麦尔维尔心里突然萌生的。《白鲸》充满各种各样的含义；关于它的含义是另一个问题。把"喜悦号"或者那口棺材视为象征是错误的，因为这种象征主义观点如果是正确的，那这部小说就寂静无声了。关于《白鲸》没什么可说，除了说它是一场抗争。还有就是歌声。

麦尔维尔作品的影响力大多得之于他的关于邪恶的观念。一般说来，小说中历来都不怎么敢正视邪恶，极少有比行为不当更严重的事情发生，或者说极少能避免神秘兮兮的疑云。对大多数小说家来说，所谓邪恶无非就是性行为和社交行为不当，或者就是某种模糊不清的东西，这种东西被认为要用某种特殊的方式加上诗歌暗示才能表现出来[①]。他们需要邪恶，因为邪恶也许会仁慈地帮助他们推动情节发展，

---

① 此处"某种模糊不清的东西"即指意识或者心理，"某种特殊的方式加上诗歌暗示"即指意识流小说所用的方式。

然而邪恶本身不是仁慈，通常会逼迫他们去面对一个坏蛋——一个洛夫莱斯或者一个尤利亚·希普①——这个坏蛋伤害其他人物，更伤害作者②。要找一个真实的坏蛋，我们还得来看看麦尔维尔的一个叫作《比利·波德》的故事。

这是个短篇小说，但必须讲一讲，因为这有助于理解麦尔维尔的其他作品。故事发生在诺尔哗变③后不久的一艘英国军舰上——一艘充当舞台但又非常真实的船。主人公——一个年轻英俊的水手——心地善良、嫉恶如仇。他为人并不怒气冲冲。但他心里却火光闪闪。表面上他是个轻松愉快、有点懵懂的年轻人，体格健壮完美，只是有点口吃，而正是这个小小的缺陷，最后竟置他于死地。他——

> 落到了一个并非没有害人陷阱的世界里，要对付那些鬼魅伎俩，单靠勇气……没有一点防身的诡计，是不太行的；在那儿固然可以做这样一个老实人，但是到了大是大非的紧要关头就总是无能为力或者手足无措了。

克拉加特——一个低级军官——见到他就把他视为敌

---

① 洛夫莱斯：理查生小说《克拉丽莎》中的反面人物。尤利亚·希普：狄更斯小说《大卫·科波菲尔》中的反面人物。
② "伤害作者"意为这样的反面人物往往很不真实而使小说作者的信誉受损。
③ 诺尔哗变：1797年英国皇家海军的一次兵变，发生在诺尔地区，故称。

人——他的私敌,因为克拉加特就是邪恶。这是亚哈和莫比·狄克之争的重演,只是双方的身份更为明确,因而我们离启示比较远,离道德和常识比较近。但也近不了多少。克拉加特和其他坏蛋都不一样。

> 天生的邪恶……还有某些恶劣品质无声相随……说这种邪恶并不是什么缺点或者小罪过是一点不过分的。它还有一种明显的傲气,所以它并不图谋钱财或者贪得无厌。总之,这种邪恶一点没有利欲熏心或者好色淫乱的意味。它是严厉的,但并不刁钻刻毒。

他指控比利试图煽动哗变。虽然这一指控荒唐可笑,但却是致命的。因为那年轻人被人叫去证明自己无罪时吓得说不出话来,口吃得更加厉害,心里的怒火顿时爆发,于是一拳击倒诽谤他的人,杀了他,自己则被吊死了。

《比利·波德》是个不着边际的荒诞故事,但却是一首并非没有歌词的歌,它值得一读有两方面原因:一是它本身就很美,二是它能引导我们去读较为难懂的作品。在这里,邪恶是被标明和被人格化的,而不是在海洋里环绕着世界到处漫游①,因而可以比较容易地了解麦尔维尔的想法。在他那里值得注意的是,他的忧虑不是个人烦恼,所以在得知

---

① 暗指白鲸。

他的忧虑后，我们会变得更大，而不是更小。他从不采用那个无聊的小东西——良心，也就是霍桑或者马克·卢瑟福①笔下的那种良心，因为那东西在严肃作家那里往往是一种累赘而影响他们的效果。麦尔维尔——用他那种粗线条的现实主义开始后——直接倒退到全人类主题，倒退到一种远远超过我们所能体验的、因而和辉煌没有什么区别的黑暗与悲伤之中。他说："在某些境况中，没有人能衡量这个世界，除非投入某种东西，某种多少有点像原罪那样的东西，去干扰那个不平衡的天平。"他投入了，投入了某种难以名状的东西，那天平正常了，他给了我们和谐与暂时的救助。

无怪乎 D. H. 劳伦斯会写两篇文章来深入研究麦尔维尔，因为据我所知，D. H. 劳伦斯自己就是当今仅有的启示小说家，当今还活着的以唱歌为主的小说家——其余的都是幻想家或说教家——他具有游吟诗人般即兴高歌的性质，所以对他进行分析研究是很无聊的。他受到评论是因为他还是个说教家——正是这个次要的一面使他显得那么难懂和误导别人——而且是个特别聪明的说教家，懂得怎样挑动朝拜者的神经。这样说吧，在这位启示者面前，你只是坐着，一点也不紧张，他就会突然在你肚皮上踢一脚。"他妈的，这我怎么受得了！"你大叫起来，接着你就打起精神来没完没了地抱怨了。也就是说，他的宣讲主题是令人焦躁不安的——

---

① 马克·卢瑟福：19世纪英国宗教家、小说家。

不是关于性的猛烈抨击，就是关于性的热切指导——最后使你连自己是不是应该有一个肉体也记不清了，只知道自己无能之极。这种威胁，以及对威胁作出的一种反应——温柔甜蜜，分别在 D. H. 劳伦斯的作品中占据最显著的地位；不过，他的伟大之处却远远不在这里，而是基于某种与美学有关的东西——并非像陀思妥耶夫斯基那样基于基督教，也不像麦尔维尔那样基于抗争。他的声音是巴尔德尔的声音，虽则他的手是以扫的手①。这位启示者从其内心发出自然之光，所以每一种色彩都很耀眼，每一种形式都很独特，这在别处是难以做到的。就以一个令人难忘的场景为例：即《恋爱中的女人》中的一个场景，其中有个人物在夜里往湖里扔石头而砸碎了水中月影。他为什么要扔石头，这个场景象征什么，都不重要。重要的是，不这么写就写不出这样的月亮和这样的湖水；他用他独特的方式把月亮和湖水渲染得比我们想象的还要奇妙。这里，这位启示者回到了他的起点，回到了湖边上那个我们正在那里等着的地方，但他使用的是一种我们绝不会有的再创造力和感召力。

与这位易怒和令人恼怒的作者在一起是不容易谦逊的，

---

① 巴尔德尔（Balder）：古斯堪的纳维亚神话中主神奥丁之子，英俊而正直。以扫（Esau）：《圣经·旧约》中的人物，和雅各是孪生兄弟。先是雅各用欺骗手段买得以扫的长子名分，后雅各又在父亲以撒临终时借母亲利百加之助想抢先骗得父亲的祝福。以撒老眼昏花，摸着雅各的手说："声音是雅各的声音，手却是以扫的手。"误以为眼前是自己的长子以扫，就给了他祝福。此处套用《圣经》中的这句话，意思是：D. H. 劳伦斯表面上在说基督教，实质上是在宣扬古代异教。见下句，意为古代异教比基督教更为自然。

因为我们越谦逊，他就越蛮横。但是我不知道除此之外还能怎样来读他的作品。如果我们一开始就嫌恶或者嘲讽他，那么他的宝藏肯定会像我们一开始就服从他一样消失不见。他的可贵之处无法用语言来表述：那是人物和事物的色彩、姿势和轮廓，小说家的常备库存，但却是用那样不寻常的方式展现的，可说属于一个新的世界。

那么艾米莉·勃朗特又怎样呢？为什么要在这里讲到《呼啸山庄》？这是个关于几个人的故事，并没有对全人类的看法。

我的回答是，希刺克利夫和凯瑟琳·恩肖①的激情不同于其他小说中的激情。不是栖居在这两个人物身上，而是像雷电云一样裹挟着他们，而且其发出的轰鸣声充满整部小说——从洛克伍德梦见窗口中有只手，直到希刺克利夫被发现死在同一个窗口下。《呼啸山庄》充满声响——充满狂风暴雨——充满一种比语词和思想更重要的声响②。这部小说之伟大，就在于读完之后什么都不会记住，只记得希刺克利夫和凯瑟琳·恩肖。他们的分离生发出情节；他们的死后相聚结束了小说。无怪乎他们"游魂"：这样的灵魂还能做什么？就是他们活着的时候，他们的爱和恨也已超越他们自身。

艾米莉·勃朗特在有些方面是小心谨慎的。她甚至比奥

---

① 希刺克利夫和凯瑟琳·恩肖：《呼啸山庄》中的男女主人公。
② 一种比语词和思想更重要的声响：即指激情。

斯丁小姐更精心地按一张时间表构筑她的小说；她不仅把林淳和恩肖两家安排得互相对称，而且对希剌克利夫获取两家财产的各种法律程序也弄得很清楚。那么，她为什么要执意引入混沌与骚乱呢？因为在我们看来，她是个女启示者；因为她所暗示的东西比她所说的东西更重要；因为唯有在混乱之中，希剌克利夫和凯瑟琳的形象才能凸显出来，才能使他们的激情淹没整个庄园乃至整个荒原。除了这两个人物，《呼啸山庄》没有神话；没有哪部伟大小说比它更少提及天国和地狱了。它是地域性的，就如它里面的那两个灵魂①，我们只有在他们那个郡里的风信子和石灰岩之间才能遇到他们，而与此不同，我们在任何一个小池塘里或许都会碰到莫比·狄克。

  总结一下。在我内心深处，我对这类启示作品总有所保留，一种有人会比我更多、有人则根本不会有的保留。幻想要求我们额外付出点东西，现在启示要求的是谦逊，甚至是幽默感缺失，所以当一个悲剧被称作《比利·波德》时，我们也是不可以偷偷地笑的。实际上，我们不得不抛开我们用来看待大多数文学作品和日常生活的单纯看法，这种看法虽然也是我们在讨论小说时尽力采用的，但在这一讲中不得不抛开而改用一套完全不同的工具。这样做对不对呢？有位启示者，布莱克②，毫不怀疑这是对的。"愿上帝使我们远离╱

---

① 那两个灵魂：即指希剌克利夫和凯瑟琳。
② 布莱克：19世纪英国诗人。

单纯的看法，和牛顿的睡眠！"① 他大声说，还画了一幅画，画面上：牛顿背对着莫比·狄克掀起的惊涛骇浪，手里拿着圆规，在画一个简单的三角形。很少有人会同意布莱克。更少有人会同意布莱克笔下的牛顿。我们大多数人会按我们的性情成为倒来倒去的折衷派。是的，人的心灵并不是什么威风凛凛的组织，除了通过倒来倒去的折中做法，我不知道怎样才能真正地发挥心灵的作用。所以，我对我的折中派伙伴提出的唯一忠告是："不要以你们的态度不一贯为荣。这很遗憾，很遗憾我们生来就是这样。很遗憾人类不能既卓越又诚实。"

在本次讲座的前面五讲中，我们使用的是一套多少有点相同的工具。在这一讲和上一讲中，我们不得不把这套工具扔在一边。在下一讲中，我们又会把它捡回来，但没法肯定它是用于批评的最佳装备，甚至都没法肯定这样的东西就是批评用的装备。

---

① 引自布莱克"With happiness stretchd across the hills"一诗，原诗无题，以首句命名。

第八章　图形与节奏

　　我们的插曲①——一段轻快，一段庄严——已经奏完，我们要返回本讲座的主曲。我们从故事开始，接着讨论人物，然后又讲到源自故事的情节。现在，我们必须考虑某种主要源自情节、同时也得益于人物和其他因素的东西。这是个新的层面，对此显然没有文学术语可用——实际上，各门艺术越是发展，就越是依靠相互解释。我们首先要从绘画中借用术语，称这个层面为"图形"②。然后我们要从音乐中借用术语，称它为"节奏"。不幸的是，这两个术语都很含糊——当人们把节奏或图形用于文学时，他们往往不是说它们是什么意思，甚至连话都不说完，譬如："哦，但可以肯定那节奏……"或者"哦，但你如果称其为图形……"

　　在讨论图形有何种含义以及读者在欣赏图形时需要有何素质之前，我要先举两部其中的图形非常清晰甚至可以用某

---

① 两段插曲：指幻想和启示。
② 原文为pattern，常译作"模式""样式"等，但鉴于此处说是从绘画中借用的术语，故译作"图形"，意即一幅画的大致轮廓。

种形状来表示的小说作为实例：一部是钟漏形的，另一部是老式兰谢舞①中的长链形。

阿纳托尔·法朗士②的《泰伊丝》是钟漏形的。其中有两个主要人物：苦行僧帕弗尼斯、交际花泰伊丝。帕弗尼斯住在沙漠里，他在小说开始的时候就已经得到救赎而倍感幸福。泰伊丝在亚历山大城过着有罪的生活，帕弗尼斯的责任就是要拯救她。在小说的核心场景中，他们相遇，他成功了；她进了一家修道院而得到救赎，因为她遇到了他；但是他呢，因为遇到了她，却要下地狱了。这两个人物是以数学的精确性相互遇见、相互交往和相互分离的，我们读这部小说所得到的大部分乐趣都要归功于此。《泰伊丝》的图形就是这样——简单明了，可说是讨论难题的一个好的起点。《泰伊丝》中的故事也是这样，其中的事件是按时间顺序展现的；《泰伊丝》中的情节也是这样，我们从中看到两个人物由于他们先前的行为而联系到一起，然后踏出关键的几步而分头走向他们自己料不到的终点③。不过，就如故事要求我们有好奇心、情节要求我们有智力，图形要求我们有审美感，它使我们把这部小说看作一个整体。我们并不真的把它看作一个钟漏——那不过是课堂上的一个牵强说法，在像我们这样的高级学术探讨中是绝对不能当真的。我们只是有一

---

① 兰谢舞：一种四人组的舞蹈。
② 阿纳托尔·法朗士：法国小说家，曾获1921年诺贝尔文学奖。
③ 这句话描述了钟漏形，即两条平行线渐渐合拢又渐渐分开。

种乐趣而不知道为什么,所以当乐趣过后,像现在这样,我们就静下心来加以解释,这才发现用这样一个钟漏的几何图形来比喻是很有帮助的。如果没有这钟漏形,那么故事、情节,还有泰伊丝和帕弗尼斯的性格,就全都不会充分发挥它们的感染力,全都不会像现在这样生动。"图形"似乎那么僵硬,而与大气层相联系,似乎又那么飘逸。

接下来看一部形状像长链的小说——珀西·卢伯克的《罗马图景》。

《罗马图景》是一部社会喜剧。故事叙述者是一个到罗马旅游的观光客;他在那里遇到他的一个热心但可鄙的朋友狄林,他自以为是地批评他老盯着教堂,还自以为是地要带他去考察社会。他恭恭敬敬地听从了;一个人把自己交给了另一个人;咖啡馆、画廊、梵蒂冈和皇宫周围都去了,直到最后,到了他觉得自己的旅程已经彻底结束之时,在一座最有贵族气派而又最破败不堪的宅邸中,他又遇到了本该在那里遇到的二流子狄林;原来,狄林是他的女房东的侄子,只是由于势利心作怪,他把这隐瞒了。这样兜了一圈,两个人以本来面目再次相见,颇为尴尬地相互打招呼,转而便哈哈大笑。

《罗马图景》的出色之处并非"长链"图形的呈现——任何人都能编织一条长链——而是这种图形和作者意图的相辅相成。卢伯克始终致力于制造一系列小小的震惊,致力于额外赋予他的人物一种装模作样的宽宏大量,这使他们显得比一点都不宽宏大量还要小气。这就是喜剧气氛，就是略有讽意，也是用心良苦。到小说结束时，我们又高兴地发现喜剧气氛的具体化：那两人在侯爵夫人的客厅里突然碰头时，他们的表现正是小说要达到的目的，一开始就要达到的目的，而且还像一根用他们自身材料编成的绳索把前面分散的事件捆扎在一起。

《泰伊丝》和《罗马图景》提供了两个关于图形的简易范例；一部小说和一幅画并不总是能精确加以比较的，虽然曲线之类的说法动不动就出现在批评家嘴里，但他们并不知道自己想说什么。（至此）我们只能说图形是小说的一个美学层面，只能说，虽然它在小说中可能得益于任何东西——人物、场景、词句，都有可能——但它最多得益于情节。在讨论情节时，我们曾讲到，情节为自身增加美感，美神对她自己会来到这里还有点诧异；讲到细心的读者会从精巧的细木工艺中看到缪斯的身影；讲到逻辑在建好自己的府邸之时就为一种新的东西打好了基础①。这儿，就在这儿的这个点上，被称作图形的层面和构成图形的材料最为紧密地连接在一起；这儿就是我们谈论图形的起点。图形主要来自情节，它就像云层里的一道光伴随着情节。所谓美，时常是指小说的形式，指小说的完整、统一；如果总是这样，我们考察起

---

① 参见第五章"情节"。此处，"细木工艺"喻情节；"逻辑"，也就是因果律，在本书中通常是指情节（因为情节所表现的就是有因果关系的事情）；"一种新的东西"即指情节。

来就容易多了。问题是,有时并不这样。那时,我就只好称其为节奏了。现在我们只关注图形。

让我们在某种程度上再来考察一部形式严谨的小说,一部前后统一的小说,这部小说虽说是亨利·詹姆斯写的,但在这个意义上说却是一部浅显的小说①。我们将在其中看到图形的胜利,还可以看到一个作家若想让图形一家获胜就必须作出牺牲。

和《泰伊丝》一样,《使节》② 也是钟漏形的。和帕弗尼斯和泰伊丝一样,斯特瑞塞和查德也相互换位,而且正是这种相互换位使得这部小说最后那么令人满意。小说的情节精巧而微妙,通过每个段落中的动作、对话或者思考而予以推进。每一件事件都是计划好的,每一事情都恰如其分:就是次要人物也没有一个像尼西亚斯宴会上的那些啰里啰唆的亚历山大城居民一样③只是摆设;他们烘托主题,他们是有用的——小说的最后效果是预先安排好的,然后一步步地逐渐展示给读者,所以当这一效果出现时也就完全成功了。小说中关于私通的细节可能会被人忘记,但小说的对称结构却是令人难忘的。

让我们来看看这一对称结构是如何形成的。

斯特瑞塞是个敏感的中年美国人,他受他的老朋友、他

---

① 由于亨利·詹姆斯采用非传统的角度讲述故事,他的小说通常被认为比较难懂。
② 《使节》:或译《奉使记》《大使》,亨利·詹姆斯的著名小说。
③ 尼西亚斯:古希腊将军。尼西亚斯的宴会是修昔底德《伯罗奔尼撒战争史》中的著名篇章,后成典故。

想与之结婚的纽瑟姆太太之托,前往巴黎去拯救她那个在这堕落之城里堕落的儿子。纽瑟姆一家是富有的商人,靠制造一种日常小用品发了财。那小用品到底是什么,亨利·詹姆斯始终没有告诉我们,不过我们随即就明白了他为什么不说。威尔斯在《托诺-邦盖》中是把它说出来的,梅瑞狄斯在《伊万·哈灵顿》中也毫不避讳,特罗洛普还大大方方地把它推荐给了邓斯特波尔小姐①,但对亨利·詹姆斯来说,要他明说他的人物是靠什么发的财——这不可能。那小用品有点不上台面,有点滑稽可笑——知道这就够了。如果你偏要粗鲁莽撞,自以为是地想象,说是纽扣钩②,那当然可以,但你这么做是你自己在冒险,和作者毫不相干。

不管是什么,反正查德·纽瑟姆应该回来协助制造那东西,所以斯特瑞塞奉命去抓捕他。他必须从一种既不道德又不赢利的生活中被拯救出来。

斯特瑞塞是典型的詹姆斯式人物——这种人物几乎在詹姆斯的所有小说中反复出现,是构成他的小说的关键部分。他是个试图对事件有所影响的旁观者,而且由于他的失败而额外得到旁观机会。其他人物都是斯特瑞塞这样的旁观者的旁观对象——通过由超一流配镜师配备的镜片来旁观③。所

---

① 邓斯特波尔小姐:特罗洛普小说《索恩医生》中的人物。
② 纽扣钩:一种用来把纽扣钩过纽扣孔的钩子,特别是在穿毛料大衣时有用。
③ "由超一流配镜师配备的镜片"喻指亨利·詹姆斯小说中独特的叙事角度。

有事物都进入他的视野,而他还不是一个静止不动的旁观者——不是,这才是这种方法①的力量所在;他使我们随他同行,我们也在动。

当他在英国登陆时(对詹姆斯来说,登陆是兴奋而难忘的经历,就像笛福对新门监狱那样刻骨铭心②;诗意和生活都围绕着登陆)③——当斯特瑞塞登陆时,虽然登上的只是古老的英国,但他却开始怀疑自己的使命;到达巴黎后,他更加怀疑了。因为查德·纽瑟姆并没有堕落,而是大有长进:他才华出众,信心满满地对奉命前来抓捕他的人真诚而热情;他结交的都是高雅之士,至于他母亲预料的"那些有关系的女人",根本连影子都没有。正是在巴黎,他长了见识,赎回了自己——对此,斯特瑞塞也是那么深有体会!

> 他最感不安的似乎是他无意中可能得到了这样一种印象:几乎任何人到了巴黎后都会抛弃自己的先入之见。今天早上,巴黎就呈现在他眼前,这宽敞而光明的巴比伦④,就像一个灿烂辉煌的庞然大物,一块璀璨而坚实的宝石,各部分都难以区分,都令人赏心悦目。它闪闪

---

① 这种方法:即指亨利·詹姆斯的角度论。
② 笛福曾由于多种原因几次入狱。
③ 这里的"他"是双关语,既指斯特瑞塞,又指亨利·詹姆斯。后面括号里的话意谓亨利·詹姆斯离开美国,横渡大西洋登陆英国,这才功成名就。
④ 巴比伦:公元前2世纪中东古城,史称极其繁华,后世用其泛指大都市。

发光，微微震动，浑然一体；任何地方在这一刻看似表面，下一刻便尽显深度。就是这个地方，没错，是查德所钟爱的；因此，如果他，斯特瑞塞，也喜欢得不得了，那么这样一来，他们两人究竟还分得出你我吗？

就这样，既精妙又稳重，詹姆斯营造出他的氛围——巴黎始终是小说中的亮点，始终是一个并不人格化的角色，一个可以衡量人类感受力的尺度，而当我们读完这部小说后，小说中的事件会变得模糊而小说的图形则会看得更清楚，这时我们会看到，在钟漏形中央闪耀的就是巴黎——既不纯善也不纯恶的巴黎。斯特瑞塞看到了这一点，同时看出查德也看到了这一点，而就在这时，小说来了个转折：终究，有关系的女人还是有一个的，即令人羡慕、受人尊敬的德·维奥内夫人，她指点查德从巴黎背后认识巴黎。至此，斯特瑞塞再要做什么事已不可能了。德·维奥内夫人集高贵和优雅于一身，更有悲天悯人之心。她恳求他不要带走查德。他答应了——并不勉强，因为他自己的内心已提出同样的恳求——他留在巴黎，并不和它争斗，而是为它而争斗。

现在，从新世界①来了第二批使节。因为纽瑟姆太太被莫名其妙的拖延弄得既恼怒又困惑，便派来了查德的姐姐和姐夫，还有玛米，一个被认为查德应该和她结婚的年轻姑

---

① 新世界：即美国。

娘。现在,小说在其自身限度内显得最为有趣。这儿有查德的姐姐和德·维奥内夫人之间的一场好戏,至于玛米——下面就是斯特瑞塞眼中的玛米:

在童年时,在"蓓蕾"之时,以及后来的如花绽放之时,玛米在他看来一直都很活泼,很随便的,几乎会不间断地出现在家门口;在那儿,他记得她起先很大方,后来又很拘束——因为有一段时间他在纽瑟姆太太的客厅里……起劲地温习英国文学课程,因为要考试,又喝着茶——那是最后再一次温习功课,就像以前许多次一样。不过,他记不得和她有过多少接触;因为在伍莱特镇上,刚开的鲜花和冬天的皱皮苹果放在一个篮子里是很不自然的事情……然而,当他和这个迷人的姑娘一起坐着时,他觉得信任感明显增加了。她很迷人,再怎么说也是——然而,却是有那种自由放任的行为习惯。她很迷人,他觉得即使他没有发现她很迷人,也会发现她有某种他可以冒险地称为"滑稽"的东西。是的,她是滑稽的、奇异的玛米,这是做梦也想不到的;她是温顺的,她是——这是他早就想到的——没有新郎搀扶的新娘;她是漂亮的、丰满的、轻松的、饶舌的,她是温柔的、甜蜜的,可亲近得几乎令人尴尬。如果我们硬要挑剔,她的穿着不太像一位年轻女士,而像一个老妇人——一个在斯特瑞塞看来肯定是难免虚荣的老妇人；还有她的发型很考究，不像年轻姑娘那样一头散发；还有当她把一双特别光洁的手轻轻地握在胸前时，她显得有点弯腰屈背似的老态，像是在给人发奖章；而这一切合在一起就是她的"接待客人"时的风采，它不仅永久地将她置于窗台之间和冰激凌盘子发出的叮当声中，还不断地使她想起一系列属于同一种类的、她乐于"相见"的社交爱好者的名字……

玛米是另一类亨利·詹姆斯式的人物，几乎在他的每部小说中都会出现——譬如《波英顿的珍藏》中的格瑞斯太太，或者《一位女士的画像》中的亨丽爱塔·斯塔克波尔。亨利·詹姆斯擅长寥寥数笔直接表现人物，因而即使是次要的、愚昧迟钝的、俗里俗气的人物，他也照样能把他们写得那么生动，以致他们的荒唐行为也使人觉得趣味盎然。

这样，斯特瑞塞改变了立场，从而失去了和纽瑟姆太太结婚的所有希望。巴黎赢了——而此时他却有了新的发现。查德看上去很正派，会不会是他故意装出来的？巴黎对查德来说会不会真的是个寻欢作乐的地方？他的担心得到了证实。有一次他独自在乡间散步，到黄昏时他偶尔看到了查德和德·维奥内夫人。他们在一只小船上，装着没有看见他，因为他们的关系其实就是寻常的男女私情，所以羞于被人看到。他们此时正想到一个乡间客栈里去过一个秘密周末，以此延续他们的激情；如果激情不能延续，查德就会厌倦这个衣着优雅的法国女人，因为她利用了他的一时冲动；如果这样，查德就会回到他母亲身边去经营那种家庭小用品，就会和玛米结婚。他们两人对此都心知肚明，虽然他们竭力隐瞒，却还是被斯特瑞塞发现了；他们在说谎，他们卑劣低贱——甚至德·维奥内夫人，甚至她的悲天悯人，也沾满了鄙俗之尘。

  这对他来说就像一阵阴风，这简直使人毛骨悚然，一个这么优秀的人，出于神秘的原因，竟会是一个这么不堪的人。因为，归根结底，他们是神秘的；她不过是把查德教成他这个样子——她为什么还会以为她把他教得完美无缺了？她以为她把他教得更好了，她把他教得最好了，她把他教得再好没有了；然而在我们的朋友看来却是奇怪之极，他不过就是查德……她所做的事，虽然值得称道，但不管怎么说还是俗人之事；简单说来，令人惊叹的是它以世间凡俗的欢愉、享受和越轨——反正是诸如此类的东西——为伴，竟然还会那么超凡脱俗地受到赞誉……

  他觉得她今晚变老了，显然少不了岁月的印痕；但她和以往一样仍是他这几年来遇到的最优雅、最精明的女人，最快乐的精灵；然而，他千真万确地看到，她像一个为自己的小情人哭泣的女仆一样在那儿俗里俗气地伤心。只不过她自己能判断而女仆不能；但同样，这种软弱的聪明才智,这种不光彩的判断能力,似乎也只会使她更消沉。

这样,斯特瑞塞又失去了他们。就如他自己所说:"你看,这就是我的命运。整个这件事,我从中一无所获。"这不是他们背弃他。这是他舍弃了他们。他们向他展示了巴黎——现在,如果他们有眼力看的话,他也可以向他们展示巴黎,因为有些事情比他们所能注意到的更为美好,他的想象力比他们的年轻更有精神价值。这样,钟漏图形便完成了:他和查德互换了位置,其步骤比泰伊丝和帕弗尼斯的互换位置更为精妙,那道云层里的光[①]不是来自灯火辉煌的亚历山大城,而是来自那块"闪闪发光,微微震动,浑然一体;任何地方在这一刻看似表面,下一刻便尽显深度"的宝石[②]。

《使节》中充满美感,这是对一位优秀艺术家辛勤劳作的报偿。亨利·詹姆斯非常清楚自己想要什么,他踏上了那条狭窄的美学之路,而他所获得的最大可能的成功使他声名遐迩。他的图形是自动生成的,协调一致而且有所预示,这在阿纳托尔·法朗士那里是不可能有的。但为此要作出怎样的牺牲!

牺牲如此之大,以致许多读者在读亨利·詹姆斯的作品时虽然都读得下去(他的作品难懂是过于夸大的),也很赏

---

① 那道云层里的光:喻图形。参见前文。
② 那块……宝石:喻巴黎。参见前文中的引文。

识他的努力，但就是提不起兴趣。他们不能同意他的前提，即：在他能为我们写出一部小说之前，人类生活的大部分必须消失①。

首先，他的人物很少。我已说到过两种——试图对事件有所影响的旁观者，和次要的局外人（譬如，《梅西所知道的》中非常出色的开头部分写的就是这种人物）。此外还有心怀关切的陪衬人物——很活跃而且频繁出现的女性人物——在《使节》中，玛利亚·高斯特里扮演的就是这种角色；还有神奇而罕见的女主人公，德·维奥内夫人近似这种人物，而《鸽翼》中的米莉则是地地道道的这种人物；有时还会有个坏蛋，有时还会有个慷慨激昂的青年艺术家；这大概就是全部了。对于这样一位优秀小说家来说，这是个可怜巴巴的人物阵容。

其次，除了数量少，他的人物还是用很少几根线条描绘出来的。他们不会开玩笑，不会莽莽撞撞，既不淫荡，也不好色，而且十分之九没有一点英雄气概。他们的衣服从不脱下；他们患上的疾病都是无名的，就如他们的收入来源也是无名的；他们的仆人都是无声无息的，要不就和他们一样；没有一种我们知道的社会理论对他们来说是必要的，因为他们那里没有愚昧的民众，没有语言障碍，也没有穷人。甚至

---

① 此句意为亨利·詹姆斯并不以模仿生活为写作宗旨，而是致力于小说自身的艺术（很大程度上就是小说的叙事角度，即怎样通过变换叙事角度而产生艺术幻觉，或艺术效果）。

他们的感受力也很有限。他们会登陆欧洲，会去观看艺术品，或者会相互观看，但也仅此而已。残缺不全的人物唯有在亨利·詹姆斯的小说中才能生存——他们残缺不全，但被专门处理过。他们使人想起阿克那顿①王朝时古埃及艺术中流行的一种精美的畸形雕像——巨大的头颅和细小的双腿，但依然很迷人。只是到了下一个王朝，这种畸形雕像就销声匿迹了。

这种人物数量和人物作用的大幅减少，都是为图形着想的。亨利·詹姆斯写作时间越久，他越是确信一部小说应该是一个整体——虽然没必要一定要像《使节》那样成几何形，但小说应该围绕一个主题、一种情境、一种态势展开，应该由这些东西来占有人物和提供情节，同时还应该使小说紧密联系外部世界——把分散的叙述收入一张网内，使其像一颗行星一样，旋转着穿越记忆的太空。因而，某种图形必须呈现，任何脱离图形而呈现的东西必须被视为胡闹而清除掉。那么，谁在这样胡闹呢？把汤姆·琼斯或者爱玛甚至卡苏朋先生②放入亨利·詹姆斯的某部小说，这部小说会烧成灰烬，然而我们却可以把他们相互放入对方的小说，结果只是局部起火。只有亨利·詹姆斯的人物才适合亨利·詹姆斯的小说，虽然他们并非都是死人——对某些特定的人生经

---

① 阿克那顿：古埃及法老（前1379—前1362在位）。
② 汤姆·琼斯：菲尔丁同名小说主人公。爱玛：简·奥斯丁同名小说主人公。卡苏朋先生：乔治·爱略特《米德尔马契》中的重要人物。

历,亨利·詹姆斯还是作了很好的探讨——但其他小说中的人物所共有的东西在他们身上被去除了。这样的阉割并非为天国着想,他的小说中没有哲学,没有宗教(除了偶尔有点迷信),没有启示,毫无超常之处。他只是为了达到某种特殊的审美效果而且确实达到了,但付出了如此沉重的代价。

H. G. 威尔斯一直在思考这一点,也许还很深刻。在他的一部最生动有趣的论著《恩惠》中,他非常重视亨利·詹姆斯,写了一篇极好的文章来调侃他。

> 亨利·詹姆斯理所当然地认为一部小说就是一部艺术作品,必须根据它的独特性来加以评判。其实,这种看法最初是由某人告诉他的,只是他一直没有发现。他从不发现什么。他甚至都不想发现什么……他轻易接受了,就加以发挥……唯一留在亨利·詹姆斯小说中的人类欲念是某种热切的期待和某种非常肤浅的好奇心……暗示接着暗示,联想接着联想,他的人物嗅出种种疑点。有谁见过这样的活人?他的小说所讲的东西总是那么一套。它就像一座只有烛光没有信徒聚集的教堂,每一道光线都集中到高高的祭坛上。而在那祭坛上,非常虔诚地、非常热切地,放着一只死猫、一个蛋壳、一截绳子……就如他的《死者的祭坛》,和死者根本没有关系……因为,如果有什么关系,那些东西就没法全被烛光照亮,效果就没了……

威尔斯把《恩惠》当作礼物寄给詹姆斯，显然以为这位小说大师会像他自己一样对这样的真心诚意感到高兴。但这位大师一点也不高兴，而是开始了两人间极有意思的书信往来。詹姆斯彬彬有礼、顾念旧情，但又困惑不解、深为恼怒，而且怒不可遏：他直言不讳地说威尔斯的调侃没有"使我觉得欣喜有趣"，而且最后还抱歉地表示他只能署名为"您忠实的，亨利·詹姆斯"①。威尔斯也困惑不解，但原因不同：他不明白那人为什么要发火。这里，不仅是私人间的吵闹，还有意义重大的文学问题。正是这个问题，牵涉到小说中的固定图形：钟漏形也好，长链形也好，大教堂式的双线交叉形也好，凯瑟琳车轮②式的多线条辐射形也好，普罗克拉斯提斯之床形③也好——只要能自成一体，不管什么形状都可以。那么，图形能和来自生活中的各种各样的素材结合在一起吗？威尔斯和詹姆斯都会同意，这不可能。威尔斯还会进一步说，生活应该给予优先考虑，决不能因为图形的缘故而被压缩或者夸大。我和威尔斯一样存有这种偏见。詹姆斯的小说是一种独特的成就，不能接受他的前提的读者将错失某些有益和精美的享受。但是，就像我不希望阿克那顿王朝的艺术延续到图坦卡蒙④王朝，我不希望他再写出更多

---

① 这是公文式署名，表示他断绝了和威尔斯的朋友关系。
② 凯瑟琳车轮：一种轮圈外缘装有倒钩的车轮。
③ 普罗克拉斯提斯：古希腊神话中的阿卡蒂巨人，传说他有一张床，人躺上去，比床长的他就截短，比床短的他就拉长。
④ 图坦卡蒙：古埃及法老（前1361—前1352在位），阿克那顿的继任者。

小说，尤其不希望其他作家也去写这种小说。

这就是固定图形的坏处。它也许可以使小说氛围具体化，而且从情节中自然产生，但是它关掉了生活之门，使小说家往往只能在客厅里施展才能①。美神是到来了，但一副专横霸道的样子。在戏剧中——譬如在拉辛②的戏剧中——她也许是正当的，因为美神可以做舞台上的伟大女皇，可以使我们不计较失去我们的熟人③。但是在小说中，她越是专横霸道，就越是卑微低贱，令人遗憾，这种遗憾有时就会在像《恩惠》这样的著述中表达出来。换句话说，小说是不可能像戏剧那样偏重于艺术展示的，因为它受阻于它的世俗性或者说它的素材的粗杂性（你们想换种说法也可以，反正就是这个意思）。在大多数小说读者看来，得自图形的那点感觉和为此而作出的牺牲是不相称的，所以他们的结论是："美是美的，但不值得。"

至此，我们的讨论并未结束。我们还不会放弃对美的希求。要把美引入小说，除了图形还有其他方式吗？有的，让我们小心翼翼地靠近那个叫作"节奏"的概念。

节奏有时很容易懂。譬如，贝多芬《第五交响曲》④ 就

---

① 意即图形（即某种人为的情节结构）可使小说具有某种审美形态（"小说氛围具体化"），但很可能会使小说太"人为"而不像是真实的生活，小说家只是在自己设定的图形内写小说（这里的"客厅"即喻小说家自己设定的图形）。
② 拉辛：17世纪法国古典主义戏剧代表人物。
③ 失去我们的熟人：意为远离日常生活。
④ 贝多芬《第五交响曲》：即通常说的《命运交响曲》。

是以"diddidy dum"的节奏开始的，我们谁都听得出而且打得出拍子。但是整部交响曲也有节奏——主要来自各乐章之间的联系——有些人听得出，但没有人打得出拍子。这第二种节奏很难懂，它本质上是否和第一种节奏一样，只有音乐家才能告诉我们。不过，一个搞文学的人所要说的是，第一种节奏，即"diddidy dum"，在有些小说中也有，而且可能还使小说具有美感。至于另一种节奏，即难懂的一种——整部《第五交响曲》的节奏——我说不出小说中有没有与之相对应的节奏，说不定有，我不知道。

容易懂的节奏可以用马塞尔·普鲁斯特的作品来说明。

普鲁斯特的最后一卷尚未出版①，他的崇拜者说，等到他的各卷全部出齐，似水年华将重新流回而且被冻结住，我们将有一个完美的整体。我不相信这种说法。在我看来，这部作品与其说是一部审美忏悔录，不如说是一个行进过程，因为作者在精心描述阿尔贝蒂娜时已经有点疲倦了。或许会有点新东西等着我们，但是说我们到时不得不修正自己对整部作品的看法，那是危言耸听。这部小说是无秩无序的，结构松散，迄今没有、将来也不会有外在的形状②；然而它却聚拢在一起，因为它是内在联结的，因为它具有节奏。

可以举几个例子（外祖母照相就是其中之一），但是从

---

① 普鲁斯特《追忆似水年华》的最后一卷《重现的时光》出版于1927年，福斯特的这个讲座也是在1927年，可能早于前者。也可能他指的是英译本，这一卷的英译本要两年后即1929年才出版。

② 外在的形状：意即看得见的结构（即图形）。

联结的角度看,最好的例子是凡特伊音乐中"短乐句"。这短乐句比任何其他东西——甚至比先后毁掉斯万、主人公①和夏吕斯的妒忌——更使我们觉得处身于一个同性质的世界。我们最初听到凡特伊的名字时情况就很糟。这个乐师已经死了——一个卑微矮小的乡村风琴师,默默无闻——他的女儿还在败坏人们对他的记忆。这可怕的情景是可以朝好几个方向散射出去的,但它就这样过去了。

接着我们就到了巴黎的一个沙龙。那里正在演奏一首小提琴协奏曲,行板中的一个短乐句抓住斯万的耳朵并潜入他的生活。它始终是一个活物,但有不同的外形。有一段时间,它伴随他一起爱上了奥黛特。恋爱出了错,短乐句被他忘记,我们也忘了它。后来在他受妒忌折磨时它又蹦了出来,同时伴随他忍受痛苦和告别幸福,但又不失其自身的非凡性质。这首协奏曲是谁写的?听说是凡特伊写的,斯万说:"我曾认识一个可怜巴巴的矮小风琴师叫这个名字——这不可能是他写的。"但就是他写的,凡特伊的女儿和她的朋友把它誊清后发表了。

似乎就这些。那短乐句一次又一次出现在小说中,但只是作为一种回声、一种记忆;我们乐于碰到它,但它却没有一点束缚力②。然后,翻过好几百页,此时凡特伊成了国宝,人们在谈论要在他的故乡——他生前在那里是那么凄惨、那

---

① 主人公:即小说中的叙述者(或回忆者)"我"。
② 没有一点束缚力:意为并非小说中的重要因素。

么卑微——为他立一座塑像，他的另一部遗作——一部七重奏——也上演了。主人公听着——仿佛置身于一个未知的、颇为可怕的世界，只见一抹不祥的朝霞映红了大海。突然之间，他听到，读者也听到，那奏鸣曲中的短乐句又出现了——不太清晰，有所变化，但出现的是完整的曲调，这使他回想起童年时代的乡间生活，同时又意识到这属于未来世界。

我们不必同意普鲁斯特对音乐的具体描述（我觉得他描述得太图像化），但我们必须赞赏他在文学中使用节奏，赞赏他使用某种本质上和小说所要产生的效果密切相关的东西——即：乐句。凡特伊的那个短乐句虽有不同的人——先是斯万，后来是主人公——听到，但并不是固定不变的：它不是像我们在乔治·梅瑞狄斯那里发现他所用的一种标志——不是伴随着克兰拉·米德尔顿出现的一棵双花樱桃树，也不是为塞西丽娅·霍尔基特准备的一只平静水面上的小船①。标志只会重现，节奏却会发展，那个短乐句有其自身的生命，就像它无关乎它的谱写者的生活，它和它的聆听者的生活也毫不相关。它几乎就是一个角色，却又不全是，这"不全是"的意思就是，它所具有的功能不仅可以从内部把普鲁斯特的小说整合为一体，还可以产生美感和挑逗读者的记忆力。有时，那个短乐句——它忧郁地诞生，经由那首协奏曲，进入现在的七重奏——对读者来说即意味着一切。有

---

① 克兰拉·米德尔顿：梅瑞狄斯《利己主义者》中的女主人公。塞西丽娅·霍尔基特：梅瑞狄斯《比彻姆的事业》中的女主人公。

时，它又毫无意义而被忘记，这在我看来就是节奏在小说中的功能：它不像图形那样时时存在，而是以其调皮的时有时无使我们充满惊奇、新意和期待。

弄得不好，节奏是最令人厌烦的，它僵化为一种符号，不但不引领我们，反而绊倒我们。我们会怒不可遏地发现，高尔斯华绥的长耳狗约翰①或者什么东西，又躺到我们脚边来了；甚至是梅瑞狄斯的樱桃树和小船，虽则优雅，也只是开向诗歌的窗户②而已。我很怀疑那些事先把作品规划好的作家笔下会有节奏，因为必须依靠一种不常见的本能冲动才有可能产生适当的间隔③。不过，节奏的效果可说是很精妙的，它可以获得效果而不损害人物，还可以减少我们对小说外部形式的要求。

关于小说中的简单节奏，这么说肯定足够了：它也许可以定义为重复加变化，而且可以举例说明。接下来是个比较难的问题。当管弦乐队演奏完《第五交响曲》时，我们听到了某种实际上并没有演奏出来的东西④，这是《第五交响曲》整体上的效果；那么，小说中有没有可与之相比拟的效果呢？第一乐章、行板⑤，和构成第三部分的三重奏-谐谑曲-

---

① 高尔斯华绥：19世纪与20世纪之际英国小说家，曾获1932年诺贝尔文学奖。长耳狗约翰：高尔斯华绥《乡宅》中的一只狗，特别令人讨厌。
② 开向诗歌的窗户：意为把小说引向诗歌。
③ 适当的间隔：意即节奏。
④ 某种实际上并没有演奏出来的东西：即指节奏。
⑤ 行板：即第二乐章。

三重奏-终曲-三重奏-终曲①,一下子全都进入我们心中,而且相互延伸而形成一个共同体。这个共同体,这个新东西,就是这部交响曲的整体,它的形成主要(虽不是全部)是靠管弦乐队奏出的三个乐章之间的联系。我把这称为"有节奏的"联系。如果准确的音乐术语不是这么说的,那也没关系;因为我们现在要问自己的是小说中有没有类似的联系。

我没有发现任何类似的东西。但说不定有;在音乐小说②中大概能找到与之最为对应的某种联系。

戏剧的情况有所不同。戏剧或许可以参照绘画艺术,或许可以让亚里士多德来为它制定规则③,因为戏剧并不那么深地牵扯到普通人的诉求。小说则不然,处处都要为普通人创造机会。普通人对小说家说:"你可以重塑我们,但我们必须进入小说。"所以,就如我们所见,小说家面临的问题是既要让普通人得到充分表现,同时又要获取其他什么东西④。他会转身到哪里去呢?他其实不需要帮助,而是要找同类。音乐虽然不表现普通人,虽然受制于复杂的规则,但它最终会给人一种美感,这种美感或许小说也能以自己的方式获得。扩张!这是小说家必须抓住不放的一个想法。不是

---

① 贝多芬《第五交响曲》总共三个乐章。
② 音乐小说:music fiction,指与音乐密切相关的小说,大概有三种:第一种是大量写到音乐和音乐家的小说;第二种是在结构上模仿乐曲结构的小说(一种特殊的抒情小说);第三种是既大量写到音乐和音乐家、又在结构上模仿乐曲结构的小说。此处说到的应该是第二和第三种音乐小说。
③ 西方戏剧的基本规则源自亚里士多德的《诗学》。
④ 其他什么东西:指艺术成就。

固守!不是团团转,而是破门而出。既然听完交响曲后我们会觉得组成交响乐曲的音符和曲调都已经获释,已经各自在整首交响乐曲的节奏中得到自由①,那么,小说就不能这样吗?《战争与和平》不是有点像这样吗?——是的,我们一开始就提到过这部小说,现在就用它来结束。一部多么庞杂的小说啊。但是,当我们读它的时候,不是有洪亮的音乐声在我们身后响起吗?当我们读完它之后,其中的每一种事物——甚至战略图——不是全都超越当时的可能性而得到了一个更大的存在空间②吗?

---

① 此句意为交响曲的最后效果主要在于它的整体节奏,而不是其中的音符和音调;听完交响曲后,音符和音调都会被忘记,留下来的是节奏。
② 得到了一个更大的存在空间:意即存在于小说给人的节奏感中。

第九章 结 语

以预测小说的未来作为结束是很有吸引力的：譬如，小说会不会变得更加写实，还是更不写实；小说会不会被电影扼杀，等等。预测，不管是悲观的，还是乐观的，总有一种了不起的意思，这是一种非常便利于为人提供帮助或者使人印象深刻的方法。不过，我们没有权利享受这种便利。我们既不接受过去的束缚，也就没有未来的福利。我们把过去两百年间的小说家看作是在一个房间里写作的，他们服从同样的激情而把发生在各自时代的事情放进了灵感的熔炉；不管结果如何，我们的这种看法是合理的——至少对于像我们这样的一批假学者来说是合理的。只是，我们还必须把未来两百年间的小说家也看作是在一个房间里写作的。他们的题材会千变万化；他们自己则会一成不变。我们或许会利用原子能，我们或许会登上月球，我们或许会消灭战争或者强调战争，我们或许会理解动物的心理；但所有这些都是区区小事，它们属于历史，不属于艺术。历史是发展的，艺术是静止的。不管有多少创新机制，未来的小说家也会放弃新事物而追寻旧事物。

然而,有一个问题和我们的主题有关,而且只有心理学家才能回答。但不妨由我们来问。创作过程本身会不会变?镜子会不会重新涂上一层水银?也就是说,人性会不会变?让我们考虑一下这种可能性——我们也应该放松放松了。

听听老年人谈论这个问题很有意思。有时,有人信心十足地说:"人性在所有时代都是一样的。原始穴居人始终躺在我们所有人的内心深处。文明——呸!只是摆设。你没法改事实。"他这么说的时候他自我感觉很好,洋洋得意。当他自我感觉不好、被年轻人弄得恼怒时,或者伤心地想到年轻人会成功而他已经失败时,他又会持相反的观点,神秘兮兮地说:"人性从来就不一样。我这一辈子就看到人性彻底变了。你必须面对事实。"他就这样一天又一天地活着,时而说要面对人性会变的事实,时而又拒绝承认人性会变的事实。

我想做的只是陈述一种可能性。说人性会变,可能只是因为有些个人①用一种新的方式看待自己。这儿那儿总有人——很少,但其中有几个是小说家——试图这么做。每一种惯例和每一种既得利益都和这种意图相对立,因为无论是宗教组织、政府,还是家庭经济,都不会因此而有所得;只有当外部禁令减弱时,这种意图才会有所展示;但它历来都被限制

---

① 有些个人:指否定传统文学的现代派作家。

在有限范围内。有此种意图的人也许会失败，思维工具思维自身也许是不可能的，如若可能也许就意味着想象性文学的终结——如果我没有弄错的话，这是那位敏锐的探寻家 I. A. 瑞恰慈①先生的观点。不管怎样，那种新的方式会使小说发生变动甚至爆炸，因为小说家一旦以不同以往的方式看待自己，他就会以不同以往的方式看待他的人物，由此一种新的照明系统②便会产生。

我不知道以上所说是不是冒犯了哪种哲学或者哪些相互竞争的哲学，但当我反省自己的零星知识和审视自己的内心时，我看到这样两种人类智性的运动，即：被称作历史的宏大而沉闷的急流，和一种羞怯的、螃蟹似的侧面运动③。这两种运动在我们的讲座中都被忽视了：历史被忽视，是因为它仅仅携人而行，只是一列满载旅客的火车；螃蟹似的运动被忽视，是因为它在我们讲到的短短两百年间显然动得太慢、太拘谨。所以，当我们讲到人性不变、讲到这使得一系列散文虚构作品迅速产生、讲到五万字以上才可称作长篇小说时，我们理所当然地把它搁下了。如果我们有能力或者有权利作一更为广泛的考察，纵览全人类和前人类④的所有活

---

① I. A. 瑞恰慈：20 世纪初英国著名学者、西方现代文艺学奠基人之一，他的理论强调文学的语言学和心理学功能，因而要求重新审视历来被认为不变的人性。
② 照明系统：喻小说（因小说的主要功能是探索和揭示人性）。
③ 一种羞怯的、螃蟹似的侧面运动：喻艺术运动。
④ 前人类：pre-human，意即人类之前。

动,我们很可能就不会有这样的结果了;螃蟹似的运动,旅客的上上下下①,可能都会历历在目,"小说的发展"这一短语也可能不再是假学术的标志或者一种技术上的琐事,而会变得很重要,因为它意味着人性的发展。

---

① 旅客的上上下下:喻历史(见前文"历史……只是一列满载旅客的火车")。

Edward Morgan Forster

Aspects of the Novel

1927

Contents

Chapter 1   Introductory   187

Chapter 2   The Story   212

Chapter 3   People   232

Chapter 4   People (Continued)   257

Chapter 5   The Plot   278

Chapter 6   Fantasy   301

Chapter 7   Prophecy   322

Chapter 8   Pattern and Rhythm   349

Chapter 9   Conclusion   373

Chapter 1   Introductory

This lectureship is connected with the name of William George Clark, a Fellow of Trinity. It is through him we meet today, and through him we shall approach our subject.

Clark was, I believe, a Yorkshireman. He was born in 1821, was at school at Sedbergh and Shrewsbury, entered Trinity as an undergraduate in 1840, became Fellow four years later, and made the college his home for nearly thirty years, only leaving it when his health broke, shortly before his death. He is best known as a Shakespearian scholar, but he published two books on other subjects to which we must here refer. He went as a young man to Spain and wrote a pleasant lively account of his holiday called *Gazpacho*: gazpacho being the name of a certain cold soup which he ate and appears to have enjoyed among the peasants of Andalusia; indeed he appears to have enjoyed everything. Eight years later, as a result of a holiday in Greece, he published a second book, *Peloponnesus*. *Peloponnesus* is a graver work and a duller. Greece was a serious place in those days, more serious than Spain, besides, Clark had by now not only taken Orders but become Public Orator, and he was, above all, travelling with Dr. Thompson, the then Master of the college, who was not at all the sort of person to be involved in a cold soup. The jests about mules and fleas are consequently few, and we are increasingly confronted with the remains of classical antiquity and the sites of battles. What survives in the book — apart from its learning — is its feeling for Greek countryside. Clark also travelled in Italy and Poland.

To turn to his academic career. He planned the great Cambridge Shakespeare, first with Glover, then with Aldis Wright (both librarians of Trinity), and, helped by Aldis Wright, he issued the popular Globe Shakespeare. He collected much material for an edition of Aristophanes. He also published some sermons, but in 1869 he gave up Holy Orders — which, by the way, will exempt us from excessive orthodoxy. Like his friend and biographer Leslie Stephen, like Henry Sidgwick and others of that generation, he did not find it possible to remain in the Church, and he has explained his reasons in a pamphlet entitled *The Present Dangers of the Church of England*. He resigned his post of Public Orator in consequence, while retaining his college tutorship. He died at the age of fifty-seven, esteemed by all who knew him as a lovable, scholarly and honest man. You will have realized that he is a Cambridge figure. Not a figure in the great world or even at Oxford, but a spirit peculiar to these courts, which perhaps only you who tread them after him can justly appreciate: the spirit of integrity. Out of a bequest in his will, his old college has provided for a series of lectures, to be delivered annually "on some period or periods of English Literature not earlier than Chaucer," and that is why we meet here now.

Invocations are out of fashion, yet I wanted to make this small one, for two reasons. Firstly, may a little of Clark's integrity be with us through this course; and secondly, may he accord us a little inattention! For I am not keeping quite strictly to the terms laid down. "Period or periods of English Literature." This condition, though it sounds liberal and is liberal enough in spirit, happens verbally not quite to suit our subject, and the introductory lecture will be occupied in explaining why this is. The points raised may seem trivial. But they will lead us to a convenient vantage-post from which we can begin our main attack.

We need a vantage-post, for the novel is a formidable mass, and it is so amorphous — no mountain in it to climb, no Parnassus or Helicon, not even a Pisgah. It is most distinctly one of the moister areas of literature — irrigated by a hundred rills and occasionally degenerating into a swamp. I do not wonder that the poets despise it, though they sometimes find themselves in it by accident. And I am not surprised at the annoyance of the historians when by accident it finds itself among them. Perhaps we ought to define what a novel is before starting. This will not take a second. M. Abel Chevalley has, in his brilliant little manual, provided a definition, and if a French critic cannot define the English novel, who can? It is, he says, "a fiction in prose of a certain extent" (une fiction en prose d'une certain étendue). That is quite good enough for us, and we may perhaps go so far as to add that the extent should not be less than 50,000 words. Any fictitious prose work over 50,000 words will be a novel for the purposes of these lectures, and if this seems to you unphilosophic will you think of an alternative definition, which will include *The Pilgrim's Progress*, *Marius the Epicurean*, *The Adventures of a Younger Son*, *The Magic Flute*, *A Journal of the Plague Year*, *Zuleika Dobson*, *Rasselas*, *Ulysses*, and *Green Mansions*, or else will give reasons for their exclusion? Parts of our spongy tract seem more fictitious than other pans, it is true: near the middle, on a tump of grass, stand Miss Austen with the figure of Emma by her side, and Thackeray holding up Esmond. But no intelligent remark known to me will define the tract as a whole. All we can say of it is that it is bounded by two chains of mountains neither of which rises very abruptly — the opposing ranges of Poetry and of History — and bounded on the third side by a sea — a sea that we shall encounter when we come to *Moby Dick*.

Let us begin by considering the proviso " English Literature." "English" we shall of course interpret as written in English, not as published south of the Tweed or east of the Atlantic, or north of the Equator: we need not attend to geographical accidents, they can be left to the politicians. Yet, even with this interpretation, are we as free as we wish? Can we, while discussing English fiction, quite ignore fiction written in other languages, particularly French and Russian? As far as influence goes, we could ignore it, for our writers have never been much influenced by the continentals. But — for reasons soon to be explained — I want to talk as little as possible about influence during these lectures. My subject is a particular kind of book and the aspects that book has assumed in English. Can we ignore its collateral aspects on the continent? Not entirely. An unpleasant and unpatriotic truth has here to be faced. No English novelist is as great as Tolstoy — that is to say, has given so complete a picture of man's life, both on its domestic and heroic side. No English novelist has explored man's soul as deeply as

Dostoevsky. And no novelist anywhere has analysed the modem consciousness as successfully as Marcel Proust. Before these triumphs we must pause. English poetry fears no one — excels in quality as well as quantity. But English fiction is less triumphant: it does not contain the best stuff yet written, and if we deny this we become guilty of provincialism.

Now, provincialism does not signify in a writer, and may indeed be the chief source of his strength: only a prig or a fool would complain that Defoe is cockneyfied or Thomas Hardy countrified. But provincialism in a critic is a serious fault. A critic has no right to the narrowness which is the frequent prerogative of the creative artist. He has to have a wide outlook or he has not anything at all. Although the novel exercises the rights of a created object, criticism has not those rights, and too many little mansions in English fiction have been acclaimed to their own detriment as important edifices. Take four at random: *Cranford*, *The Heart of Midlothian*, *Jane Eyre*, *The Ordeal of Richard Feverel*. For various personal and local reasons we may be attached to these four books. Cranford radiates the humour of the urban midlands, *Midlothian* is a handful out of Edinburgh, *Jane Eyre* is the passionate dream of a fine but still undeveloped woman, *Richard Feverel* exudes farmhouse lyricism and flickers with modish wit. But all four are little mansions, not mighty edifices, and we shall see and respect them for what they are if we stand them for an instant in the colonnades of *War and Peace*, or the vaults of The *Brothers Karamazov*.

I shall not often refer to foreign novels in these lectures, still less would I pose as an expert on them who is debarred from discussing them by his terms of reference. But I do want to emphasize their greatness before we start; to cast, so to speak, this preliminary shadow over our subject, so that when we look back on it at the end we may have the better chance of seeing it in its true lights.

So much for the proviso "English". Now for a more important point, the proviso of "period or periods". This idea of a period or a development in time, with its consequent emphasis on influences and schools, happens to be exactly what I am hoping to avoid during our brief survey, and I believe that the author of *Gazpacho* will be lenient. Time, all the way through, is to be our enemy. We are to visualize the English novelists not as floating down that stream which bears all its sons away unless they are careful, but as seated together in a room, a circular room, a sort of British Museum reading-room — all writing their novels simultaneously. They do not, as they sit there, think: "I live under Queen Victoria, I under Anne, I carry on the tradition of Trollope, I am reacting against Aldous Huxley." The fact that their pens are in their hands is far more vivid to them. They are half mesmerized, their sorrows and joys are pouring out through the ink, they are approximated by the act of creation, and when Professor Oliver Elton says, as he does, that "after 1847 the novel of passion was never to be the same again" none of them understands what he means. That is to be our vision of them — an imperfect vision, but it is suited to our powers, it will preserve us from a serious danger, the danger of pseudo-scholar — ship.

Genuine scholarship is one of the highest successes which our race can achieve. No one is more triumphant than the man who chooses a worthy subject and masters all its facts and the leading facts of the subjects neighbouring. He can then do what he likes. He can, if his subject is the novel, lecture on it chronologically if he wishes, because he has read all the important novels of the past four centuries, many of the unimportant ones, and has adequate knowledge of any collateral facts that bear upon English fiction. The late Sir Walter Raleigh (who once held this lectureship) was such a scholar. Raleigh knew so many facts that he was able to proceed to influences, and his monograph on the English novel adopts the treatment by period which his unworthy successor must avoid. The scholar, like the philosopher, can contemplate the river of time. He contemplates it not as a whole, but he can see the facts, the personalities, floating past him, and estimate the relations between them, and if his conclusions could be as valuable to us as they are to himself he would long ago have civilized the human race. As you know, he has failed. True scholarship is incommunicable, true scholars rare. There are a few scholars, actual or potential, in the audience today, but only a few, and there is certainly none on the platform. Most of us are pseudo-scholars, and I want to consider our characteristics with sympathy and respect, for we are a very large and quite a powerful class, eminent in Church and State, we control the education of the Empire, we lend to the Press such distinction as it consents to receive, and we are a welcome asset at dinner-parties.

Pseudo-scholarship is, on its good side, the homage paid by ignorance to learning. It also has an economic side, on which we need not be hard. Most of us must get a job before thirty, or sponge on our relatives, and many jobs can only be got by passing an exam. The pseudo-scholar often does well in examinations (real scholars are not much good), and even when he fails he appreciates their innate majesty. They are gateways to employment, they have power to ban and bless. A paper on *King Lear* may lead somewhere, unlike the rather far-fetched play of the same name. It may be a stepping-stone to the Local Government Board. He does not often put it to himself openly and say: "That's the use of knowing things, they help you to get on." The economic pressure he feels is more often subconscious, and he goes to his exam merely feeling that a paper on King Lear is a very tempestuous and terrible experience but an intensely real one. And whether he be cynical or naive, he is not to be blamed. As long as learning is connected with earning, as long as certain jobs can only be reached through exams, so long must we take the examination system seriously. If another ladder to employment was contrived, much so-called education would disappear, and no one be a penny the stupider.

It is when he comes to criticism — to a job like the present — that he can be so pernicious, because he follows the method of a true scholar without having his equipment. He classes books before he has understood or read them; that is his first crime. Classification by chronology. Books written before 1847, books written after it, books written after or before 1848. The novel in the reign of Queen Anne, the pre-novel, the Ur-novel, the novel of the future. Classification by subject-matter — sillier still. The literature of Inns, beginning with *Tom Jones*; the literature of the Woman's Movement, beginning with *Shirley*; the literature of Desert Islands, from *Robinson Crusoe* to *The Blue Lagoon*; the literature of Rogues — dreariest of all, though the Open Road runs it pretty close; the literature of Sussex (perhaps the most devoted of the Home Counties); improper books — a serious though dreadful branch of enquiry, only to be pursued by pseudo-scholars of riper years; novels relating to industrialism, aviation, chiropody, the weather. I include the weather on the authority of the most amazing work on the novel that I have met for many years. It came over the Atlantic to me, nor shall I ever forget it. It was a literary manual entitled *Materials and Methods of Fiction*. The writer's name shall be concealed. He was a pseudo-scholar and a good one. He classified novels by their dates, their length, their locality, their sex, their point of view, till no more seemed possible. But he still had the weather up his sleeve, and when he brought it out it had nine heads. He gave an example under each head, for he was anything but slovenly, and we will run through his list. In the first place the weather can be "decorative", as in Pierre Loti; then "utilitarian", as in *The Mill on the Floss* (no Floss, no Mill; no Mill, no Tullivers); "illustrative", as in *The Egoist*; "planned in pre-established harmony", as by Fiona MacLeod; "in emotional contrast", as in *The Master of Ballantrae*; "determinative of action", as in a certain Kipling story, where a man proposes to the wrong girl on account of a sandstorm; "a controlling influence", *Richard Feverel*; "itself a hero", like Vesuvius in *The Last Days of Pompeii*; and ninthly, it can be "non-existent", as in a nursery tale. I liked him flinging in nonexistence. It made everything so scientific and trim. But he himself remained a little dissatisfied, and having finished his classification he said yes, of course there was one more thing, and that was genius; it was useless for a novelist to know that there are nine sorts of weather, unless he has genius also. Cheered by this reflection, he classified novels by their tones. There are only two tones, personal and impersonal, and having given examples of each he grew pensive again and said: "Yes, but you must have genius too, or neither tone will profit."

This reference to genius is, again, typical of the pseudo-scholar. He loves mentioning genius, because the sound of the word exempts him from trying to discover its meaning. Literature is written by geniuses. Novelists are geniuses. There we are; now let us classify them. Which he does. Everything he says may be accurate but all is useless, because he is moving round books instead of through them, he either has not read them or cannot read them properly. Books have to be read (worse luck, for it takes a long time); it is the only way of discovering what they contain. A few savage tribes eat them, but reading is the only method of assimilation revealed to the West. The reader must sit down alone and struggle with the writer, and this the pseudo-scholar will not do. He would rather relate a book to the history of its time, to events in the life of its author, to the events it describes, above all to some tendency. As soon as he can use the word "tendency" his spirits rise, and though those of his audience may sink they often pull out their pencils at this point and make a note, under the belief that a tendency is portable.

That is why, in the rather ramshackly course that lies ahead of us, we cannot consider fiction by periods, we must not contemplate the stream of time. Another image better suits our powers: that of all the novelists writing their novels at once. They come from different ages and ranks, they have different temperaments and aims, but they all hold pens in their hands, and are in the process of creation. Let us look over their shoulders for a moment and see what they are writing. It may exorcise that demon of chronology which is at present our enemy and which (we shall discover next week) is sometimes their enemy too. "Oh, what quenchless feud is this, that Time hath with the sons of Men," cries Herman Melville, and the feud goes on not only in life and death but in the byways of literary creation and criticism. Let us avoid it by imagining that all the novelists are at work together in a circular room. I shall not mention their names until we have heard their words, because a name brings associations with it, dates, gossip, all the furniture of the method we are discarding.

They have been instructed to group themselves in pairs. We approach the first pair, and read as follows:

I. I don't know what to do, not I! — God forgive me, but I am very impatient! I wish — But I don't know what to wish, without a sin! — Yet I wish it would please God to take me to his mercy! — I can meet with none here. — What a world is this! — What is there in it desirable? The good we hope for, so strangely mixed, that one knows not what to wish for! And one half of mankind tormenting the other, and being tormented themselves in tormenting!

II. What I hate is myself — when I think that one has to take so much, to be happy, out of the lives of others, and that one isn't happy even then. One does it to cheat one's self and to stop one's mouth — but that is only, at the best, for a little. The wretched self is always there, always making us somehow a fresh anxiety. What it comes to is that it's not, that it's never, a happiness, any happiness at all, to take. The only safe thing is to give. It's what plays you least false.

It is obvious that here sit two novelists who are looking at life from much the same angle, yet the first of them is Samuel Richardson, and the second you will have already identified as

Henry James. Each is an anxious rather than an ardent psychologist. Each is sensitive to suffering and appreciates self-sacrifice; each falls short of the tragic, though a close approach is made. A sort of tremulous nobility — that is the spirit that dominates them — and oh how well they write! — not a word out of place in their copious flows. A hundred and fifty years of time divide them, but are not they close together in other ways, and may not their neighbourliness profit us? Of course as I say this I hear Henry James beginning to express his regret — no, not his regret but his surprise — no, not even his surprise but his awareness that neighbourliness is being postulated of him, and postulated, must he add, in relation to a shopkeeper. And I hear Richardson, equally cautious, wondering whether any writer born outside England can be chaste. But these are surface differences, are indeed no differences at all, but additional points of contact. We leave them sitting in harmony, and proceed to our next pair.

I. All the preparations for the funeral ran easily and happily under Mrs. Johnson's skilful hands. On the eve of the sad occasion she produced a reserve of black sateen, the kitchen steps, and a box of Stacks, and decorated the house with festoons and bows of black in the best possible taste.

She tied up the knocker with black crepe, and put a large bow over the corner of the steel engraving of Garibaldi, and swathed the bust of Mr. Gladstone that had belonged to the deceased with inky swathings. She turned the two vases that had views of Tivoli and the Bay of Naples round, so that these rather brilliant landscapes were hidden and only the plain blue enamel showed, and she anticipated the long contemplated purchase of a tablecloth for the front room, and substituted a violet purple cover for the now very worn and faded raptures and roses in plushette that had hitherto done duty there. Everything that loving consideration could do to impart a dignified solemnity to her little home was done.

II. The air of the parlour being faint with the smell of sweet cake, I looked about for the table of refreshments; it was scarcely visible until one had got accustomed to the gloom, but there was a cut-up plum-cake upon it, and there were cut-up oranges, and sandwiches, and biscuits, and two decanters that I knew very well as ornaments, but had never seen used in all my life: one full of port, and one of sherry. Standing at this table, I became conscious of the servile Pumblechook in a black cloak and several yards of hatband, who was alternately stuffing himself, and making obsequious movements to catch ray attention. The moment he succeeded, he cane over to me (breathing sherry and crumbs), and said in a subdued voice, "May I, dear sir?" and did.

These two funerals did not by any means happen on the same day. One is that of Mr. Polly's father (1910), the other Mrs. Gargery's in *Great Expectations* (1861). Yet Wells and Dickens have the same point of view and even use the same tricks of style (cf. the two vases and the two decanters). They are, both, humorists and visualizers who get an effect by cataloguing details and whisking the page over irritably. They are generous-minded; they hate shams and enjoy being indignant about them; they are valuable social reformers; they have no notion of confining books to a library shelf. Sometimes the lively surface of their prose scratches like a cheap gramophone record, a certain poorness of quality appears, and the face of the author draws rather too near to that of the reader. In other words, neither of them has much taste; the world of beauty was largely closed to Dickens, and is entirely closed to Wells. And there are other parallels — for instance their method of drawing character. And perhaps the main difference between them is the difference of opportunity offered to an obscure boy of genius a hundred years ago and forty years ago. The difference is in Wells's favour. He is better educated than his predecessor; in particular the addition of science has strengthened his mind and subdued his hysteria. He registers an improvement in society — Dotheboys Hall has been superseded by the Polytechnic — not any change in the novelist's art.

What about our next pair?

I. But for that mark, I'm not sure about it; I don't believe it was made by a nail after all; it's too big, too round, for that. I might get up, but if I got up and looked at it, ten to one I shouldn't be able to say for certain; because once a thing's done, no one ever knows how it happened. Oh! dear me, the mystery of life; the inaccuracy of thought! The ignorance of humanity! To show how very little control of our possessions we have — what an accidental affair this living is after all our civilization — let me just count over a few of the things lost in one lifetime, beginning, for that always seems the most mysterious of losses — what cat would gnaw, what rat would nibble — three pale blue canisters of book-binding tools? Then there were the bird cages, the iron hoops, the steel skates, the Queen Anne coal-scuttle, the bagatelle board, the hand organ — all gone, and jewels, too. Opals and emeralds, they lie about the roots of turnips. What a scraping paring affair it is to be sure! The wonder is that I've any clothes on my back, that I sit surrounded by solid furniture at this moment. Why, if one wants to compare life to anything, one must liken it to being blown through the Tube at fifty miles an hour ...

II. Every day for at least ten years together did my father resolve to have it mended — 'tis not mended yet; — no family but ours would have borne with it an hour — and what is most astonishing, there was not a subject in the world upon which my father was so eloquent, as upon that of door-hinges. — And yet at the same time, he was certainly one of the greatest bubbles to them, I think, that history can produce: his rhetoric and conduct were at perpetual handy-cuffi. Never did the parlour-door open — but his philosophy or his principles fell a victim to it; — three drops of oil with a feather, and a smart stroke of a hammer, had saved his honour for ever.

— Inconsistent soul that man is! — languishing under wounds, which he has the power to heal! — his whole life a contradiction to his knowledge! — his reason, that precious gift of God to him — (instead of pouring in oil) serving but to sharpen his sensibilities — to multiply his pains, and render him more melancholy and uneasy under them! — Poor unhappy creature, that he should do so! — Are not the necessary causes of misery in this life enow, but he must add voluntary ones to his stock of sorrow; — struggle against evils which cannot be avoided, and submit to others, which a tenth part of the trouble they create him would remove from his heart for ever?

By all that is good and virtuous, if three are three drops of oil to be got, and a hammer to be found within ten miles of Shandy Hall — the parlour door hinge shall be mended this reign.

The passage last quoted is, of course, out of *Tristram Shandy*. The other passage was from Virginia Woolf. She and Sterne are both fantasists. They start with a little object, take a flutter from it, and settle on it again. They combine a humorous appreciation of the muddle of life with a keen sense of its beauty. There is even the same tone in their voices — a rather deliberate bewilderment, an announcement to all and sundry that they do not know where they are going. No doubt their scales of value are not the same. Sterne is a sentimentalist, Virginia Woolf (except perhaps in her latest work, *To the Lighthouse*) is extremely aloof. Nor are their achievements on the same scale. But their medium is similar, the same odd effects are obtained by it, the parlour door is never mended, the mark on the wall turns out to be a snail, life is such a muddle, oh, dear, the will is so weak, the sensations fidgety ... philosophy... God ... oh, dear, look at the mark ... listen to the door — existence is really too ... what were we saying?

Does not chronology seem less important now that we have visualized six novelists at their jobs? If the novel develops, is it not likely to develop on different lines from the British Constitution, or even the Women's Movement? I say "even the Women's Movement" because there happened to be a close association between fiction in England and that movement during the nineteenth century — a connection so close that it has misled some critics into thinking it an organic connection. As women bettered their position, the novel, they asserted, became better too. Quite wrong. A minor does not develop because an historical pageant passes in front of it. It only develops when it gets a fresh coat of quicksilver — in other words, when it acquires new sensitiveness; and the novel's success lies in its own sensitiveness, not in the success of its subject-matter. Empires fall, votes are accorded, but to those people writing in the circular room it is the feel of the pen between their fingers that matters most. They may decide to write a novel upon the French or the Russian Revolution, but memories, associations, passions, rise up and cloud their objectivity, so that at the close, when they re-read, someone else seems to have been holding their pen and to have relegated their theme to the background. That "someone else" is their self no doubt, but not the self that is so active in time and lives under George IV or V. All through history writers while writing have felt more or less the same. They have entered a common state which it is convenient to call inspiration, and, having regard to that state, we may say that History develops, Art stands still.

History develops, Art stands still, is a crude motto, indeed it is almost a slogan, and though forced to adopt it we must not do so without admitting its vulgarity. It contains only a partial truth.

It debars us in the first place from considering whether the human mind alters from generation to generation; whether, for instance, Thomas Deloney, who wrote humorously about shops and pubs in the reign of Queen Elizabeth, differs fundamentally from his modern representative — who would be someone of the calibre of Neil Lyons or Pett Ridge. As a matter of fact I believe Deloney did not differ; differed as an individual, but not fundamentally, not because he lived four hundred years ago. Four thousand, fourteen thousand years, might give us pause, but four hundred years is nothing in the life of our race, and does not allow room for any measurable change. So our slogan there is no practical hindrance. We can chant it without shame.

It is more serious when we turn to the development of tradition and see what we lose through being debarred from examining that. Apart from schools and influences and fashions, there has been a technique in English fiction, and this does alter from generation to generation. The technique of laughing at characters for instance: to smoke and to rag are not identical; the Elizabethan humorist picks up his victim in a different way from the modem, raises his laugh by other tricks. Or the technique of fantasy: Virginia Woolf, though her aim and general effect both resemble Sterne's, differs from him in execution; she belongs to the same tradition but to a later phase of it. Or the technique of conversation: in my pairs of examples I could not include a couple of dialogues, though I wanted to, for the reason that the use of the "he said" and "she said" varies so much through the centuries that it colours its surroundings, and though the speakers may be similarly conceived they will not seem so in an extract. Well, we cannot examine questions like these, and must admit we are the poorer, though we can abandon the development of subject-matter and the development of the human race without regret. Literary tradition is the borderland lying between literature and history, and the well-equipped critic will spend much time there and enrich his judgement accordingly. We cannot go there because we have not read enough. We must pretend it belongs to history and cut it off accordingly. We must refuse to have anything to do with chronology.

Let me quote here for our comfort from my immediate predecessor in this lectureship, Mr. T. S. Eliot. Mr. Eliot enumerates, in the introduction to *The Sacred Wood*, the duties of the critic:

> It is part of the business of the critic to preserve tradition — where a good tradition exists. It is part of his business to see literature steadily and to see it whole; and this is eminently to see it not as consecrated by time, but to see it beyond time ...

The first duty we cannot perform, the second we must try to perform. We can neither examine nor preserve tradition. But we can visualize the novelists as sitting in one room, and force them, by our very ignorance, from the limitations of date and place. I think that is worth doing, or I should not have ventured to undertake this course.

How then are we to attack the novel — that spongy tract,

those fictions in prose of a certain extent which extend so indeterminately? Not with any elaborate apparatus. Principles and systems may suit other forms of art, but they cannot be applicable here — or if applied their results must be subjected to re-examination. And who is the re-examiner? Well, I am afraid it will be the human heart, it will be this man-to-man business, justly suspect in its cruder forms. The final test of a novel will be our affection for it, as it is the test of our friends, and of anything else which we cannot define. Sentimentality to some a worse demon than chronology — will lurk in the background saying, "Oh, but I like that," "Oh, but that doesn't appeal to me," and all I can promise is that sentimentality shall not speak too loudly or too soon. The intensely, stiflingly human quality of the novel is not to be avoided; the novel is sogged with humanity; there is no escaping the uplift or the downpour, nor can they be kept out of criticism. We may hate humanity, but if it is exorcised or even purified the novel wilts; little is left but a bunch of words.

And I have chosen the title Aspects because it is unscientific and vague, because it leaves us the maximum of freedom, because it means both the different ways we can look at a novel and the different ways a novelist can look at his work. And the aspects selected for discussion are seven in number: The Story; People; The Plot; Fantasy; Prophecy; Pattern and Rhythm.

Chapter 2 The Story

We shall all agree that the fundamental aspect of the novel is its story-telling aspect, but we shall voice our assent in different tones, and it is on the precise tone of voice we employ now that our subsequent conclusions will depend.

Let us listen to three voices. If you ask one type of man, "What does a novel do?" he will reply placidly: "Well — I don't know — it seems a funny sort of question to ask — a novel's a novel — well, I don't know — I suppose it kind of tells a story, so to speak." He is quite good-tempered and vague, and probably driving a motor-bus at the same time and paying no more attention to literature than it merits. Another man, whom I visualize as on a golf-course, will be aggressive and brisk. He will reply: "What does a novel do? Why, tell a story of course, and I've no use for it if it didn't. I like a story. Very bad taste on my part, no doubt, but I like a story. You can take your art, you can take your literature, you can take your music, but give me a good story. And I like a story to be a story, mind, and my wife's the same." And a third man, he says in a sort of drooping regretful voice: "Yes — oh dear yes — the novel tells a story." I respect and admire the first speaker. I detest and fear the second. And the third is myself. Yes — oh dear yes — the novel tells a story. That is the fundamental aspect without which it could not exist. That is the highest factor common to all novels, and I wish that it was not so, that it could be something different — melody, or perception of the truth, not this low atavistic form.

For, the more we look at the story (the story that is a story, mind), the more we disentangle it from the finer growths that it supports, the less shall we find to admire. It runs like a backbone — or may I say a tapeworm, for its beginning and end are arbitrary. It is immensely old — goes back to neolithic times, perhaps to paleolithic. Neanderthal man listened to stories, if one may judge by the shape of his skull. The primitive audience was an audience of shock-heads, gaping round the campfire, fatigued with contending against the mammoth or the woolly rhinoceros, and only kept awake by suspense. What would happen next? The novelist droned on, and as soon as the audience guessed what happened next they either fell asleep or killed him. We can estimate the dangers incurred when we think of the career of

Scheherazade in somewhat later times. Scheherazade avoided her fate because she knew how to wield the weapon of suspense — the only literary tool that has any effect upon tyrants and savages. Great novelist though she was — exquisite in her descriptions, tolerant in her judgements, ingenious in her incidents, advanced in her morality, vivid in her delineations of character, expert in her knowledge of three oriental capitals — it was yet on none of these gifts that she relied when trying to save her life from her intolerable husband. They were but incidental. She only survived because she managed to keep the king wondering what would happen next. Each time she saw the sun rising she stopped in the middle of a sentence, and left him gaping. "At this moment Scheherazade saw the morning appearing and, discreet, was silent." This uninteresting little phrase is the backbone of the *One Thousand and One Nights*, the tapeworm by which they are tied together and the life of a most accomplished princess was preserved.

We are all like Scheherazade's husband, in that we want to know what happens next. That is universal and that is why the backbone of a novel has to be a story. Some of us want to know nothing else — there is nothing in us but primeval curiosity, and consequently our other literary judgements are ludicrous. And now the story can be defined. It is a narrative of events arranged in their time sequence — dinner coming after breakfast, Tuesday after Monday, decay after death, and so on. Qua story, it can only have one merit: that of making the audience want to know what happens next. And conversely it can only have one fault: that of making the audience not want to know what happens next. These are the only two criticisms that can be made on the story that is a story. It is the lowest and simplest of literary organisms. Yet it is the highest factor common to all the very complicated organisms known as novels.

When we isolate the story like this from the nobler aspects through which it moves, and hold it out on the forceps — wriggling and interminable, the naked worm of time — it presents an appearance that is both unlovely and dull. But we have much to learn from it. Let us begin by considering it in connection with daily life.

Daily life is also full of the time-sense. We think one event occurs after or before another, the thought is often in our minds, and much of our talk and action proceeds on the assumption. Much of our talk and action, but not all; there seems something else in life besides time, something which may conveniently be called "value", something which is measured not by minutes or hours, but by intensity, so that when we look at our past it does not stretch back evenly but piles up into a few notable pinnacles, and when we look at the future it seems sometimes a wall, sometimes a cloud, sometimes a sun, but never a chronological chart. Neither memory nor anticipation is much interested in Father Time, and all dreamers, artists and lovers are partially delivered from his tyranny; he can kill them, but he cannot secure their attention, and at the very moment of doom, when the clock collected in the tower its strength and struck, they may be looking the other way. So daily life, whatever it may be really, is practically composed of two lives — the life in time and the life by values — and our conduct reveals a double allegiance. "I only saw her for five minutes, but it was worth it." There you have both allegiances in a single sentence. And what the story does is to narrate the life in time. And what the entire novel does — if it is a good novel — is to include the life by values as well; using devices hereafter to be examined. It, also, pays a double allegiance. But in it, in the novel, the allegiance to time is imperative: no novel could be written without it. Whereas in daily life the allegiance may not be necessary: we do not know, and the experience of certain mystics suggests, indeed, that it is not necessary, and that we are quite mistaken in supposing that Monday is followed by Tuesday, or death by decay. It is always possible for you or me in daily life to deny that time exists and act accordingly even if we become unintelligible and are sent by our fellow citizens to what they choose to call a lunatic-asylum. But it is never possible for a novelist to deny time inside the fabric of his novel: he must cling, however lightly, to the thread of his story, he must touch the interminable tapeworm, otherwise he becomes unintelligible, which, in his case, is a blunder.

I am trying not to be philosophic about time, for it is (experts assure us) a most dangerous hobby for an outsider, far more fatal than place; and quite eminent metaphysicians have been dethroned through referring to it improperly. I am only trying to explain that as I lecture now I hear that clock ticking or do not hear it ticking, I retain or lose the time sense; whereas in a novel there is always a clock. The author may dislike his clock. Emily Bronte in *Wruthering Heights* tried to hide hers. Sterne, in *Tristram Shandy*, turned his upside down. Marcel Proust, still more ingenious, kept altering the hands, so that his hero was at the same period entertaining a mistress to supper and playing ball with his nurse in the park. All these devices are legitimate, but none of them contravene our thesis: the basis of a novel is a story, and a story is a narrative of events arranged in time sequence. (A story, by the way, is not the same as a plot. It may form the basis of one, but the plot is an organism of a higher type, and will be defined and discussed in a future lecture.)

Who shall tell us a story?

Sir Walter Scott of course.

Scott is a novelist over whom we shall violently divide. For my own part I don't care for him, and find it difficult to understand his continued reputation. His reputation in his day — that is easy to understand. There are important historical reasons for it, which we should discuss if our scheme was chronological. But when we fish him out of the river of time, and set him to write in that circular room with the other novelists, he presents a less impressive figure. He is seen to have a trivial mind and a heavy style. He cannot construct. He has neither artistic detachment nor passion, and how can a writer who is devoid of both create characters who will move us deeply? Artistic detachment — perhaps it is priggish to ask for that. But passion — surely passion is lowbrow enough, and think how all Scott's laborious mountains and scooped-out glens and carefully ruined abbeys call out for passion, passion, and how it is never there! If he had passion he would be a great writer — no amount of clumsiness or artificiality would matter then. But he only has a temperate heart and gentlemanly feelings, and an intelligent affection for the countryside; and this is not basis enough for great novels. And his integrity — that is worse than nothing, for it was a purely moral and commercial integrity. It satisfied his highest needs and he never dreamt that another sort of loyalty exists.

His fame is due to two causes. In the first place, many of the elder generation had him read aloud to them when they were young; he is entangled with happy sentimental memories, with holidays in or residence in Scotland. They love him indeed for the same reason that I loved and still love *The Swiss Family Robinson*. I could lecture to you now on *The Swiss Family Robinson* and it would be a glowing lecture, because of the emotions felt in boyhood. When my brain decays entirely I shall not bother any more over great literature. I shall go back to the romantic shore where the "ship struck with a frightful shock", emitting four demigods named Fritz, Ernest, Jack and little Franz, together with their father, their mother, and a cushion, which contained all the appliances necessary for a ten years' residence in the tropics. That is my eternal summer, — that is what *The Swiss Family Robinson* means to me, and is not it all that Sir Walter Scott means to some of you? Is he really more than a reminder of early happiness? And until our brains do decay must not we put all this aside when we attempt to understand books?

In the second place, Scott's fame rests upon one genuine basis. He could tell a story. He had the primitive power of keeping the reader in suspense and playing on his curiosity. Let us paraphrase *The Antiquary* — not analyze it, analysis is the wrong method, but paraphrase. Then we shall see the story unrolling itself, and be able to study its simply devices.

The Antiquary
Chapter 1

It was early in a fine summer's day, near the end of the eighteenth century, when a young man, of genteel appearance, journeying towards the north-east of Scotland, provided himself with a ticket in one of those public carriages which travel between Edinburgh and the Queensferry, at which place, as the name implies, and as is well known to all my northern readers, there is a passage-boat for crossing the Firth of Forth.

That is the first sentence in *The Antiquary* — not an exciting sentence, but it gives us the time, the place, and a young man — it sets the story-teller's scene. We feel a moderate interest in what the young man will do next. His name is Lovel, and there is a mystery about him. He is the hero, or Scott would not call him genteel, and he is sure to make the heroine happy. He meets the Antiquary, Jonathan Oldbuck. They get into the coach, not too quickly, become acquainted, Lovel visits Oldbuck at his house.

Near it they meet a new character, Edie Ochiltree. Scott is good at introducing fresh characters. He slides them in very naturally, and with a promising air. Edie Ochiltree promises a good deal. He is a beggar — no ordinary beggar, a romantic and reliable rogue, and will he not help to solve the mystery of which we saw the tip in Lovel? More introductions: to Sir Arthur Wardour (old family, bad manager); to his daughter Isabella (haughty), whom the hero loves unrequited; to Oldhuck's sister Miss Grizzle. Miss Grizzle is introduced with the same air of promise. As a matter of fact she is just a comic turn — she leads nowhere, and your story-teller is full of these turns. He need not hammer away all the time at cause and effect. He keeps just as well within the simple boundaries of his art if he says things that have no bearing on the development. The audience thinks they will develop, but the audience is shock-headed and tired and easily forgets. Unlike the weaver of plots, the story-teller profits by ragged ends. Miss Grizzle is a small example of a ragged end; for a big one I would refer to a novel that professes to be lean and tragic: *The Bride of Lammermoor*. Scott presents the Lord High Keeper in this book with great emphasis and with endless suggestions that the defects of his character will lead to the tragedy, while as a matter of fact the tragedy would occur in almost the same form if he did not exist — the only necessary ingredients in it being Edgar, Lucy, Lady Ashton and Bucklaw. Well, to return to *The Antiquary*, then there is a dinner, Oldbuck and Sir Arthur quarrel, Sir Arthur is offended and leaves with his daughter, and they walk back across the sands. The tide rises. Sir Aurthur and Isabella are cut off, and are confronted by Edie Ochiltree. This is the first serious moment in the story and this is how the story-teller who is a story-teller handles it:

> While they exchanged these words, they paused upon the highest ledge of rock to which they could attain; for it seemed that any further attempt to move forward could only serve to anticipate their fate. Here, then, they were to await the sure though slow progress of the raging element, something in the situation of the martyrs of the Early Church, who, exposed by heathen tyrants to be slain by wild beasts, were compelled for a time to witness the impatience and rage by which the animals were agitated, while awaiting the signal for undoing their grates and letting them loose upon the victims.
>
> Yet even this fearful pause gave Isabella time to collect the powers of a mind naturally strong and courageous, and which rallied itself at this terrible juncture. "Must we yield

life," she said, "without a struggle? Is there no path, however dreadful, by which we could climb the crag, or at least attain some height above the tide, where we could remain till morning, or till help comes? They must be aware of our situation, and will raise the country to relieve us."

Thus speaks the heroine, in accents which certainly chill the reader. Yet we want to know what happens next. The rocks are of cardboard, like those in my dear Swiss Family; the tempest is turned on with one hand while Scott scribbles away about Early Christians with the other; there is no sincerity, no sense of danger in the whole affair; it is all passionless, perfunctory, yet we do just want to know what happens next.

Why — Lovel rescues them. Yes; we ought to have thought of that; and what then?

Another ragged end. Lovel is put by the Antiquary to sleep in a haunted room, where he has a dream or vision of his host's ancestor, who says to him, "Kunst macht Gunst," words which he does not understand at the time, owing to his ignorance of German, and learns afterwards that they mean "Skill wins Favour": he must pursue the siege of Isabella's heart. That is to say, the supernatural contributes nothing to the story. It is introduced with tapestries and storm, but only a copybook maxim results. The reader does not know this, though. When he hears "Kunst macht Gunst" his attention reawakens ... then his attention is diverted to something else, and the time-sequence goes on.

Picnic in the ruins of St. Ruth. Introduction of Dousterswivel, a wicked foreigner, who has involved Sir Arthur in mining schemes and whose superstitions are ridiculed because not of the genuine Border brand. Arrival of Hector McIntyre, the Antiquary's nephew, who suspects Lovel of being an impostor. The two fight a duel; Lovel, thinking he has killed his opponent, flies with Edie Ochiltree, who has turned up as usual. They hide in the ruins of St. Ruth, where they watch Dousterswivel gulling Sir Arthur in a treasure-hunt. Lovel gets away on a boat and — out of sight, out of mind; we do not worry about him until he turns up again. Second treasure-hunt at St Ruth. Sir Arthur finds a hoard of silver. Third treasure-hunt. Dousterswivel is soundly cudgelled, and when he comes to himself sees the funeral rites of the old Countess of Glenallan, who is being buried there at midnight and with secrecy, that family being of the Romish persuasion.

Now the Glenallans are very important in the story, yet how casually they are introduced! They are hooked on to Dousterswivel in the most artless away. His pair of eyes happened to be handy, so Scott had a peep through them. And the reader by now is getting so docile under the succession of episodes that he just gapes, like a primitive cave-man. Now the Glenallan interest gets to work, the ruins of St Ruth are switched off, and we enter what may be called the "pre-story", where two new characters intervene, and talk wildly and darkly about a sinful past. Their names are: Elspeth Mucklebackit, a Sibyl of a fisherwoman, and Lord Glenallan, son of the dead countess. Their dialogue is interrupted by other events — by the arrest, trial and release of Edie Ochiltree, by the death by drowning of another new character, and by the humours of Hector McIntyre's convalescence at his uncle's house. But the gist is that Lord Glenallan many years ago had married a lady called Evelina Nevile, against his mother's wish, and had then been given to understand that she was his half-sister. Maddened with horror, he had left her before she gave birth to a child. Elspeth, formerly his mother's servant, now explains to him that Evelina was no relation to him, that she died in childbirth — Elspeth and another woman attending — and that the child disappeared. Lord Glenallan then goes to consult the Antiquary, who, as a Justice of the Peace, knew something of the events of the time, and who had also loved Evelina. And what happens next? Sir Arthur Wardour's goods are sold up, for Dousterswivel has ruined him.

And then? The French are reported to be landing. And then? Lovel rides into the district leading the British troops. He calls himself Major Nevile now. But even Major Nevile is not his right name, for he is who but the lost child of Lord Glenallan, he is none other than the legitimate heir to an earldom. Partly through Elspeth Mucklebackit, partly through her fellow servant whom he meets as a nun abroad, partly through an uncle who has died, partly through Edie Ochiltree, the truth has come out. There are indeed plenty of reasons for the denouement, but Scott is not interested in reasons; he dumps them down without bothering to elucidate them; to make one thing happen after another is his only serious aim. And then? Isabella Wardour relents and marries the hero. And then? That is the end of the story. We must not ask "And then?" too often. If the time-sequence is pursued one second too far it leads us into quite another country.

The Antiquary is a book in which the life in time is celebrated instinctively by the novelist, and this must lead to slackening of emotion and shallowness of judgement, and in particular to that idiotic use of marriage as a finale. Time can be celebrated consciously also, and we shall find an example of this in a very different sort of book, a memorable book: Arnold Bennett's *The Old Wives' Tale*. Time is the real hero of *The Old Wives' Tale*. He is installed as the lord of creation — excepting indeed of Mr. Critchlow, whose bizarre exemption only gives added force. Sophia and Constance are the children of Time from the instant we see them romping with their mother's dresses; they are doomed to decay with a completeness that is very rare in literature. They are girls, Sophia runs away and marries, the mother dies, Constance marries, her husband dies, Sophia's husband dies, Sophia dies, Constance dies, their old rheumatic dog lumbers up to see whether anything remains in the saucer. Our daily life in time is exactly this business of getting old which clogs the arteries of Sophia and Constance, and the story that is a story and sounded so healthy and stood no nonsense cannot sincerely lead to any conclusion but the grave. It is an unsatisfactory conclusion. Of course we grow old. But a great book must rest on something more than an "of course," and though *The Old Wives' Tale* is very strong, sincere, sad, it misses greatness.

What about *War and Peace*? That is certainly great, that likewise emphasizes the effects of time and the waxing and waning of a generation. Tolstoy, like Bennett, has the courage to show us people getting old — the partial decay of Nicolay and Natasha is really more sinister than the complete decay of Constance and Sophia: more of our own youth seems to have perished in it. Then why is *War and Peace* not depressing?

Probably because it has extended over space as well as over time, and the sense of space until it terrifies us is exhilarating, and leaves behind it an effect like music. After one has read *War and Peace* for a bit, great chords begin to sound, and we cannot say exactly what struck them. They do not arise from the story, though Tolstoy is quite as interested in what comes next as Scott, and quite as sincere as Bennett. They do not come from the episodes nor yet from the characters. They come from the immense area of Russia, over which episodes and characters have been scattered, from the sum total of bridges and frozen rivers, forests, roads, gardens, fields, which accumulate grandeur and sonority after we have passed them. Many novelists have the feeling for place — Five Towns, Auld Reekie, and so on. Very few have the sense of space, and the possession of it ranks high in Tolstoy's divine equipment. Space is the lord of *War and Peace*, not time.

A word in conclusion about the story as the repository of a voice. It is the aspect of the novelist's work which asks to be read out loud, which appeals not to the eye, like most prose, but to the ear; having indeed this much in common with oratory. It does not offer melody or cadence. For these, strange as it may seem, the eye is sufficient; the eye, backed by a mind that transmutes, can easily gather up the sounds of a paragraph or dialogue when they have aesthetic value, and refer them to our enjoyment — yes, can even telescope them up so that we get them quicker than we should do if they were recited, just as some people can look through a musical score quicker than it can be rapped out on the piano. But the eye is not equally quick at catching a voice. That opening sentence of *The Antiquary* has no beauty of sound, yet we should lose something if it was not read aloud. Our mind would commune with Walter Scott's silently, and less profitably. The story, besides saying one thing after another, adds something because of its connection with a voice.

It does not add much. It does not give us anything as important as the author's personality. His personality — when he has one — is conveyed through nobler agencies, such as the characters or the plot or his comments on life. What the story does do in this particular capacity, all it can do, is to transform us from readers into listeners, to whom "a" voice speaks, the voice of the tribal narrator, squatting in the middle of the cave, and saying one thing after another until the audience falls asleep among their offal and bones. The story is primitive, it reaches back to the origins of literature, before reading was discovered, and it appeals to what is primitive in us. That is why we are so unreasonable over the stories we like, and so ready to bully those who like something else. For instance, I am annoyed when people laugh at me for loving *The Swiss Family Robinson*, and I hope that I have annoyed some of you over Scott! You see what I mean. Intolerance is the atmosphere stories generate. The story is neither moral nor is it favourable to the understanding of the novel in its other aspects. If we want to do that we must come out of the cave.

We shall not come out of it yet, but observe already how that other life — the life by value — presses against the novel from all sides, how it is ready to fill and indeed distort it, offering it people, plots, fantasies, views of the universe, anything except this constant "and then ... and then", which is the sole contribution of our present enquiry. The life in time is so obviously base and inferior that the question naturally occurs: cannot the novelist abolish it from his work, even as the mystic asserts he has abolished it from his experience, and install its radiant alternative alone?

Well, there is one novelist who has tried to abolish time, and her failure is instructive: Gertrude Stein. Going much further than Emily Bronte, Sterne or Proust, Gertrude Stein has smashed up and pulverized her clock and scattered its fragments over the world like the limbs of Osiris, and she has done this not from naughtiness but from a noble motive: she has hoped to emancipate fiction from the tyranny of time and to express in it the life by values only. She fails, because as soon as fiction is completely delivered from time it cannot express anything at all, and in her later writing we can see the slope down which she is slipping. She wants to abolish this whole aspect of the story, this sequence in chronology, and my heart goes out to her. She cannot do it without abolishing the sequence between the sentences. But this is not effective unless the order of the words in the sentences is also abolished, which in its turn entails the abolition of the order of the letters or sounds in the words. And now she is over the precipice. There is nothing to ridicule in such an experiment as hers. It is much more important to play about like this than to rewrite the Waverley Novels. Yet the experiment is doomed to failure. The time-sequence cannot be destroyed without carrying in its ruin all that should have taken its place; the novel that would express values only becomes unintelligible and therefore valueless.

That is why I must ask you to join me in repeating it in exactly the right tone of voice the words with which this lecture opened. Do not say them vaguely and good temperedly like a busman; you have not the right. Do not say them briskly and aggressively like a golfer; you know better. Say them a little sadly, and you will be correct. Yes — oh dear yes — the novel tells a story.

Chapter 3   People

Having discussed the story that simple and fundamental aspect of the novel — we can turn to a more interesting topic: the actors. We need not ask what happened next, but to whom did it happen; the novelist will be appealing to our intelligence and imagination, not merely to our curiosity. A new emphasis enters his voice: emphasis upon value.

Since the actors in a story are usually human, it seemed convenient to entitle this aspect People. Other animals have been introduced, but with limited success, for we know too little so far about their psychology. There may be, probably will be, an alteration here in the future, comparable to the alteration in the novelist's rendering of savages in the past. The gulf that separates Man Friday from Batouala may be paralleled by the gulf that will separate Kipling's wolves from their literary descendants two hundred years hence, and we shall have animals who are neither symbolic, nor little men disguised, nor as four-legged tables moving, nor as painted scraps of paper that fly. It is one of the ways where science may enlarge the novel, by giving it fresh subject-matter. But the help has not been given yet, and until it comes we may say that the actors in a story are, or pretend to be, human beings.

Since the novelist is himself a human being, there is an affinity between him and his subject-matter which is absent in many other forms of art. The historian is also linked, though as we shall see, less intimately. The painter and sculptor need not be linked: that is to say, they need not represent human beings unless they wish, no more need the poet, while the musician cannot represent them even if he wishes, without the help of a programme. The novelist, unlike many of his colleagues, makes up a number of word-masses roughly describing himself (roughly: niceties shall come later), gives them names and sex, assigns them plausible gestures, and causes them to speak by the use of inverted commas, and perhaps to behave consistently. These word-masses are his characters. They do not come thus coldly to his mind, they may be created in delirious excitement; still, their nature is conditioned by what he guesses about other people, and about himself, and is further modified by the other aspects of his work. This last point — the relation of characters to the other aspects of the novel — will form the subject of a future enquiry. At present we are occupied with their relation to actual life. What is the difference between people in a novel and people like the novelist or like you, or like me, or Queen Victoria?

There is bound to be a difference. If a character in a novel is exactly like Queen Victoria — not rather like but exactly like — then it actually is Queen Victoria, and the novel, or all of it that the character touches, becomes a memoir. A memoir is history, it is based on evidence. A novel is based on evidence + or — χ, the unknown quantity being the temperament of the novelist; and the unknown quantity always modifies the effect of the evidence, and sometimes transforms it entirely.

The historian deals with actions, and with the characters of men only so far as he can deduce them from their actions. He is quite as much concerned with character as the novelist, but he can only know of its existence when it shows on the surface. If Queen Victoria had not said, "We are not amused," her neighbours at table would not have known she was not amused, and her ennui could never have been announced to the public. She might have frowned, so that they would have deduced her state from that — looks and gestures are also historical evidence. But if she remained impassive — what would anyone know? The hidden life is, by definition, hidden. The hidden life that appears in external signs is hidden no longer, has entered the realm of action. And it is the function of the novelist to reveal the hidden life at its source; to tell us more about Queen Victoria than could be known, and thus to produce a character who is not the Queen Victoria of history.

The interesting and sensitive French critic who writes under the name of Alain has some helpful if slightly fantastic remarks on this point. He gets a little out of his depth, but not as much as I feel myself out of mine, and perhaps together we may move towards the shore. Alain examines in turn the various forms of aesthetic activity, and coming in time to the novel (le roman) he asserts that each human being has two sides, appropriate to history and fiction. All that is observable in a man — that is to say, his actions and such of his spiritual existence as can be deduced from his actions — falls into the domain of history. But his romanceful or romantic side (sa partie romanesque ou romantique) includes "the pure passions, that is to say, the dreams, joys, sorrows and self-communings which politeness or shame prevent him from mentioning"; and to express this side of human nature is one of the chief functions of the novel.

What is fictitious in a novel is not so much the story as the method by which thought develops into action, a method which never occurs in daily life ... . History, with its emphasis on external causes, is dominated by the notion of fatality, whereas there is no fatality in the novel; there, everything is founded on human nature, and the dominating feeling is of an existence where everything is intentional, even passions and crimes, even misery.

This is perhaps a roundabout way of saying what every British schoolboy knew, that the historian records whereas the novelist must create. Still, it is a profitable round-about, for it brings out the fundamental difference between people in daily life and people in books. In daily life we never understand each other, neither complete clairvoyance nor complete confessional exists. We know each other approximately, by external signs, and these serve well enough as a basis for society and even for intimacy. But people in a novel can be understood completely by the reader, if the novelist wishes; their inner as well as their outer life can be exposed. And this is why they often seem more definite than characters in history, or even our own friends; we have been told all about them that can be told; even if they are imperfect or unreal they do not contain any secrets, whereas our friends do and must, mutual secrecy being one of the conditions of life upon this globe.

Now let us re-state the problem in a more schoolboyish way. You and I are people. Had not we better glance through the main facts in our own lives — not in our individual careers but in our make-up as human beings? Then we shall have something definite to start from.

The main facts in human life are five: birth, food, sleep, love and death. One could increase the number — add breathing for instance — but these five are the most obvious. Let us briefly ask ourselves what part they play in our lives, and what in novels. Does the novelist tend to reproduce them accurately or does he tend to exaggerate, minimize, ignore, and to exhibit his characters going through processes which are not the same through which you and I go, though they bear the same names?

To consider the two strangest first: birth and death; strange because they are at the same time experiences and not experiences. We only know of them by report. We were all born, but we cannot remember what it was like. And death is coming even as birth has come, but, similarly, we do not know what it is like. Our final experience, like our first, is conjectural. We move between two darknesses. Certain people pretend to tell us what birth and death are like: a mother, for instance, has her point of view about birth; a doctor, a religious, have their points of view about both. But it is all from the outside, and the two entities who might enlighten us, the baby and the corpse, cannot do so, because their apparatus for communicating their experiences is not attuned to our apparatus for reception.

So let us think of people as starting life with an experience they forget and ending it with one which they anticipate but cannot understand. These are the creatures whom the novelist proposes to introduce as characters into books; these, or creatures plausibly like them. The novelist is allowed to remember and understand everything, if it suits him. He knows all the hidden life. How soon will he pick up his characters after birth, how close to the grave will he follow them? And what will he say, or cause to be felt, about these two queer experiences?

Then food, the stoking-up process, the keeping alive of an individual flame, the process that begins before birth and is continued after it by the mother, and finally taken over by the individual himself, who goes on day after day putting an assortment of objects into a hole in his face without becoming surprised or bored: food is a link between the known and the forgotten; closely connected with birth, which none of us remembers, and coming down to this morning's breakfast. Like sleep — which in many ways it resembles — food does not merely restore our strength, it has also an aesthetic side, it can taste good or bad. What will happen to this double-faced commodity in books?

And fourthly, sleep. On the average, about a third of our time is not spent in society or civilization or even in what is usually called solitude. We enter a world of which little is known and which seems to us after leaving it to have been partly oblivion, partly a caricature of this world and partly a revelation. "I dreamt of nothing" or "I dreamt of a ladder" or "I dreamt of heaven," we say when we wake. I do not want to discuss the nature of sleep and dreams — only to point out that they occupy much time and that what is called "History" only busies itself with about two-thirds of the human cycle, and theorizes accordingly. Does fiction take up a similar attitude?

And lastly, love. I am using this celebrated word in its widest and dullest sense. Let me be very dry and brief about sex in the first place. Some years after a human being is born, certain changes occur in it, as in other animals, which changes often lead to union with another human being, and to the production of more human beings. And our race goes on. Sex begins before adolescence, and survives sterility; it is indeed coeval with our lives, although at the mating age its effects are more obvious to society. And besides sex there are other emotions, also strengthening towards maturity: the various upliftings of the spirit, such as affection, friendship, patriotism, mysticism — and as soon as we try to determine the relation between sex and these other emotions we shall of course begin to quarrel as violently as we ever could about Walter Scott, perhaps even more violently. Let me only tabulate the various points of view. Some people say that sex is basic and underlies all these other loves — love of friends, of God, of country. Others say that it is connected with them, but laterally, it is not their root. Others say that it is not connected at all. All I suggest is that we call the whole bundle of emotions love, and regard them as the fifth great experience through which human beings have to pass. When human beings love they try to get something. They also try to give something, and this double aim makes love more complicated than food or sleep. It is selfish and altruistic at the same time, and no amount of specialization in one direction quite atrophies the other. How much time does love take? This question sounds gross but it bears on our present enquiry. Sleep takes about eight hours out of the twenty-four, food about two more. Shall we put down love for another two? Surely that is a handsome allowance. Love may weave itself into our other activities — so may drowsiness and hunger. Love may start various secondary activities: for instance, a man's love for his family may cause him to spend a good deal of time on the Stock Exchange, or his love for God a good deal of time in church. But that he has emotional communion with any beloved object for more than two hours a day may be gravely doubted, and it is this emotional communion, this desire to give and to get, this mixture of generosity and expectation, that distinguishes love from the other experiences on our list.

That is the human make-up — or part of it. Made up like this himself, the novelist takes his pen in his hand, gets into the abnormal state which it is convenient to call "inspiration", and tries to create characters. Perhaps the characters have to fall in with something else in his novel; this often happens (the books of Henry James are an extreme case), and then the characters have, of course, to modify the make-up accordingly. However, we are considering now the more simple case of the novelist whose main passion is human beings and who will sacrifice a great deal to their convenience — story, plot, form, incidental beauty.

Well, in what senses do the nations of fiction differ from those of the earth? One cannot generalize about them, because they have nothing in common in the scientific sense; they need not have glands, for example, whereas all human beings have glands. Nevertheless, though incapable of strict definition, they tend to behave along the same lines.

In the first place, they come into the world more like

parcels than human beings. When a baby arrives in a novel it usually has the air of having been posted. It is delivered "off"; one of the elder characters goes and picks it up and shows it to the reader, after which it is usually laid in cold storage until it can talk or otherwise assist in the action.

There is both a good and a bad reason for this and for all other deviations from earthly practice; these we will note in a minute, but do just observe in what a very perfunctory way the population of noveldom is recruited. Between Sterne and James Joyce, scarcely any writer has tried either to use the facts of birth or to invent a new set of facts, and no one, except in a sort of auntish wistful way, has tried to work back towards the psychology of the baby's mind and to utilize the literary wealth that must lie there. Perhaps it cannot be done. We shall decide in a moment.

Death. The treatment of death, on the other hand, is nourished much more on observation, and has a variety about it which suggests that the novelist finds it congenial. He does, for the reason that death ends a book neatly, and for the less obvious reason that working as he does in time he finds it easier to work from the known towards the darkness rather than from the darkness of birth towards the known. By the time his characters die, he understands them, he can be both appropriate and imaginative about them — strongest of combinations. Take a little death — the death of Mrs. Proudie in *The Last Chronicle of Barset*. All is in keeping, yet the effect is terrifying, because Trollope has ambled Mrs. Proudie down many a diocesan bypath, showing her paces, making her snap, accustoming us, even to boredom, to her character and tricks, to her "Bishop, consider the souls of the people", and then she has a heart-attack by the edge of her bed, she has ambled far enough — end of Mrs. Proudie. There is scarcely anything that the novelist cannot borrow from "daily death"; scarcely anything he may not profitably invent. The doors of that darkness lie open to him and he can even follow his characters through it, provided he is shod with imagination and does not try to bring us back scraps of seance information about the "life beyond".

What of food, the third fact upon our list? Food in fiction is mainly social. It draws characters together, but they seldom require it physiologically, seldom enjoy it, and never digest it unless specially asked to do so. They hunger for each other, as we do in life, but our equally constant longing for breakfast and lunch does not get reflected. Even poetry has made more of it — at least of its aesthetic side. Milton and Keats have both come nearer to the sensuousness of swallowing than George Meredith.

Sleep. Also perfunctory. No attempt to indicate oblivion or

the actual dream-world. Dreams are either logical or else mosaics made out of hard little fragments of the past and future. They are introduced with a purpose, and that purpose is not the character's life as a whole, but that part of it he lives while awake. He is never conceived as a creature, a third of whose time is spend in the darkness. It is the limited daylight vision of the historian, which the novelist elsewhere avoids. Why should he not understand or reconstruct sleep? For remember, he has the right to invent, and. we know when he is inventing truly, because his passion floats us over improbabilities. Yet he has neither copied sleep nor created it. It is just an amalgam.

Love. You all know how enormously love bulks in novels, and will probably agree with me that it has done them harm and made them monotonous. Why has this particular experience, especially in its sex form, been transplanted in such generous qualities? If you think of a novel in the vague you think of a love interest — of a man and woman who want to be united and perhaps succeed. If you think of your own life in the vague, or of a group of lives, you are left with a very different and a more complex impression.

There would seem to be two reasons why love, even in good sincere novels, is unduly prominent.

Firstly, when the novelist ceases to design his characters and begins to create them, "love" in any or all of its aspects becomes important in his mind, and without intending to do so he makes his characters unduly sensitive to it — unduly in the sense that they would not trouble so much in life. The constant sensitiveness of characters for each other — even in writers called robust like Fielding — is remarkable, and has no parallel in life, except among people who have plenty of leisure. Passion, intensity at moments — yes, but not this constant awareness, this endless readjusting, this ceaseless hunger. I believe that these are the reflections of the novelist's own state of mind while he composes, and that the predominance of love in novels is partly because of this.

A second reason; which logically comes into another part of our enquiry, but it shall be noted here. Love, like death, is congenial to a novelist because it ends a book conveniently. He can make it a permanency, and his readers easily acquiesce, because one of the illusions attached to love is that it will be permanent. Not has been — will be. All history, all our experience, teaches us that no human relationship is constant, it is as unstable as the living beings who compose it, and they must balance like jugglers if it is to remain; if it is constant it is no longer a human relationship but a social habit, the emphasis in it has passed from love to marriage. All this we know, yet we cannot bear to apply our bitter knowledge to the future; the future is to be so different; the perfect person is to come along, or the person we know already is to become perfect. There are to be no changes, no necessity for alertness. We are to be happy or even perhaps miserable for ever and ever. Any strong emotion brings with it the illusion of permanence, and the novelists have seized upon this. They usually end their books with marriage, and we do not object because we lend them our dreams.

Here we must conclude our comparison of those two allied species, Homo Sapiens and Homo Fictus. Homo Fictus is more elusive than his cousin. He is created in the minds of hundreds of different novelists, who have conflicting methods of gestation, so one must not generalize. Still, one can say a little about him. He is generally born off, he is capable of dying on, he wants little food or sleep, he is tirelessly occupied with human relationships. And — most important — we can know more about him than we can know about any of our fellow creatures, because his creator and narrator are one. Were we equipped for hyperbole, we might exclaim at this point: "If God could tell the story of the Universe, the Universe would become fictitious." For this is the principle involved.

Let us, after these high speculations, take an easy character and study it for a little. Moll Flanders will do. She fills the book that bears her name, or rather stands alone in it, like a tree in a park, so that we can see her from every aspect and are not bothered by rival growths. Defoe is telling a story, like Scott, and we shall find stray threads left about in much the same way, on the chance of the writer wanting to pick them up afterwards: Moll's early batch of children for instance. But the parallel between Scott and Defoe cannot be pressed. What interested Defoe was the heroine, and the form of his book proceeds naturally out of her character. Seduced by a younger brother and married to an elder, she takes to husbands in the earlier and brighter part of her career; not to prostitution, which she detests with all the force of a decent and affectionate heart. She and most of the characters in Defoe's underworld are kind to one another, they save each other's feelings and run risks through personal loyalty. Their innate goodness is always flourishing despite the author's better judgement, the reason evidently being that the author had some great experience himself while in Newgate. We do not know what it was, probably he himself did not know afterwards, for he was a busy slipshod journalist and a keen politician. But something occurred to him in prison, and out of its vague, powerful emotion Moll and Roxana are born. Moll is a character physically, with hard plump limbs that get into bed and pick pockets. She lays no stress upon her appearance, yet she moves us as having height and weight, as breathing and eating, and doing many of the things that are usually missed out. Husbands were her earlier employ: she was trigamous if not quadrigamous, and one of her husbands turned out to be a brother. She was happy with all of them, they were nice to her, she nice to them. Listen to the pleasant jaunt her draper husband took her:

> "Come, my dear," says he to me one day, "shall we go and take a turn into the country for about a week?" "Ay, my dear," says I, "whither would you go?" "I care not whither," says he, "but I have a mind to look like quality for a week. We'll go to Oxford," says he. "How," says I, "shall we go? I am no horsewoman, and 'tis too far for a coach." "Too far!" says he; "no place is too far for a coach-and-six. If I carry you out, you shall travel like a duchess." "Hum," says I, "my dear, 'tis a frolic; but if you have a mind to it, I don't care." Well, the time was appointed, we had a rich coach, very good hones, a coachman, postilion, and two footmen in very good liveries; a gentleman on horseback, and a page with a feather in his hat upon another horse. The servants all called him my lord, and the inn keepers, you may be sure, did the

like, and I was her honour the Countess, and thus we travelled to Oxford, and a very pleasant journey we had; for, give him his due, not a beggar alive knew better how to be a lord than my husband. We saw all the rarities at Oxford, talked with two or three Fellows of colleges about putting out a young nephew, that was left to his lordship's care, to the University, and of their being his tutors. We diverted ourselves with bantering several other poor scholars, with hopes of being at least his lordship's chaplains, and putting on a scarf; and thus having lived like quality, indeed, as to expense, we went away for Northampton, and, in a word, in about twelve days' ramble came home again, to the tune of about £ 93 expense.

Contrast with this the scene with her Lancashire husband, whom she deeply loved. He is a highwayman, and each by pretending to wealth has trapped the other into marriage. After the ceremony, they are mutually unmasked, and if Defoe were writing mechanically he would set them to upbraid one another, like Mr. and Mrs. Lammle in *Our Mutual Friends*. But he has given himself over to the humour and good sense of his heroine.

"Truly," said I to him, "I found you would soon have

conquered me; and it is my affliction now, that I am not in a condition to let you see how easily I should have been reconciled to you, and have passed by all the tricks you had put upon me, in recompense of so much good-humour. But, my dear," said I, "what can we do now? We are both undone, and what better are we for our being reconciled together, seeing we have nothing to live on?"

We proposed a great many things, but nothing could offer where there was nothing to begin with. He begged me at last to talk no more of it, for, he said, I would break his heart; so we talked of other things a little, till at last he took a husband's leave of me, and so we went to sleep.

Which is both truer to daily life and pleasanter to read than Dickens. The couple are up against facts, not against the author's theory of morality, and being sensible good-hearted rogues, they do not make a fuss. In the later part of her career she turns from husbands to thieving; she thinks this a change for the worse and a natural darkness spreads over the scene. But she is as firm and amusing as ever. How just are her reflections when she robs of her gold necklace the little girl returning from the dancing-class! The deed is done in the little passage leading to St. Bartholomew's, Smithfield (you can visit the place today — Defoe haunts

London), and her impulse is to kill the child as well. She does not, the impulse is very feeble, but conscious of the risk the child has run she becomes most indignant with the parents for "leaving the poor little lamb to come home by itself, and it would teach them to take more care of it another time". How heavily and pretentiously a modern psychologist would labour to express this! It just runs off Defoe's pen, and so in another passage, where Moll cheats a man, and then tells him pleasantly afterwards that she has done so, with the result that she slides still further into his good graces, and cannot bear to cheat him any more. Whatever she does gives us a slight shock — not the jolt of disillusionment, but the thrill that proceeds from a living being. We laugh at her, but without bitterness or superiority. She is neither hypocrite nor fool.

Towards the end of the book she is caught in a draper's shop by two young ladies from behind the counter: "I would have given them good words, but there was no room for it: two fiery dragons could not have been more furious than they were." — they call for the police, she is arrested and sentenced to death and then transported to Virginia instead. The clouds of misfortune lift with indecent rapidity. The voyage is a very pleasant one, owing to the kindness of the old woman who had originally taught her to steal. And (better still) her Lancashire husband happens to be transported also. They land at Virginia where, much to her distress, her brother-husband proves to be in residence. She conceals this, he dies, and the Lancashire husband only blames her for concealing it from him; he has no other grievance, for the reason that he and she are still in love. So the book closes prosperously, and firm as at the opening sentence the heroine's voice rings out: "... we resolve to spend the remainder of our years in sincere penitence for the wicked lives we have led."

Her penitence is sincere, and only a superficial judge will condemn her as a hypocrite. A nature such as hers cannot for long distinguish between doing wrong and getting caught — for a sentence or two she disentangles them but they insist on blending, and that is why her outlook is so cockneyfied and natural, with "such is life" for a philosophy and Newgate in the place of Hell. If we were to press her or her creator Defoe and say, "Come, be serious. Do you believe in Infinity?" they would say (in the parlance of their modern descendants), "Of course I believe in Infinity — what do you take me for?" — a confession of faith that slams the door on Infinity more completely than could any denial.

Moll Flanders, then, shall stand as our example of a novel in which a character is everything and is given freest play. Defoe makes a slight attempt at a plot with the brother-husband as a centre, but he is quite perfunctory, and her legal husband (the one who took her on the jaunt to Oxford) just disappears and is heard of no more. Nothing matters but the heroine; she stands in an open space like a tree, and, having said that she seems absolutely real from every point of view, we must ask ourselves whether we should recognize her if we met her in daily life. For that is the point we are still considering: the difference between people in life and people in books. And the odd thing is, that even though we take a character as natural and untheoretical as Moll, who would coincide with daily life in every detail, we should not find her there as a whole. Suppose I suddenly altered my voice from a lecturing voice into an ordinary one and said to you, "Look out — I can see Moll in the audience — look out, Mr." — naming one of you by name — "she as near as could be got your watch." — well, you would know at once that I was wrong, that I was sinning not only against probabilities, which does not signify, but against daily life and books and the gulf that divides them. If I said, "Look out, there's someone like Moll in the audience," you might not believe me but you would not be annoyed by my imbecile lack of taste: I should only be sinning against probability. To suggest that Moll is in Cambridge this afternoon or anywhere in England, or has been anywhere in

England, is idiotic. Why?

This particular question will be easy to answer next week, when we shall deal with more complicated novels, where the character has to fit in with other aspects of fiction. We shall then be able to make the usual reply, which we find in all manuals of literature, and which should always be given in an examination paper, the aesthetic reply, to the effect that a novel is a work of art, with its own laws, which are not those of daily life, and that a character in a novel is real when it lives in accordance with such laws. Amelia or Emma, we shall then say, cannot be at this lecture because they exist only in the books called after them, only in worlds of Fielding or Jane Austen. The bather of art divides them from us. They are real not because they are like ourselves (though they may be like us) but because they are convincing.

It is a good answer, it will lead on to some sound conclusions. Yet it is not satisfactory for a novel like *Moll Flanders*, where the character is everything and can do what it likes. We want a reply that is less aesthetic and more psychological. Why cannot she be here? What separates her from us? Our answer has already been implied in that quotation from Alain: she cannot be here because she belongs to a world where the secret life is visible, to a world that is not and cannot be ours, to a world where the narrator and the creator are one. And now we can get a definition as to when a character in a book is real: it is real when the novelist knows everything about it. He may not choose to tell us all he knows — many of the facts, even of the kind we call obvious, may be hidden. But he will give us the feeling that though the character has not been explained it is explicable, and we get from this a reality of a kind we can never get in daily life.

For human intercourse, as soon as we look at it for its own sake and not as a social adjunct, is seen to be haunted by a spectre. We cannot understand each other, except in a rough and ready way; we cannot reveal ourselves, even when we want to; what we call intimacy is only a makeshift; perfect knowledge is an illusion. But in the novel we can know people perfectly, and, apart from the general pleasure of reading, we can find here a compensation for their dimness in life. In this direction fiction is truer than history, because it goes beyond the evidence, and each of us knows from his own experience that there is something beyond the evidence, and, even if the novelist has not got it correctly, well — he has tried. He can post his people in as babies, he can cause them to go on without sleep or food, he can make them be in love, love and nothing but love, provided he seems to know everything about them, provided they are his creations. That is why Moll Flanders cannot be here, that is one of the reasons why Amelia and Emma cannot be here. They are people whose secret lives are visible or might be visible; we are people whose secret lives are invisible.

And that is why novels, even when they are about wicked people, can solace us: they suggest a more comprehensible and thus a more manageable human race, they give us the illusion of perspicacity and of power.

Chapter 4 People (Continued)

We now turn from transplantation to acclimatization. We have discussed whether people could be taken out of life and put into a book, and conversely whether they could come out of books and sit down in this room. The answer suggested was in the negative and led to a more vital question: can we, in daily life, understand each other? Today our problems are more academic. We are concerned with the characters in their relation to other aspects of the novel; to a plot, a moral, their fellow characters, atmosphere, etc. They will have to adapt themselves to other requirements of their creator.

It follows that we shall no longer expect them to coincide as a whole with daily life, only to parallel it. When we say that a character in Jane Austen, Miss Bates for instance, is "so like life" we mean that each bit of her coincides with a bit of life, but that she as a whole only parallels the chatty spinster we met at tea. Miss Bates is bound by a hundred threads to Highbury.

We cannot tear her away without bringing her mother too, and Jane Fairfax and Frank Churchill, and the whole of Box Hill; whereas we could tear Moll Flanders away, at least for the purposes of experiment. A Jane Austen novel is more complicated than a Defoe, because the characters are interdependent, and there is the additional complication of a plot. The plot in Emma is not prominent and Miss Bates contributes little. Still, it is there, she is connected with the principals, and the result is a closely woven fabric from which nothing can be removed. Miss Bates and Emma herself are like bushes in a shrubbery — not isolated trees like Moll — and anyone who has tried to thin out a shrubbery knows how wretched the bushes look if they are transplanted elsewhere, and how wretched is the look of the bushes that remain. In most books the characters cannot spread themselves. They must exercise a mutual restraint.

The novelist, we are beginning to see, has a very mixed lot of ingredients to handle. There is the story, with its time-sequence of "and then ... and then ..."; there are ninepins about whom he might tell the story, and tell a rattling good one, but no, he prefers to tell his story about human beings; he takes over the life by values as well as the life in time. The characters arrive when evoked, but full of the spirit of mutiny. For they have these numerous parallels with people like ourselves, they try to live their own lives and are consequently often engaged in treason against the main scheme of the book. They "run away", they "get out of hand"; they are creations inside a creation, and often inharmonious towards it; if they are given complete freedom they kick the book to pieces, and if they are kept too sternly in check, they revenge themselves by dying, and destroy it by intestinal decay.

These trials beset the dramatist also, and he has yet another set of ingredients to cope with — the actors and actresses — and they appear to side sometimes with the characters they represent, sometimes with the play as a whole, and more often to be the mortal enemies of both. The weight they throw is incalculable, and how any work of art survives their arrival I do not understand. Concerned with a lower form of art, we need not worry — but, in passing, is it not extraordinary that plays on the stage are often better than they are in the study, and that the introduction of a bunch of rather ambitious and nervous men and women should add anything to our understanding of Shakespeare and Chekov? No, the novelist has difficulties enough, and today we shall examine two of his devices for solving them — instinctive devices, for his methods when working are seldom the same as the methods we use when examining his work. The first device is the use of different kinds of characters. The second is connected with the point of view.

1

We may divide characters into flat and round.

Flat characters were called "humorous" in the seventeenth century, and are sometimes called types, and sometimes caricatures. In their purest form, they are constructed round a single idea or quality; when there is more than one factor in them, we get the beginning of the curve towards the round. The really flat character can be expressed in one sentence such as "I never will desert Mr. Micawber". There is Mrs. Micawber — she says she won't desert Mr. Micawber; she doesn't, and there she is. Or: "I must conceal, even by subterfuges, the poverty of my master's house." There is Caleb Balderstone in *The Bride of Lammermoor*. He does not use the actual phrase, but it completely describes him; he has no existence outside it, no pleasures, none of the private lusts and aches that must complicate the most consistent of servitors. Whatever he does, wherever he goes, whatever lies he tells or plates he breaks, it is to conceal the poverty of his master's house. It is not his *idée fixe*, because there is nothing in him into which the idea can be fixed. He is the idea, and such life as he possesses radiates from its edges and from the scintillations it strikes when other elements in the novel impinge. Or take Proust. There are numerous flat characters in Proust, such as the Princess of Parma, or Legrandin. Each can be expressed in a single sentence, the Princess's sentence being, "I must be particularly careful to be kind." She does nothing except to be particularly careful, and those of the other characters who are more complex than herself easily see through the kindness, since it is only a by-product of the carefulness.

One great advantage of flat characters is that they are easily recognized whenever they come in — recognized by the reader's emotional eye, not by the visual eye, which merely notes the recurrence of a proper name. In Russian novels, where they so seldom occur, they would be a decided help. It is a convenience for an author when he can strike with his full force at once, and flat characters are very useful to him, since they never need reintroducing, never run away, have not to be watched for development, and provide their own atmosphere — little luminous disks of a pre-arranged size, pushed hither and thither like counters across the void or between the stars; most satisfactory.

A second advantage is that they are easily remembered by the reader afterwards. They remain in his mind as unalterable for the reason that they were not changed by circumstances; they moved through circumstances, which gives them in retrospect a comforting quality, and preserves them when the book that produced them may decay. The Countess in *Evan Harrington* furnishes a good little example here. Let us compare our memories of her with our memories of Becky Sharp. We do not remember what the Countess did or what she passed through. What is clear is her figure and the formula that surrounds it, namely, "Proud as we are of dear papa, we must conceal his memory." All her rich humour proceeds from this. She is a flat character. Becky is round. She, too, is on the make, but she cannot be summed up in a single phrase, and we remember her in connection with the great scenes through which she passed and as modified by those scenes — that is to say, we do not remember her so easily because she waxes and wanes and has facets like a human being. All of us, even the sophisticated, yearn for permanence, and to the unsophisticated permanence is the chief excuse for a work of art. We all want books to endure, to be refuges, and their inhabitants to be always the same, and flat characters tend to justify themselves on this account.

All the same, critics who have their eyes fixed severely upon daily life — as were our eyes last week — have very little patience with such renderings of human nature. Queen Victoria, they argue, cannot be summed up in a single sentence, so what excuse remains for Mrs. Mieawber? One of our foremost writers, Mr. Norman Douglas, is a critic of this type, and the passage from him which I will quote puts the case against flat characters in a forcible fashion. The passage occurs in an open letter to D. H. Lawrence, with whom he is quarrelling: a doughty pair of combatants, the hardness of whose hitting make the rest of us feel like a lot of ladies up in a pavilion. He complaints that Lawrence, in a biography of a mutual friend, has falsified the picture by employing "the novelist's touch", and he goes on to define what this is:

> It consists, I should say, in a failure to realize the profundities and complexities of the ordinary human mind; it selects for literary purposes two or three frets of a man or woman, generally the most spectacular and therefore 'useful' ingredients of their character, and disregards all the others. Whatever fails to fit in with these specially chosen traits is eliminated; must be eliminated, for otherwise the description would not hold water. Such and such are the data; everything incompatible with those data has to go by the board. It follows that the novelist's touch argues, often logically, from a wrong premise; it takes what it likes and leaves the rest. The facets may be correct as far as they go,

but there are too few of them; what the author says may be true, and yet by no means the truth. That is the novelist's touch. It falsifies life.

Well, the novelist's touch as thus defined is, of course, bad in biography, for no human being is simple. But in a novel it has its place: a novel that is at all complex often requires flat people as well as round, and the outcome of their collisions parallels life more accurately than Mr. Douglas implies. The case of Dickens is significant. Dickens's people are nearly all flat (Pip and David Copperfield attempt roundness, but so diffidently that they seem more like bubbles than solids). Nearly every one can be summed up in a sentence, and yet there is this wonderful feeling of human depth. Probably the immense vitality of Dickens causes his characters to vibrate a little, so that they borrow his life and appear to lead one of their own. It is a conjuring-trick; at any moment we may look at Mr. Pickwick edgeways and find him no thicker than a gramophone record. But we never get the sideway view. Mr. Pickwick is far too adroit and well-trained. He always has the air of weighing something, and when he is put into the cupboard of the young ladies' school he seems as heavy as Falstaff in the buck-basket at Windsor. Part of the genius of Dickens is that he does use types and caricatures, people whom we recognize the instant they re-enter, and yet achieves effects that are not mechanical and a vision of humanity that is not shallow. Those who dislike Dickens have an excellent case. He ought to be bad. He is actually one of our big writers, and his immense success with types suggests that there may be more in flatness than the severer critics admit.

Or take H. G. Wells. With the possible exceptions of Kipps and the aunt in *Tono Bungay*, all Wells' characters are as flat as a photograph. But the photographs are agitated with such vigour that we forget their complexities lie on the surface and would disappear if it were scratched or curled up. A Wells character cannot indeed be summed up in a single phrase; he is tethered much more to observation, he does not create types. Nevertheless his people seldom pulsate by their own strength. It is the deft and powerful hands of their maker that shake them and trick the reader into a sense of depth. Good but imperfect novelists, like Wells and Dickens, are very clever at transmitting force.

The part of their novel that is alive galvanizes the part that is not, and causes the characters to jump about and speak in a convincing way. They are quite different from the perfect novelist who touches all his material directly, who seems to pass the creative finger down every sentence and into every word. Richardson, Defoe, Jane Austen, are perfect in this particular way; their work may not be great but their hands are always upon it; there is not the tiny interval between the touching of the button and the sound of the bell which occurs in novels where the characters are not under direct control.

For we must admit that flat people are not in themselves as big achievements as round ones, and also that they are best when they are comic. A serious or tragic flat character is apt to be a bore. Each time he enters crying "Revenge!" or "My heart bleeds for humanity!" or whatever his formula is, our hearts sink. One of the romances of a popular contemporary writer is constructed round a Sussex farmer who says, "I'll plough up that bit of gorse." There is the farmer, there is the gorse; he says he'll plough it up, he does plough it up, but it is not like saying "I'll never desert Mr. Micawber," because we are so bored by his consistency that we do not care whether he succeeds with the gone or fails. If his formula were analysed and connected up with the rest of the human outfit, we should not be bored any longer, the formula would cease to be the man and become an obsession in the man; that is to say he would have turned from a flat famer into a round one. It is only round people who are fit to perform tragically for any length of time and can move us to any feelings except humour and appropriateness.

So now let us desert these two-dimensional people, and, by

way of transition to the round, let us go to Mansfield Park, and look at Lady Bertram, sitting on her sofa with pug. Pug is flat, like most animals in fiction. He is once represented as straying into a rose-bed in a cardboard kind of way, but that is all, and during most of the book his mistress seems to be cut out of the same simple material as her dog. Lady Bertram's formula is, "I am kindly, but must not be fatigued", and she functions out of it. But at the end there is a catastrophe. Her two daughters come to grief — to the worst grief known to Miss Austen's universe, far worse than the Napoleonic wars. Julia elopes; Maria, who is unhappily married, runs off with a lover. What is Lady Bertram's reaction? The sentence describing it is significant:

> Lady Bertram did not think deeply, but, guided by Sir Thomas, she thought justly on all important points; and she saw, therefore, in all its enormity, what had happened, and neither endeavoured herself, nor required Fanny to advise her, to think lithe of guilt and infamy.

These are strong words, and they used to worry me because I thought Jane Austen's moral sense was getting out of hand. She may, and of course does, deprecate guilt and infamy herself, and she duly causes all possible distress in the minds of Edmund and Fanny, but has she any right to agitate calm, consistent Lady Bertram? Is not it like giving pug three faces and setting him to guard the gates of Hell? Ought not her ladyship to remain on the sofa saying, "This is a dreadful and sadly exhausting business about Julia and Maria, but where is Fanny gone? I have dropped another stitch"?

I used to think this, through misunderstanding Jane Austen's method — exactly as Scott misunderstood it when he congratulated her for painting on a square of ivory. She is a miniaturist, but never two-dimensional. All her characters are round, or capable of rotundity. Even Miss Bates has a mind, even Elizabeth Elliot a heart, and Lady Bertram's moral fervour ceases to vex us when we realize this; the disc has suddenly extended and become a little globe. When the novel is closed, Lady Bertram goes back to the flat, it is true; the dominant impression she leaves can be summed up in a formula. But that is not how Jane Austen conceived her, and the freshness of her reappearances is due to this. Why do the characters in Jane Austen give us a slightly new pleasure each time they come in, as opposed to the merely repetitive pleasure that is caused by a character in Dickens? Why do they combine so well in a conversation, and draw one another out without seeming to do so, and never perform? The answer to this question can be put in several ways: that, unlike Dickens, she was a real artist, that she never stooped to caricature, etc. But the best reply is that her characters though smaller than his, are more highly organized. They function all round, and even if her plot made greater demands on them than it does they would still be adequate. Suppose that Louisa Musgrove had broken her neck on the Cobb. The description of her death would have been feeble and ladylike — physical violence is quite beyond Miss Austen's power — but the survivors would have reacted properly as soon as the corpse was carried away, they would have brought into view new sides of their character, and, though *Persuasion* would have been spoiled as a book, we should know more than we do about Captain Wentworth and Anne. All the Jane Austen characters are ready for an extended life, for a life which the scheme of her books seldom requires them to lead, and that is why they lead their actual lives so satisfactorily.

Let us return to Lady Bertram and the crucial sentence. See how subtly it modulates from her formula into an area where the formula does not work. "Lady Bertram did not think deeply." Exactly: as her formula. "But guided by Sir Thomas, she thought justly on all important points." Sir Thomas's guidance, which is part of the formula, remains, but it pushes her ladyship towards an independent and undesired morality. " She saw, therefore, in all its enormity, what had happened." This is the moral fortissimo — very strong but carefully introduced. And then follows a most artful decrescendo, by means of negatives. She "neither endeavoured herself, nor required Fanny to advise her, to think little of guilt and infamy." The formula is reappearing, because as a rule she does try to minimize trouble, and does require Fanny to advise her how to do this; indeed Fanny has done nothing else for the last ten years. The words, though they are negatived, remind us of this, her normal state is again in view, and she has in a single sentence been inflated into a round character and collapsed back into a flat one. How Jane Austen can write! In a few words she has extended Lady Bertram, and by so doing she has increased the probability of the elopements of Maria and Julia. I say probability because the elopements belong to the domain of violent physical action, and here, as already indicated, Jane Austen is feeble and ladylike. Except in her schoolgirl novels, she cannot stage a crash. Everything violent has to take place " off " — Louisa's accident and Marianne Dashwood's putrid throat are the nearest exceptions — and consequently all the comments on the elopement must be sincere and convincing, otherwise we should doubt whether it occurred. Lady Bertram helps us to believe that her daughters have run away, and they have to run away, or there would be no apotheosis for Fanny. It is a little point, and a little sentence, yet it shows us how delicately a great novelist can modulate into the round.

All through her works we find these characters, apparently so simple and flat, never needing reintroduction and yet never out of their depth — Henry Tilney, Mr. Woodhouse, Charlotte Lucas. She may label her characters "Sense," "Pride," "Sensibility," "Prejudice," but they are not tethered to those qualities.

As for the round characters proper, they have already been defined by implication and no more need be said. All I need do is to give some examples of people in books who seem to me round, so that the definition can be tested afterwards.

All the principal characters in *War and Peace*, all the Dostoevsky characters, and some of the Proust — for example, the old family servant, the Duchess of Guermantes, M. de Charlus, and Saint-Loup; Madame Bovary — who, like Moll Flanders, has her book to herself, and can expand and secrete unchecked; some people in Thackeray — for instance, Becky and Beatrix; some in Fielding — Parson Adams, or Jones; and some in Charlotte Bronte, most particularly Lucy Snowe. (And many more — this is not a catalogue.) The test of a round character is whether it is capable of surprising in a convincing way. If it never surprises, it is flat. If it does not convince, it is a flat pretending to be round. It has the incalculability of life about it — life within the pages of a book. And by using it sometimes alone, more often in combination with the other kind, the novelist achieves his task of acclimatization, and harmonizes the human race with the other aspects of his work.

2

Now for the second device: the point of view from which the story may be told.

To some critics this is the fundamental device.

> The whole intricate question of method, in the craft of fiction, [says Mr. Percy Lubbock], I take to be governed by the question of the point of view — the question of the relation in which the narrator stands to the story.

And his book *The Craft of Fiction* examines various points of view with genius and insight. The novelist, he says, can either describe the characters from outside, as an impartial or partial onlooker; or he can assume omniscience and describe them from within; or he can place himself in the position of one of them and affect to be in the dark as to the motives of the rest; or there are certain intermediate attitudes.

Those who follow him will lay a sure foundation for the aesthetics of fiction — a foundation which I cannot for a moment promise. This is a ramshackly survey, and for me the whole intricate question of method resolves itself not into formulae but into the power of the writer to bounce the reader into accepting what he says — a power which Mr. Lubbock admits and admires, but locates at the edge of the problem instead of at the centre. I should put it plumb in the centre. Look how Dickens bounces us in *Bleak House*. Chapter I of *Bleak House* is omniscient. Dickens takes us into the Court of Chancery and rapidly explains all the people there. In Chapter II he is partially omniscient. We still use his eyes, but for some unexplained reason they begin to grow weak: he can explain Sir Leicester Dedlock to us, part of Lady Dedlock but not all, and nothing of Mr. Tulkinghorn. In Chapter III he is even more reprehensible: he goes straight across into the dramatic method and inhabits a young lady, Esther Summerson. "I have a great deal of difficulty in beginning to write my portion of these pages, for I know I am not clever," pipes up Esther, and continues in this strain with consistency and competence, so long as she is allowed to hold the pen. At any moment the author of her being may snatch it from her, and run about taking notes himself, leaving her seated goodness knows where, and employed we do not care how. Logically, Bleak House is all to pieces, but Dickens bounces us, so that we do not mind the shillings of the viewpoint.

Critics are more apt to object than readers. Zealous for the novel's eminence, they are a little too apt to look out for problems that shall be peculiar to it, and differentiate it from the drama; they feel it ought to have its own technical troubles before it can be accepted as an independent art; and since the problem of a point of view certainly is peculiar to the novel they have rather overstressed it. I do not myself think it is so important as a proper mixture of characters — a problem which the dramatist is up against also. And the novelist must bounce us; that is imperative.

Let us glance at two other examples of a shifting viewpoint.

The eminent French writer, André Gide, has published a novel called *Les Faux-Monnayeurs* of which there will be more to say next week: a novel for all its modernity, has one aspect in common with *Bleak House*: it is all to pieces logically. Sometimes the author is omniscient: he explains everything, he stands back, "il juge ses personages"; at other times his omniscience is partial; yet again he is dramatic, and causes the story to be told through the diary of one of the characters. There is the same absence of viewpoint, but whereas in Dickens it was instinctive, in Gide it is sophisticated; he expatiates too much about the jolts. The novelist who betrays too much interest in his own method can never be more than interesting; he has given up the creation of character and summoned us to help analyse his own mind, and a heavy drop in the emotional thermometer results. *Les Faux-Monnayeurs* is among the more interesting of recent works; not among the vital ; and greatly as we shall have to admire it as a fabric we cannot praise it unrestrictedly now.

For our second example we must again glance at *War and Peace*. Here the result is vital: we are bounced up and down Russia — omniscient, semi-omniscient, dramatized here or there as the moment dictates — and at the end we have accepted it all. Mr. Lubbock does not, it is true: great as he finds the book, he would find it greater if it had a viewpoint; he feels Tolstoy has not pulled his full weight. I feel that the rules of the game of writing are not like this. A novelist can shift his viewpoint if it comes off, and it came off with Dickens and Tolstoy. Indeed this power to expand and contract perception (of which the shifting viewpoint is a symptom), this right to intermittent knowledge — I find it one of the great advantages of the novel-form, and it has a parallel in our perception of life. We are stupider at some times than others; we can enter into people's minds occasionally but not always, because our own minds get tired; and this intermittence lends in the long run variety and colour to the experiences we receive. A quantity of novelists, English novelists especially, have behaved like this to the people in their books: played fast and loose with them, and I cannot see why they should be censured.

They must be censured if we catch them at it at the time. That is quite true, and out of it arises another question: may the writer take the reader into his confidence about his characters? Answer has already been indicated: better not. It is dangerous, it generally leads to a drop in the temperature, to intellectual and emotional laxity, and worse still to facetiousness, and to a friendly invitation to see how the figures hook up behind. "Doesn't A look nice — she always was my favourite." "Let's think of why B does that — perhaps there's more in him than meets the eye — yes, see — he has a heart of gold — having given you this peep at it I'll pop it back — I don't think he's noticed." "And C — he always was the mystery man." Intimacy is gained but at the expense of illusion and nobility. It is like standing a man a drink so that he may not criticize your opinions. With all respect to Fielding and Thackeray, it is devastating, it is bar-parlour chattiness, and nothing has been more harmful to the novels of the past. To take your reader into your confidence about the universe is a different thing. It is not dangerous for a novelist to draw back from his characters, as Hardy and Conrad do, and to generalize about the conditions under which he thinks life is carried on. It is confidences about individual people that do harm, and beckon the reader away from the people to an examination of the novelist's mind. Not much is ever found in it at such a moment, for it is never in the creative state: the mere process of saying, "Come along, let's have a chat" has cooled it down.

Our comments on human beings must now come to an end. They may take fuller shape when we come to discuss the plot.

Chapter 5   The Plot

"Character," says Aristotle, "gives us qualities, but it is in actions — what we do — that we are happy or the reverse." We have already decided that Aristotle is wrong, and now we must face the consequences of disagreeing with him. "All human happiness and misery," says Aristotle, "take the form of action." We know better. We believe that happiness and misery exist in the secret life, which each of us leads privately and to which (in his characters) the novelist has access. And by the secret life we mean the life for which there is no external evidence, not, as is vulgarly supposed, that which is revealed by a chance word or a sigh. A chance word or sigh are just as much evidence as a speech or a murder: the life they reveal ceases to be secret and enters the realm of action.

There is, however, no occasion to be hard on Aristotle. He had read few novels and no modern ones — the *Odyssey* but not *Ulysses* — he was by temperament apathetic to secrecy, and indeed regarded the human mind as a sort of tub from which everything can finally be extracted; and when he wrote the words quoted above he had in view the drama, where no doubt they hold true. In the drama all human happiness and misery does and must take the form of action. Otherwise its existence remains unknown, and this is the great difference between the drama and the novel.

The speciality of the novel is that the writer can talk about his characters as well as through them, or can arrange for us to listen when they talk to themselves. He has access to self-communings, and from that level he can descend even deeper and peer into the subconscious. A man does not talk to himself quite truly — not even to himself; the happiness or misery that he secretly feels proceeds from causes that he cannot quite explain, because as soon as he raises them to the level of the explicable they lose their native quality. The novelist has a real pull here. He can show the subconscious short-circuiting straight into action (the dramatist can do this too); he can also show it in its relation to soliloquy. He commands all the secret life, and he must not be robbed of his privilege. "How did the writer know that?" it is sometimes said. "What's his standpoint? He is not being consistent, he's shifting his point of view from the limited to the omniscient, and now he's edging back again."

Questions like these have too much the atmosphere of the law courts about them. All that matters to the reader is whether the shifting of attitude and the secret life are convincing, whether it is πιθανσν in fact, and with his favourite word ringing in his ears Aristotle may retire.

However, he leaves us in some confusion, for what, with this enlargement of human nature, is going to become of the plot? In most literary works there are two elements: human individuals, whom we have recently discussed, and the element vaguely called art. Art we have also dallied with, but with a very low form of it, the story: the chopped-off length of the tapeworm of time. Now we arrive at a much higher aspect, the plot; and the plot, instead of finding human beings more or less cut to its requirements, as they are in the drama, finds them. enormous, shadowy and intractable, and three-quarters hidden like an iceberg. In vain it points out to these unwieldy creatures the advantages of the triple process of complication, crisis and solution so persuasively expounded by Aristotle. A few of them rise and comply, and a novel which ought to have been a play is the result. But there is no general response. They want to sit apart and brood or something, and the plot (whom I here visualize as a sort of higher government official) is concerned at their lack of public spirit: "This will not do," it seems to say. "Individualism is a most valuable quality; indeed my own position depends upon individuals; I have always admitted as much freely. Nevertheless there are certain limits, and those limits are being overstepped. Characters must not brood too long, they must not waste time running up and down ladders in their own insides, they must contribute, or higher interests will be jeopardized." How well one knows that phrase, "a contribution to the plot"! It is accorded, and of necessity, by the people in a drama; how necessary is it in a novel?

Let us define a plot. We have defined a story as a narrative of events arranged in their time-sequence. A plot is also a narrative of events, the emphasis falling on causality. "The king died and then the queen died" is a story. "The king died, and then the queen died of grief" is a plot. The time-sequence is preserved, but the sense of causality overshadows it. Or again: "The queen died, no one knew why, until it was discovered that it was through grief at the death of the king." This is a plot with a mystery in it, a form capable of high development. It suspends the time-sequence, it moves as far away from the story as its limitations will allow. Consider the death of the queen. If it is in a story we say "And then?" If it is in a plot we ask: "Why?" That is the fundamental difference between these two aspects of the novel. A plot cannot be told to a gaping audience of cavemen or to a tyrannical sultan or to their modern descendant the movie-public. They can only be kept awake by "And then — and then —" they can only supply curiosity. But a plot demands intelligence and memory also.

Curiosity is one of the lowest of the human faculties. You will have noticed in daily life that when people are inquisitive they nearly always have bad memories and are usually stupid at bottom. The man who begins by asking you how many brothers and sisters you have is never a sympathetic character, and if you meet him in a year's time he will probably ask you how many brothers and sisters you have, his mouth again sagging open, his eyes still bulging from his head. It is difficult to be friends with such a man, and for two inquisitive people to be friends must be impossible. Curiosity by itself takes us a very little way, nor does it take us far into the novel — only as far as the story. If we would grasp the plot we must add intelligence and memory.

Intelligence first. The intelligent novel-reader, unlike the inquisitive one who just runs his eye over a new fact, mentally picks it up. He sees it from two points of view: isolated, and related to the other facts that he has read on previous pages. Probably he does not understand it, but he does not expect to do so yet awhile. The facts in a highly organized novel (like *The Egoist*) are often of the nature of cross-correspondences and the ideal spectator cannot expect to view them properly until he is sitting up on a hill at the end. This element of surprise or mystery — the detective element as it is sometimes rather emptily called — is of great importance in a plot. It occurs through a suspension of the time-sequence; a mystery is a pocket in time, and it occurs crudely, as in "Why did the queen die?", and more subtly in half-explained gestures and words, the true meaning of which only dawns pages ahead. Mystery is essential to a plot, and cannot be appreciated without intelligence. To the curious it is just another "And then?" To appreciate a mystery, part of the mind must be left behind, brooding, while the other part goes marching on.

That brings us to our second qualification: memory.

Memory and intelligence are closely connected, for unless we remember we cannot understand. If by the time the queen dies we have forgotten the existence of the king we shall never make out what killed her. The plot-maker expects us to remember, we expect him to leave no loose ends. Every action or word in a plot ought to count; it ought to be economical and spare; even when complicated it should be organic and free from dead matter. It may be difficult or easy, it may and should contain mysteries, but it ought not to mislead. And over it, as it unfolds, will hover the memory of the reader (that dull glow of the mind of which intelligence is the bright advancing edge) and will constantly rearrange and reconsider, seeing new clues, new chains of cause and effect, and the final sense (if the plot has been a fine one) will not be of clues or chains, but of something aesthetically compact, something which might have been shown by the novelist straight away, only if he had shown it straight away it would never have become beautiful. We come up against beauty here — for the first time in our enquiry: beauty at which a novelist should never aim, though he fails if he does not achieve it. I will conduct beauty to her proper place later on. Meanwhile please accept her as part of a completed plot. She looks a little surprised at being there, but beauty ought to look a little surprised; it is the emotion that best suits her face, as Botticelli knew when he painted her risen from the waves, between the winds and the flowers. The beauty who does not look surprised, who accepts her position as her due — she reminds us too much of a prima donna. But let us get back to the plot, and we will do so via George Meredith.

Meredith is not the great name he was twenty or thirty years ago, when much of the universe and all Cambridge trembled. I remember how depressed I used to be by a line in one of his poems: "We breathe but to be sword or block." I did not want to be either and I knew that I was not a sword. It seems, though, that there was no real cause for depression, for Meredith is himself now rather in the trough of a wave, and though fashion will turn and raise him a bit he will never be the spiritual power he was about the year 1900. His philosophy has not worn well. His heavy attacks on sentimentality — they bore the present generation, which pursues the same quarry but with neater instruments, and is apt to suspect anyone carrying a blunderbuss of being a sentimentalist himself. And his visions of Nature — they do not endure like Hardy's, there is too much Surrey about them, they are fluffy and lush. He could no more write the opening chapter of *The Return of the Native* than Box Hill could visit Salisbury Plain. What is really tragic and enduring in the scenery of England was hidden from him, and so is what is really tragic in life. When he gets serious and noble-minded there is a strident overtone, a bullying that becomes distressing. I feel indeed that he was like Tennyson in one respect: through not taking himself quietly enough be strained his inside. And his novels: most of the social values are faked. The tailors are not tailors, the cricket matches are not cricket, the railway trains do not even seem to be trains, the county families give the air of having been only just that moment unpacked, scarcely in position before the action starts, the straw still clinging to their beards. It is surely very odd, the social scene in which his characters are set; it is partly due to his fantasy, which is legitimate, but partly a chilly fake, and wrong. What with the faking, what with the preaching, which was never agreeable and is now said to be hollow, and what with the home counties posing as the universe, it is no wonder Meredith now lies in the trough. And yet he is in one way a great novelist. He is the finest contriver that English fiction has ever produced, and any lecture on plot must do homage to him.

Meredith's plots are not closely knit. We cannot describe the action of *Harry Richmond* in a phrase, as we can *Great Expectations*', though both books turn on the mistake made by a young man as to the sources of his fortune. A Meredithian plot is not a temple to the tragic or even to the comic Muse, but rather resembles a series of kiosks most artfully placed among wooded slopes, which his people reach by their own impetus, and from which they emerge with altered aspect. Incident springs out of character, and having occurred it alters that character. People and events are closely connected, and he does it by means of these contrivances. They are often delightful, sometimes touching, always unexpected. This shock, followed by the feeling "Oh, that's all right", is a sign that all is well with the plot ; characters, to be real, ought to run smoothly, but a plot ought to cause surprise. The horse-whipping of Dr. Shrapnel in

Beauchamp's Career is a surprise. We know that Everard Romfrey must dislike Shrapnel, must hate and misunderstand his radicalism, and be jealous of his influence over Beauchamp; we watch too the growth of the misunderstanding over Rosamund, we watch the intrigues of Cecil Baskelett. As far as characters go, Meredith plays with his cards on the table, but when the incident comes what a shock it gives us and the characters too! The tragi-comic business of one old man whipping 'another from the highest motives — it reacts upon all their world, and transforms all the personages of the book. It is not the centre of *Beauchamp's Career*, which indeed has no centre. It is essentially a contrivance, a door through which the book is made to pass, emerging in an altered form. Towards the close, when Beauchamp is drowned and Shrapnel and Romfrey are reconciled over his body, there is an attempt to elevate the plot to Aristotelean symmetry, to turn the novel into a temple wherein dwells interpretation and peace. Meredith fails here: *Beauchamp's Career* remains a series of contrivances (the visit to France is another of them), but contrivances that spring from the characters and react upon them.

And now briefly to illustrate the mystery element in the plot: the formula of " the queen died, it was afterwards discovered through grief". I will take an example, not from

Dickens (though Great Expectations provides a fine one), nor from Conan Doyle (whom my priggishness prevents me from enjoying), but again from Meredith: an example of a concealed emotion from the admirable plot of *The Egoist*: it occurs in the character of Laetitia Dale.

We are told, at first, all that passes in Laetitia's mind. Sir Willoughby has, twice jilted her, she is sad, resigned. Then, for dramatic reasons, her mind is hidden from us, it develops naturally enough, but does not re-emerge until the great midnight scene where he asks her to marry him because he is not sure about Clara, and this time, a changed woman, Laetitia says "No". Meredith has concealed the change. It would have spoiled his high comedy if we had been kept in touch with it throughout. Sir Willoughby has to have a series of crashes, to catch at this and that, and find everything rickety. We should not enjoy the fun, in fact it would be boorish, if we saw the author preparing the booby-traps beforehand, so Laetitia's apathy has been hidden from us. This is one of the countless examples in which either plot or character has to suffer, and Meredith with his unerring good sense here lets the plot triumph.

As an example of mistaken triumph, I think of a slip — it is no more than a slip — which Charlotte Bronte makes in Villette. She allows Lucy Snowe to conceal from the reader her discovery that Dr. John is the same as her old playmate Graham. When it comes out, we do get a good plot-thrill, but too much at the expense of Lucy's character. She has seemed, up to then, the spirit of integrity, and has, as it were, laid herself under a moral obligation to narrate all that she knows. That she stoops to suppress is a little distressing, though the incident is too trivial to do her any permanent harm.

Sometimes a plot triumphs too completely. The characters have to suspend their natures at every turn, or else are so swept away by the course of fate that our sense of their reality is weakened. We shall find instances of this in a writer who is far greater than Meredith, and yet less successful as a novelist — Thomas Hardy. Hardy seems to me essentially a poet, who conceives of his novels from an enormous height. They are to be tragedies or tragi-comedies, they are to give out the sound of hammer-strokes as they proceed; in other words Hardy arranges events with emphasis on causality, the ground-plan is a plot, and the characters are ordered to acquiesce in its requirements. Except in the person of Tess (who conveys the feeling that she is greater than destiny), this aspect of his work is unsatisfactory. His characters are involved in various snares, they are finally bound hand and foot, there is ceaseless emphasis on fate, and yet, for all the sacrifices made to it, we never see the action as a living thing as we see it in *Antigone or Bérénice* or *The Cherry Orchard*. The fate above us, not the fate working through us — that is what is eminent and memorable in the Wessex novels. Egdon Heath before Eustacia Vye has set foot upon it. The woods without the Woodlanders. The downs above Budmouth Regis with royal princesses, still asleep, driving across them through the dawn. Hardy's success in *The Dynasts* (where he uses another medium) is complete, there the hammer-strokes are heard, cause and effect enchain the characters despite their struggles, complete contact between the actors and the plot is established. But in the novels, though the same superb and terrible machine works, it never catches humanity in its teeth; there is some vital problem that has not been answered, or even posed, in the misfortunes of Jude the Obscure. In other words the characters have been required to contribute too much to the plot; except in their rustic humours, their vitality has been impoverished, they have gone dry and thin. This, as far as I can make out, is the flaw running through Hardy's novels: he has emphasized causality more strongly than his medium permits. As a poet and prophet and visualizer George Meredith is nothing by his side — just a suburban roarer — but Meredith did know what the novel could stand, where the plot could dun the characters for a contribution, where it must let them function as they liked. And the moral — well, I see no moral, because the work of Hardy is my home and that of Meredith cannot be: still the moral from the point of these lectures is again un favourable to Aristotle. In the novel, all human happiness and misery does not take the form of action, it seeks means of expression other than through the plot, it must not be rigidly canalized.

In the losing battle that the plot fights with the characters, it often takes a cowardly revenge. Nearly all novels are feeble at the end. This is because the plot requires to be wound up. Why is this necessary? Why is there not a convention which allows a novelist to stop as soon as he feels bored? Alas, he has to round things off, and usually the characters go dead while he is at work, and our final impression of them is through deadness. *The Vicar of Wakefield* is in this way a typical novel, so clever and fresh in the first half, up to the painting of the family group with Mrs. Primrose as Venus, and then so wooden and imbecile. Incidents and people that occurred at first for their own sake now have to contribute to the denouement. In the end even the author feels he is being a little foolish. "Nor can I go on," he says, "without a reflection on those accidental meetings which, though they happen every day, seldom excite our surprise but upon some extraordinary occasion." Goldsmith is of course a lightweight, but most novels do fail here — there is this disastrous standstill while logic takes over the command from flesh and blood. If it was not for death and marriage I do not know how the average novelist would conclude. Death and marriage are almost his only connection between his characters and his plot, and the reader is more ready to met him here, and take a bookish view of them, provided they occur later on in the book; the writer, poor fellow, must be allowed to finish up somehow, he has his living to get like anyone else, so no wonder that nothing is heard but hammering and screwing.

This, as far as one can generalize, is the inherent defect of novels: they go off at the end ; and there are two explanations: firstly, failure of pep, which threatens the novelist like all workers; and secondly, the difficulty which we have been discussing. The characters have been getting out of hand, laying foundations and declining to build on them afterwards, and now the novelist has to labour personally, in order that the job may be done to time. He pretends that the characters are acting for him. He keeps mentioning their names and using inverted commas. But the characters are gone or dead.

The plot, then, is the novel in its logical intellectual aspect; it requires mystery, but the mysteries are solved later on; the reader may be moving about in worlds unrealized, but the novelist has no misgivings. He is competent, poised above his work, throwing a beam of light here, popping on a cap of invisibility there, and (qua plot-maker) continually negotiating with himself qua character-monger as to the best effect to be produced. He plans his book beforehand; or anyhow he stands above it, his interest in cause and effect gives him an air of predetermination.

And now we must ask ourselves whether the framework thus produced is the best possible for a novel. After all, why has a novel to be planned? Cannot it grow? Why need it close, as a play closes? Cannot it open out? Instead of standing above his work and controlling it, cannot the novelist throw himself into it and be carried along to some goal that he does not foresee? The plot is exciting and may be beautiful, yet is it not a fetish, borrowed from the drama, from the spatial limitations of the stage? Cannot fiction devise a framework that is not so logical yet more suitable to its genius?

Modern writers say that it can, and we will now examine a recent example: a violent onslaught on the plot as we have defined it: a constructive attempt to put something in the place of the plot.

I have already mentioned the novel in question: *Lex Faux-Monnayeurs* by André Gide. It contains within its covers both the methods. Gide has also published the diary he kept while he was writing the novel, and there is no reason why he should not publish in the future the impressions he had when rereading both the diary and the novel, and in the future perfect a still more final synthesis in which the diary, the novel and his impressions of both will interact. He is indeed a little more solemn than an author should be about the whole caboodle, but regarded as a caboodle it is excessively interesting, and repays careful study by critics.

We have, in the first place, a plot in *Les Faux-Monnayeurs* of the logical objective type that we have been considering — a plot, or rather fragments of plots. The main fragment concerns a young man called Olivier — a charming, touching and lovable character, who misses happiness, and then recovers it after an excellently contrived denouement; confers it also; this fragment has a wonderful radiance and "lives", if I may use so coarse a word, it is a successful creation on familiar lines. But it is by no means the centre of the book. No more are the other logical fragments — that which concerns Georges, Olivier's schoolboy brother, who passes false coin, and is instrumental in driving a fellow pupil to suicide. (Gide gives us his sources for all this in his diary: he got the idea of Georges from a boy whom he caught trying to steal a book off a stall, the gang of coiners were caught at Rouen, and the suicide of children took place at Clermont-Ferrand, etc.) Neither Olivier, nor Georges, nor Vincent a third brother, nor Bernard their friend is the centre of the book. We come nearer to it in Edward. Edward is a novelist. He bears the same relation to Gide as Clissold does to Wells. I dare not be more precise. Like Gide, he keeps a diary, like Gide he is writing a book called *Les Faux-Monnayeurs*, and like Clissold he is disavowed. Edward's diary is printed in full. It begins before the plot-fragments, continues during them, and forms the bulk of Gide's book. Edward is not just a chronicler. He is an actor too; indeed it is he who rescues Olivier and is rescued by him; we leave those two in happiness.

But that is still not the centre. The nearest to the centre lies in a discussion about the art of the novel. Edward is holding forth to Bernard his secretary and some friends. He has said that truth in life and truth in a novel are not identical, and then he goes on to say that he wants to write a book which shall include both sorts of truth.

"And what is its subject?" asked Sophroniska.

"There is none," said Edward sharply. "My novel has no subject. No doubt that sounds foolish. Let us say, if you prefer, that it will not have ' a ' subject ... ' A slice of life,' the naturalistic school used to say. The mistake that school made was always to cut its slice in the same direction, always lengthwise, in the direction of time. Why not cut it up and down? Or across? As for me, I don't want to cut it at all. You see what I mean. I want to put everything into my novel and not snip off my material either here or there. I have been working for a year, and there is nothing I haven't put in: all I see, all I know, all I can learn from other people's lives and my own."

"My poor man, you will bore your readers to death," cried Laura, unable to restrain her mirth.

"Not at all. To get my effect, I am inventing, as my central character, a novelist, and the subject of my book will be the struggle between what reality offers him and what he tries to make of the offer."

"Have you planned out this book?" asked Sophroniska, trying to keep grave.

"Of course not."

"Why 'of course'?"

"For a book of this type any plan would be unsuitable. The whole of it would go wrong if I decided any detail ahead. I am waiting for reality to dictate to me."

"But I thought you wanted to get away from reality."

"My novelist wants to get away, but I keep pulling him back. To tell the truth, this is my subject: the struggle between facts as proposed by reality, and the ideal reality."

"Do tell us the name of this book," said Laura, in despair.

"Very well. Tell it them, Bernard."

"*Les Faux-Monnayeurs*," said Bernard. "And now will you please tell us who these f*aux-monnayeun* are."

"I haven't the least idea."

Bernard and Laura looked at each other and then at Sophroniska. There was the sound of a deep sigh.

The fact that ideas about money, depreciation, inflation, forgery, etc., had gradually invaded Edward's book — just as theories of clothing invade Satter Resartus and even assume the functions of characters. "Has anyone here ever had hold of a false coin?" he asked after a pause. "Imagine a ten-franc piece, gold, false. It is actually worth a couple of sous, but it will remain worth ten francs until it is found out. Suppose I begin with the idea that?"

"But why begin with an idea?" burst out Bernard, who was by now in a state of exasperation. "Why not begin with a fact? If you introduce the fact properly, the idea will follow of itself. If I was writing your *Faux-Monnayeun* I should begin with a piece of false money, with the ten-franc piece you were speaking of, and here it is!"

So saying, Bernard pulled a ten-franc piece out of his pocket and flung it on the table.

"There," he remarked. "It rings all right. I got it this morning from the grocer. It's worth more than a couple of sous, as it's coated in gold, but it's actually made of glass. It will become quite transparent in time. No — don't rub it — you're going to spoil my false coin."

Edward had taken it and was examining it with the utmost attention.

"How did the grocer get it?"

"He doesn't know. He passed it on me for a joke, and then enlightened me, being a decent fellow. He let me have it for five francs. I thought that, since you were writing *Les Faux-Monnayeurs*, you ought to see what false money is like, so I got it to show you. Now that you have looked at it, give it me back. I am sorry to see that reality has no interest for you."

"Yes," said Edward; "it interests me, but it puts me out."

"That's a pity," remarked Bernard.

This passage is the centre of the book. It contains the old thesis of truth in life versus truth in art, and illustrates it very neatly by the arrival of an actual false coin. What is new in it is the attempt to combine the two truths, the proposal that writers should mix themselves up in their material and be rolled over and over by it; they should not try to subdue any longer, they should hope to be subdued, to be carried away. As for a plot — to pot with the plot!

Break it up, boil it down. Let there be those "formidable erosions of contour" of which Nietzsche speaks. All that is prearranged is false.

Another distinguished critic has agreed with Gide — that old lady in the anecdote who was accused by her nieces of being illogical. For some time she could not be brought to understand what logic was, and when she grasped its true nature she was not so much angry as contemptuous. "Logic! Good gracious! What rubbish!" she exclaimed. "How can I tell what I think till I see what I say?" Her nieces, educated young women, thought that she was *passée*; she was really more up-to-date than they were.

Those who are in touch with contemporary France say that the present generation follows the advice of Gide and the old lady, and resolutely hurls itself into confusion; and indeed admires English novelists on the ground that they so seldom succeed in what they attempt. Compliments are always delightful, but this particular one is a bit of a backhander. It is like trying to lay an egg and being told you have produced a paraboloid — more curious than gratifying. And what results when you try to lay a paraboloid, I cannot conceive — perhaps the death of the hen. That seems the danger in Gide's position — he sets out to lay a paraboloid; he is not well advised, if he wants to write subconscious novels, to reason so luckily and patiently about the subconscious; he is introducing mysticism at the wrong stage of the process. However that is his affair. As a critic he is most stimulating, and the various bundles of words he has called *Les Faux-Monnayeurs* will be enjoyed by all who cannot tell what they think till they see what they say, or who weary of the tyranny by the plot and of its alternative, tyranny by characters.

There is clearly something else in view, some other aspect or aspects which we have yet to examine. We may suspect the claim to be consciously subconscious, nevertheless there is a vague and vast residue into which the subconscious enters. Poetry, religion, passion — we have not placed them yet, and since we are critics — only critics — we must try to place them, to catalogue the rainbow. We have already peeped and botanized upon our mothers' graves.

The numbering of the warp and woof of the rainbow must accordingly be attempted, and we must now bring our minds to bear on the subject of fantasy.

Chapter 6   Fantasy

A course of lectures, if it is to be more than a collection of remarks, must have an idea running through it. It must also have a subject, and the idea ought to run through the subject too. This is so obvious as to sound foolish, but anyone who has tried to lecture will realize that here is a genuine difficulty. A course, like any other collection of words, generates an atmosphere. It has its own apparatus — a lecturer, an audience or provision for one — it occurs at regular intervals, it is announced by printed notices, and it has a financial side, though this last is tactfully concealed. Thus it tends in its parasitic way to lead a life of its own, and it and the idea running through it are apt to move in one direction while the subject steals off in the other.

The idea running through these lectures is by now plain enough: that there are in the novel two forces: human beings and a bundle of various things not human beings, and that it is the novelist's business to adjust these two forces and con-ciliate their claims. That is plain enough, but does it run through the novel too? Perhaps our subject, namely the books we have read, has stolen away from us while we theorize, like a shadow from an ascending bird. The bird is all right — it climbs, it is consistent and eminent. The shadow is all right — it has flickered across roads and gardens. But the two things resemble one another less and less, they do not touch as they did when the bird rested its toes on the ground. Criticism, especially a critical course, is so misleading. However lofty its intentions and sound its method, its subject slides away from beneath it, imperceptibly away, and lecturer and audience may awake with a start to find that they are carrying on in a distinguished and intelligent manner, but in regions which have nothing to do with anything they have read.

It was this that was worrying Gide, or rather one of the things that was worrying him, for he has an anxious mind. When we try to translate truth out of one sphere into another, whether from life into books or from books into lectures, something happens to truth: it goes wrong, not suddenly, when it might be detected, but slowly. That long passage from *Les Faux-Monnayeurs* already quoted, may recall the bird to its shadow. It is not possible, after it, to apply the old apparatus any more. There is more in the novel than time or people or logic or any of their derivatives, more even than fate. And by more I do not mean something that excludes these aspects nor something that includes them, embraces them. I mean something that cuts across them like a bar of light, that is intimately connected with them at one place and patiently illumines all their problems, and at another place shoots over or through them as if they did not exist. We shall give that bar of light two names, fantasy and prophecy.

The novels we have now to consider all tell a story, contain characters, and have plots or bits of plots, so we could apply to them the apparatus suited for Fielding or Arnold Bennett. But when I say two of their names — *Tristram Shandy* and *Moby Dick* — it is clear that we must stop and think a moment. The bird and the shadow are too far apart. A new formula must be found; the mere fact that one can mention Tristram and Moby in a single sentence shows it. What an impossible pair! As far apart as the poles. Yes. And like the poles they have one thing in common, which the lands round the equator do not share: an axis. What is essential in Sterne and Melville belongs to this new aspect of fiction: the fantastic-prophetical axis. George Meredith touched it: he was somewhat fantastic. So did Charlotte Bronte: she was a prophetess occasionally. But in neither of these was it essential. Deprive them of it, and a book remains which still resembles *Harry Richmond* or *Shirley*. Deprive Sterne or Melville of it, deprive Peacock or Max Beerbohm or Virginia Woolf or

Walter de la Mare or William Beckford or James Joyce or D. H. Lawrence or Swift, and nothing is left at all.

Our easiest approach to a definition of any aspect of fiction is always by considering the sort of demand it makes on the reader. Curiosity for the story, human feelings and a sense of value for the characters, intelligence and memory for the plot. What does fantasy ask of us? It asks us to pay something extra. It compels us to an adjustment that is different to an adjustment required by a work of art, to an additional adjustment. The other novelists say "Here is something that might occur in your lives," the fantasist: "Here is something that could not occur. I must ask you first to accept my book as a whole, and secondly to accept certain things in my book." Many readers can grant the first request, but refuse the second. "One knows a book isn't real," they say; "still, one does expect it to be natural, and this angel or midget or ghost or silly delay about the child's birth — no, it is too much." They either retract their original concession and stop reading, or if they do go on it is with complete coldness, and they watch the gambols of the author without realizing how much they may mean to him.

No doubt the above approach is not critically sound. We all know that a work of art is an entity, etc., etc. ; it has its own laws which are not those of daily life, anything that suits it is true, so why should any question arise about the angel, etc., except whether it is suitable to its book? Why place an angel on a different basis from a stockbroker? Once in the realm of the fictitious, what difference is there between an apparition and a mortgage? I see the soundness of this argument, but my heart refuses to assent. The general tone of novels is so literal that when the fantastic is introduced it produces a special effect ; some readers are thrilled, others choked off; it demands an additional adjustment because of the oddness of its method or subject-matter — like a side-show in an exhibition where you have to pay sixpence as well as the original entrance fee. Some readers pay with delight, it is only for the side-shows that they entered the exhibition, and it is only to them I can address myself now. Others refuse with indignation, and these have our sincere regards, for to dislike the fantastic in literature is not to dislike literature. It does not even imply poverty of imagination, only a disinclination to meet certain demands that are made on it. Mr. Asquith (if gossip is correct) could not meet the demands made on him by Lady into Fox. He should not have objected, he said, if the fox had become a lady again, but as it was he was left with an uncomfortable dissatisfied feeling. This feeling reflects no discredit either upon an eminent politician or a charming book. It merely means that Mr. Asquith, though a genuine lover of literature, could not pay the additional sixpence — or rather he was willing to pay it but hoped to get it back again at the end.

So fantasy asks us to pay something extra.

Let us now distinguish between fantasy and prophecy.

They are alike in having gods, and unlike in the gods they have. There is in both the sense of mythology which differentiates them from other aspects of our subject. An invocation is again possible, therefore on behalf of fantasy let us now invoke all beings who inhabit the lower air, the shallow water, and the smaller hills, all Fauns and Dryads and slips of the memory, all verbal coincidences, Pans and puns, all that is medieval this side of the grave. When we come to prophecy, we shall utter no invocation, but it will have been to whatever transcends our abilities, even when it is human passion that transcends them, to the deities of India, Greece, Scandinavia and Judaea, to all that is medieval beyond the gave and to Lucifer son of the morning. By their mythologies we shall distinguish these two sorts of novels.

A number of rather small gods, then, should haunt us today — I would call them fairies if the word were not consecrated to imbecility. (Do you believe in fairies? No, not under any circumstances.) The stuff of daily life will be tugged and strained in various directions, the earth will be given little tilts, mischievous or pensive, spotlights will fall on objects that have no reason to anticipate or welcome them, and tragedy herself, though not excluded, will have a fortuitous air as if a word would disarm her. The power of fantasy penetrates into every corner of the universe, but not into the forces that govern it — the stars that are the brain of heaven, the army of unalterable law, remain untouched — and novels of this type have an improvised air, which is the secret of their force and charm. They may contain solid character-drawing, penetrating and bitter criticism of conduct and civilization; yet our simile of the beam of light must remain, and if one god must be invoked specially let us call upon Hermes — messenger, thief, and conductor of souls to a not too terrible hereafter.

You will expect me now to say that a fantastic book asks us to accept the supernatural. I will say it, but reluctantly, because any statement as to their subject-matter brings these novels into the claws of critical apparatus, from which it is important that they should be saved. It is truer of them than of most books that we can only know what is in them by reading them, and their appeal is specially personal — they are side-shows inside the main show. So I would rather hedge as much as possible, and say that they ask us to accept either the supernatural or its absence.

A reference to the greatest of them — *Tristram Shandy* — will make this point clear. The supernatural is absent from the Shandy ménage, yet a thousand incidents suggest that it is not far off. It would not be really odd, would it, if the furniture in Mr. Shandy's bedroom, where he retired in despair after hearing the omitted details of his son's birth, should come alive like Belinda's toilette in *The Rape of the Lock*, or that Uncle Toby's drawbridge should lead into Lilliput? There is a charmed stagnation about the whole epic — the more the characters do the less gets done, the less they have to say the more they talk, the harder they think the softer they get, facts have an unholy tendency to unwind and trip up the past instead of begetting the future, as in well-conducted books, and the obstinacy of inanimate objects, like Dr. Slop's bag, is most suspicious. Obviously a god is hidden in *Tristram Shandy*, his name is Muddle, and some readers cannot accept him. Muddle is almost incarnate — quite to reveal his awful features was not Sterne's intention; that is the deity that lurks behind his masterpiece — the army of unutterable muddle, the universe as a hot chestnut. Small wonder that another divine muddler, Dr. Johnson, writing in 1776, should remark, "Nothing odd will do long: *Tristram Shandy* did not last!" Doctor Johnson was not always happy in his literary judgements, but the inappropriateness of this one passes belief.

Well, that must serve as our definition of fantasy. It implies the supernatural, but need not express it. Often it does express it, and were that type of classification helpful, we could make a list of the devices which writers of a fantastic turn have used — such as the introduction of a god, ghost, angel, monkey, monster, midget, witch into ordinary life; or the introduction of ordinary men into no man's land, the future, the past, the interior of the earth, the fourth dimension; or divings into and dividings of personality; or finally the device of parody or adaptation. These devices need never grow stale; they will occur naturally to writers of a certain temperament, and be put to fresh use; but the fact that their number is strictly limited is of interest; and suggests that the beam of light can only be manipulated in certain ways.

I will select, as a typical example, a recent book about a witch: *Flecker's Magic*, by Norman Matson. It seemed to me good and I recommended it to a friend whose judgement I respect. He thought it poor. That is what is so tiresome about new books: they never give us that restful feeling which we have when perusing the classic. Flecker's Magic contains scarcely anything that is new — fantasies cannot ; only the old old story of the wishing-ring which brings either misery or nothing at all. Flecker, an American boy who is learning to paint in Paris, is given the ring by a girl in a café; she is a witch, she tells him; he has only to be sure what he wants and he will get it. To prove her power, a motor-bus rises slowly from the street and turns upside down in the air. The passengers, who do not fall out, try to look as if nothing was happening. The driver, who is standing on the pavement at the moment, cannot conceal his surprise, but when his bus returns safe to earth again he thinks it wiser to get into his seat and drive off as usual. Motor-buses do not revolve slowly through the air — so they do not. Flecker now accepts the ring. His character, though slightly sketched, is individual, and this definiteness causes the book to grip.

It proceeds with a growing tension, a series of little shocks. The method is Socratic. The boy starts by thinking of something obvious, like a Rolls Royce. But where shall he put the beastly thing? Or a beautiful lady. But what about her carte d'identité? Or money? Ah, that's more like it — he is almost a beggar. Say a million dollars. He prepares to turn the ring for this wish — except while one's about it two millions seem safer — or ten — or — and money blares out into madness, and the same thing happens when he thinks of long life: to die in forty years — no, in fifty — in one hundred — horrible, horrible. Then a solution occurs. He has always wanted to be a great painter. Well, he'll be it at once. But what kind of greatness? Giotto's? Cézanne's? Certainly not; his own kind, and he does not know what that is, so this wish likewise is impossible.

And now a horrible old woman begins to haunt his days and dreams. She reminds him vaguely of the girl who gave him the ring. She knows his thoughts and sidles up to say, "Dear boy, darling boy! Wish for happiness!" We learn in time that she is the real witch — the girl was a human acquaintance whom she used to get into touch with Flecker. The last of the witches — very lonely. The rest have committed suicide during the eighteenth century — they could not endure to survive into the world of Newton where two and two make four; and even the world of Einstein is not sufficiently decentralised to revive them. She has hung on in the hope of smashing this world, and she wants the boy to ask for happiness because such a wish has never been made in all the history of the ring.

Perhaps Flecker was the first modern man to find himself in this predicament? The people of the old world had so little they knew surely what they wanted. They knew about Almighty God, who wore a beard and sat in an armchair about a mile above the fields, and life was very short and very long too, for the days were so full of unthinking effort.

The people of the recorded olden times wished for a beautiful castle on a high hill and lived therein until death. But the hill was not so high one might see from the windows back along thirty centuries — as one may from a bungalow. In the castle there were no great volumes filled with words and pictures of things dug up by man's relentless curiosity from sand and soil in all corners of the world; there was a sentimental half-belief in dragons, but no knowledge that once upon a time only dragons had lived on the earth — that man's grandfather and grandmother were dragons; there were no movies flickering like thoughts against a white wall, no phonograph, no machinery with which to achieve the sensation of speed; no diagrams of the fourth dimension, no contrasts in life like that of Waterville, Minn., and Paris, France. In the castle the light was weak and flickering, hallways were dark, rooms deeply shadowed. The little outside world was full of shadow, and on the very top of the mind of him who lived in the castle played a dim light — underneath were shadows, fear, ignorance, will-to-ignorance. Most of all there was not in the castle on the hill the breathless sense of imminent revelation — that today or surely tomorrow Man would at a stroke double his power and change the world again.

The ancient tales of magic were the mumbling thoughts of a distant shabby little world — so, at least, thought Flecker, offended. The tales gave him no guidance. There was too much difference between his world and theirs ...

He wondered if he hadn't dismissed the wish for happiness rather heedlessly? He seemed to get nowhere thinking about it. He was not wise enough. In the old tales a wish for happiness was never made! He wondered why.

He might chance it — just to see what would happen. The thought made him tremble. He leaped from his bed and paced the red-tiled floor, rubbing his hands together ...

"I want to be happy for ever," he whispered, to hear the words, careful not to touch the ring. "Happy ... for ever" — the two syllables of the first word, like little hard pebbles, struck musically against the bell of his imagination, but the second was a sigh. For ever — his spirit sank under the soft, heavy impact of it. Held in his thought the word made a dreary music, fading. "Happy ... for ever" — NO!!

A true fantasist, Norman Matson merges the kingdoms of magic and common sense by using words that apply to both, and the mixture he has created comes alive. I will not tell the end of the story. You will have guessed its essentials, but there are always surprises in the working of a fresh mind, and to the end of time good literature will be made round this notion of a wish.

To turn from this simple example of the supernatural to a more complicated one — to a highly accomplished and superbly written book whose spirit is farcical: *Zuleika Dobson* by Max Beerbohm. You all know Miss Dobson — not personally, or you would not be here now. She is the damsel for love of whom all the undergraduates of Oxford except one drowned themselves during Eights Week, and he threw himself out of a window.

A superb theme for a fantasy, but all will depend on the handling. It is treated with a mixture of realism, wittiness, charm and mythology, and the mythology is most important. Max has borrowed or created a number of supernatural machines — to have entrusted Zuleika to one of them would be inept; the fantasy would become heavy or thin. But we pass from the sweating emperors to the black and pink pearls, the hooting owls, the interference of the Muse Clio, the ghosts of Chopin and George Sand, of Nellie O'Mora; just as one fails another starts, to uphold this most exquisite of funeral palls.

Through the square, across the High; down Grove

Street they passed. The Duke looked up at the tower of Merton, ως ονποτ' ανθc αλλα νον πανμσγατον. Strange that tonight it would still be standing here, in all its sober and solid beauty — still be gazing, over the roofs and chimneys, at the tower of Magdalen, its rightful bride. Through untold centuries of the future it would stand thus, gaze thus. He winced. Oxford walls have a way of belittling us; and the Duke was loth to regard his doom as trivial.

Aye, by all minerals we are mocked. Vegetables, yearly deciduous, are far more sympathetic. The lilac and laburnum, making lovely now the railed pathway to Christ Church meadow, were all a-swaying and a-nodding to the Duke as he passed by. "Adieu, adieu, your Grace," they were whispering. "We are very sorry for you, very sorry indeed. We never dared suppose you would predecease us. We think your death a very great tragedy. Adieu! Perhaps we shall meet in another world — that is, if the members of the animal kingdom have immortal souls, as we have."

The Duke was little versed in their language; yet, as he passed between these gently garrulous blooms, he caught at least the drift of their salutation, and smiled a vague but courteous acknowledgment, to the right and the left alternately, creating a very favourable impression.

Has not a passage like this a beauty unattainable by serious literature? It is funny and charming, iridescent yet profound. Criticisms of human nature fly not like arrows but upon the wings of sylphs. Towards the end — that dreadful end often so fatal to fiction — the book rather flags: the suicide of all the undergraduates of Oxford is not as delightful as it ought to be when viewed at close quarters, and the defenestration of Noels almost nasty. Still, it is a great work — the most consistent achievement of fantasy in our time, and the closing scene in Zuleika's bedroom with its menace of further disasters is impeccable.

> And now with pent breath and fast-beating heart, she stood staring at the lady of the mirror, without seeing her; and now she wheeled round and swiftly glided to that little table on which stood her two books. She snatched *Bradshaw*.
>
> We always intervene between Bradshaw and anyone whom we see consulting him. "Mademoiselle will permit me to find that which she seeks?" asked Mélisande.
>
> "Be quiet," said Zuleika. We always repulse, at first, any one who intervenes between us and Bradshaw.
>
> We always end by accepting the intervention. "See if it is possible to go direct from here to Cambridge," said Zuleika, handing the book on. "If it isn't, then — well,

see how one does get there."

We never have any confidence in the intervener. Nor is the intervener, when it comes to the point, sanguine. With mistrust mounting to exasperation Zuleika sat watching the faint and frantic researches of her maid.

"Stop!" she said suddenly. "I have a much better idea. Go down very early to the station. See the station-master. Order me a special train. For ten o'clock, say."

Rising, the stretched her arms above her head. Her lips parted in a yawn, met in a smile. With both hands she pushed back her hair from her shoulders, and twisted it into a loose knot. Very lightly she slipped up into bed, and very soon she was asleep.

So Zuleika ought to have come on to this place. She does not seem ever to have arrived and we can only suppose that through the intervention of the gods her special train failed to start, or, more likely, is still in a siding at Bletchley.

Among the devices in my list I mentioned "parody" or "adaptation" and would now examine this further. The fantasist here adopts mythology for his some earlier work and uses it as a framework or quarry for his own purposes. There is an aborted example of this in *Joseph Andrews*. Fielding set out to use

Pamela as a comic mythology. He thought it would be fun to invent a brother to Pamela, a pure-minded footman, who should repulse Lady Booby's attentions just as Pamela had repulsed Mr. B.'s, and he made Lady Booby Mr. B.'s aunt. Thus he would be able to laugh at Richardson, and incidentally express his own views of life. Fielding's view of life, however, was of the sort that only rests content with the creation of solid round characters, and with the growth of Parson Adams and Mrs.

Slipslop the fantasy ceases, and we get an independent work. *Joseph Andrews* (which is also important historically) is interesting to us as an example of a false start. Its author begins by playing the fool in a Richardsonian world, and ends by being serious in a world of his own — the world of Tom Jones and Amelia.

Parody or adaptation have enormous advantages to certain novelists, particularly to those who may have a great deal to say and abundant literary genius, but who do not see the world in terms of individual men and women — who do not, in other words, take easily to creating characters. How are such men to start writing? An already existing book or literary tradition may inspire them — they may find high up in its cornices a pattern that will serve as a beginning, they may swing about in its rafters and gain strength. That fantasy of Lowes Dickinson, *The Magic*

Flute, seems to be created thus: it has taken as its mythology the world of Mozart. Tamino, Sarastro, and the Queen of the Night stand in their enchanted kingdom ready for the author's thoughts, and when these are poured in they become alive, and a new and exquisite work is born. And the same is true of another fantasy, anything but exquisite — James Joyce's *Ulysses*. That remarkable affair — perhaps the most interesting literary experiment of our day — could not have been achieved unless Joyce had had, as his guide and butt, the world of the *Odyssey*.

I am only touching on one aspect of *Ulysses*; it is of course far more than a fantasy — it is a dogged attempt to cover the universe with mud, an inverted Victorianism, an attempt to make crossness and dirt succeed where sweetness and light failed, a simplification of the human character in the interests of Hell. All simplifications are fascinating, all lead away from the truth (which lies nearer the muddle of *Tristram Shandy*), and *Ulysses* must not detain us on the ground that it contains a morality — otherwise we shall also have to discuss Mrs. Humphry Ward. We are concerned with it because, through a mythology, Joyce has been able to create the peculiar stage and characters he required.

The action of those 400,000 words occupies a single day, the scene is Dublin, the theme is a journey — the modern man's journey from morn to midnight, from bed to the squalid tasks of mediocrity, to a funeral, newspaper office, library, pub, lavatory, lying-in hospital, a saunter by the beach, brothel, coffee-stall, and so back to bed. And it coheres because it depends from the journey of a hero through the seas of Greece, like a bat hanging to a cornice.

Ulysses himself is Mr. Leopold Bloom — a converted Jew — greedy, lascivious, timid, undignified, desultory, superficial, kindly, and always at his lowest when he pretends to aspire. He tries to explore life through the body. Penelope is Mrs. Marion Bloom, an overblown soprano, by no means harsh to her suitors. The third character is young Stephen Dedalus, whom Bloom recognizes as his spiritual son much as Ulysses recognizes Telemachus as his actual son. Stephen tries to explore life through the intellect — we have met him before in *A Portrait of the Artist as a Young Man*, and now he is worked into this epic of grubbiness and disillusion. He and Bloom meet halfway through in Night Town (which corresponds partly to Homer's Palace of Circe, partly to his Descent into Hell), and in its supernatural and filthy alleys they strike up their slight but genuine friendship. This is the crisis of the book, and here — and indeed throughout — smaller mythologies swarm and pullulate, like vermin between the scales of a poisonous snake. Heaven and earth fill with infernal life, personalities melt, sexes interchange, until the whole universe, including poor, pleasure-loving Mr. Bloom, is involved in one joyless orgy.

Does it come off? No, not quite. Indignation in literature never quite comes off either in Juvenal or Swift or Joyce; there is something in words that is alien to its simplicity. The Night Town scene does not come off except as a superfetation of fantasies, a monstrous coupling of reminiscences. Such satisfaction as can be attained in this direction is attained, and all through the book we have similar experiments — the aim of which is to degrade all things, and more particularly civilization and art, by turning them inside out and upside down. Some enthusiasts may think that *Ulysses* ought to be mentioned not here but later on, under the heading of prophecy, and I understand this criticism. But I prefer to mention it today with *Tristram Shandy*, *Flecker's Magic*, *Zuleika Dobson*, and *The Magic Flute*, because the raging of Joyce, like the happier or calmer moods of the other writers, seems essentially fantastic, and lacks the note for which we shall be listening soon.

We must pursue this notion of mythology further and more circumspectly.

Chapter 7 Prophecy

With prophecy in the narrow sense of foretelling the future we have no concern, and we have not much concern with it as an appeal for righteousness. What will interest us today — what we must respond to, for interest now becomes an inappropriate word — is an accent in the novelist's voice, an accent for which the flutes and saxophones of fantasy may have prepared us. His theme is the universe, or something universal, but he is not necessarily going to "say" anything about the universe; he proposes to sing, and the strangeness of song arising in the halls of fiction is bound to give us a shock. How will song combine with the furniture of common sense? we shall ask ourselves, and shall have to answer "not too well": the singer does not always have room for his gestures, the tables and chairs get broken, and the novel through which bardic influence has passed often has a wrecked air, like a drawing-room after an earthquake or a children's party. Readers of D. H. Lawrence will understand what I mean.

Prophecy — in our sense — is a tone of voice. It may imply any of the faiths that have haunted humanity — Christianity, Buddhism, dualism, Satanism, or the mere raising of human love and hatred to such a power that their normal receptacles no longer contain them; but what particular view of the universe is recommended — with that we are not directly concerned. It is the implication that signifies and will filter into the turns of the novelist's phrase, and in this lecture, which promises to be so vague and grandiose, we may come nearer than elsewhere to the minutiae of style. We shall have to attend to the novelist's state of mind and to the actual words he uses; we shall neglect as far as we can the problems of common sense. As far as we can: for all novels contain tables and chairs, and most readers of fiction look for them first. Before we condemn him for affectation and distortion we must realize his viewpoint. He is not looking at the tables and chairs at all, and that is why they are out of focus. We only see what he does not focus — not what he does — and in our blindness we laugh at him.

I have said that each aspect of the novel demands a different quality in the reader. Well, the prophetic aspect demands two qualifies: humility and the suspension of the sense of humour. Humility is a quality for which I have only a limited admiration.

In many phases of life it is a great mistake and degenerates into defensiveness or hypocrisy. But humility is in place just now. Without its help we shall not hear the voice of the prophet, and our eyes will behold a figure of fun instead of his glory. And the sense of humour — that is out of place; that estimable adjunct of the educated man must be laid aside. Like the schoolchildren in the Bible, one cannot help laughing at a prophet — his bald head is so absurd — but one can discount the laughter and realize that it has no critical value and is merely food for bears.

Let us distinguish between the prophet and the non-prophet.

There were two novelists, who were both brought up in Christianity. They speculated and broke away, yet they neither left nor did they want to leave the Christian spirit, which they interpreted as a loving spirit. They both held that sin is always punished, and punishment a purgation, and they saw this process not with the detachment of an ancient Greek or a modern Hindu, but with tears in their eyes. Pity, they felt, is the atmosphere in which morality exercises its logic, a logic which otherwise is crude and meaningless. What is the use of a sinner being punished and cured if there is not an addition in the cure, a heavenly bonus? And where does the addition come from? Not out of the machinery, but out of the atmosphere in which the process occurs, out of the love and pity which (they believed) are attributes of God.

How similar these two novelists must have been! Yet one of them was George Eliot and the other Dostoevsky.

It will be said that Dostoevsky had vision. Still, so had George Eliot. To classify them apart — and they must be parted — is not so easy. But the difference between them will define itself at once exactly if I read two passages from their works. To the classifier the passages will seem similar; to anyone who has an ear for song they come out of different worlds.

I will begin with a passage — fifty years ago it was a very famous passage — out of *Adam Bede*. Hetty is in prison, condemned to die for the murder of her illegitimate child. She will not confess, she is hard and impenitent. Dinah, the Methodist, comes to visit her.

> Dinah began to doubt whether Hefty was conscious who it was that sat beside her ... But she felt the Divine presence more and more, — nay, as if she herself were a part of it, and it was the Divine pity that was beating in her heart, and was willing the rescue of this helpless one. At last she was prompted to speak, and find out how far Hetty was conscious of the present.
>
> "Hetty," she said gently, "do you know who it is that

sits by your side?"

"Yes," Hetty answered slowly, "it's Dinah." ... Then, after a pause, she added, "But you can do nothing for me. You can't make 'em do anything. They'll hang me o' Monday — its Friday now." ...

"But Hetty, there is some one else in this cell besides me, some one close to you."

Hetty said, in a frightened whisper, "Who?"

"Some one who has been with you through all your hours of sin and trouble — who has known every thought you have had — has seen where you went, where you lay down and rose up again, and all the deeds you have tried to hide in darkness. And on Monday, when I can't follow you, — when my arms can't reach you, — when death has parted us, — He who is with you now, and knows all, will be with you then. It makes no difference — whether we live or die, we are in the presence of God."

"Oh, Dinah, won't nobody do anything for me? Will they hang me for certain? ... I wouldn't mind if they'd let me live ... help me ... . I can't feel anything like you ... my heart is hard."

Dinah held the clinging hand, and all her soul went forth in her voice:

"... Come, mighty Saviour! let the dead hear Thy voice; let the eyes of the blind be opened; let her see that God encompasses her; let her tremble at nothing but at the sin that cuts her off from Him. Melt the hard heart; unseal the closed lips; make her cry with her whole soul, 'Father, I have sinned.' ..."

"Dinah," Hetty sobbed out, throwing her arms round Dinah's neck, "I will speak ... I will tell ... I won't hide it any more ... I did do it, Dinah ... I. buried it in the wood ... the little baby ... and it cried ... I heard it cry ... ever such a way off ... all night ... and I went back because it cried."

She paused, and then spoke hurriedly in a louder pleading tone.

"But I thought perhaps it wouldn't die — there might somebody find it. I didn't kill it — I didn't kill it myself. I put it down there and covered it up, and when I came back it was gone ... I don't know what I felt till I saw the baby was gone. And when I'd put it there, I thought I should like somebody to find it, and save it from dying; but when I saw it was gone, I was struck like a stone, with fear. I never thought o' stirring, I felt so weak. I knew I couldn't run away, and everybody as saw me 'ud know about the baby. My heart went like a stone; I couldn't wish or try for anything; it seemed like as if I should stay there for ever, and nothing 'ud ever change. But they came and took me away."

Hetty was silent, but she shuddered again, as if there was still something behind; and Dinah waited, for her heart was so full, that tears must come before words. At last Hetty bunt out with a sob.

"Dinah, do you think God will take away that crying and the place in the wood, now I've told everything?"

"Let us pray, poor sinner: let us fall on our knees again, and pray to the God of all mercy."

I have not done justice to this scene, because I have had to cut it, and it is on her massiveness that George Eliot depends — she has no nicety of style. The scene is sincere, solid, pathetic, and penetrated with Christianity. The god whom Dinah summons is a living force to the authoress also; he is not brought in to work up the reader's feelings; he is the natural accompaniment of human error and suffering.

Now contrast with it the following scene from *The Brothers Karamazov* (Mitya is being accused of the murder of his father; he is spiritually though not technically guilty).

They proceeded to a final revision of the protocol. Mitya got up, moved from his chair to the corner by the curtain, lay down on a large chest covered by a rug, and instantly fell asleep.

He had a strange dream, utterly out of keeping with the place and the time.

He was driving somewhere in the steppes, where he had been stationed long ago, and a peasant was driving him in a cart with a pair of hones, through snow and sleet ... Not far off was a village, he could see the black huts, and half the huts were burnt down, there were only the charred beams sticking up. And as they drove in, there were peasant women drawn up along the road, a lot of women, a whole row, all thin and wan, with their faces a sort of brownish colour, especially one at the edge, a tall, bony woman, who looked forty, but might have been only twenty, with a long thin face. And in her arms was a little baby crying. And her breasts seemed so dried up that there was not a drop of milk in them. And the child cried and cried, and held out its little bare arms, with its little fists blue from cold.

"Why are they crying? Why are they crying?" Mitya asked as they dashed gaily by.

"It's the babe," answered the driver. "the babe weeping."

And Mitya was struck by his saying, in his peasant way, "the babe", and he liked the peasant's calling it "the babe". There seemed more pity in it.

"But why is it weeping?" Mitya persisted stupidly, "why are its little arms bare? Why don't they wrap it up?" ...

"Why, they're poor people, burnt out. They've no bread. They're begging because they've been burnt out."

"No, no," Mitya, as it were, still did not understand. "Tell me why it is those poor mothers stand there? Why are people poor? Why is the babe poor? Why is the steppe barren? Why don't they hug each other and kiss? Why don't they sing songs of joy? Why are they so dark from black misery? Why don't they feed the babe?"

And he felt that, though his questions were unreasonable and senseless, yet he wanted to ask just that, and he had to ask it just in that way. And he felt that a passion of pity, such as he had never known before, was rising in his heart, that he wanted to cry, that he wanted to do something for them all, so that the babe should weep no more, so that the dark-faced, dried-up mother should not weep, that no one should shed tears again from that moment, and he wanted to do it at once, at once, regardless of all obstacles, with all the recklessness of the Karamazovs ... And his heart glowed, and he struggled forward towards the light, and he longed to live, to live, to go on and on, towards the new, beckoning light, and to hasten, hasten, now, at once!

"What! Where?" he exclaimed, opening his eyes, and sitting up on the chest, as though he had revived from a swoon, smiling brightly. Nikolay Parfenovitch was standing over him, suggesting that he should hear the protocol read aloud and sign it. Mitya guessed that he had been asleep an hour or more, but he did not hear Nikolay Parfenovitch. He was suddenly struck by the fact that there was a pillow under his head, which hadn't been there when he leant back, exhausted, on the chest.

"Who put that pillow under my head? Who was so kind?" he cried, with a sort of ecstatic gratitude, and tears in his voice, as though some great kindness had been shown him.

He never found out who this kind man was, perhaps one of the peasant witnesses, or Nikolay Parfenovitch's little secretary had compassionately thought to put a pillow under his head, but his whole soul was quivering which tears. He went to the table and said he would sign whatever they liked.

"I've had a good dream, gentlemen," he said in a strange voice, with a new light, as of joy, in his face.

Now the difference between these passages is that the first writer is a preacher, and the second a prophet. George Eliot talks about God, but never alters her focus; God and the tables and chairs are all in the same plane, and in consequence we have not for a moment the feeling that the whole universe needs pity and love — they are only needed in Hetty's cell. In Dostoevsky the characters and situations always stand for more than themselves; infinity attends them, though they remain individuals they expand to embrace it and summon it to embrace them; one can apply to them the saying of St. Catherine of Siena that God is in the soul and the soul is in God as the sea is in the fish and the fish is in the sea. Every sentence he writes implies this extension, and the implication is the dominant aspect of his work. He is a great novelist in the ordinary sense — that is to say, his characters have relation to ordinary life and also live in their own surroundings, there are incidents which keep us excited, and so on; he has also the greatness of a prophet, to which our ordinary standards are inapplicable.

That is the gulf between Hetty and Mitya, though they inhabit the same moral and mythological worlds. Hetty, taken by herself, is quite adequate. She is a poor girl, brought to confess her crime, and so to a better frame of mind. But Mitya, taken by himself, is not adequate. He only becomes real through what he implies, his mind is not in a frame at all. Taken by himself he seems distorted out of drawing, intermittent; we begin explaining him away and saying he was disproportionately grateful for the pillow because he was overwrought — very like a Russian in fact. We cannot understand him until we see that he extends, and that the part of him on which Dostoevsky focused did not lie on that wooden chest or even in dreamland, but in a region where it could be joined by the rest of humanity. Mitya is — all of us. So is Alyosha, so is Smerdyakov. He is the prophetic vision; and the novelist's creation also. He does not become all of us here; he is Mitya here as Hetty is Hetty. The extension, the melting, the unity through love and pity occur in a region which can only be implied, and to which fiction is perhaps the wrong approach. The world of the Karamazovs and Myshkin and Raskolnikov, the world of Moby Dick which we shall enter shortly — it is not a veil, it is not an allegory. It is the ordinary world of fiction, but it reaches back. And that tiny humorous figure of Lady Bertram whom we considered some time ago — Lady Bertram sitting on her sofa with pug — may assist us in these deeper matters. Lady Bertram, we decided, was a flat character, capable of extending into a round when the action required it. Mitya is a round character, but he too is capable of extension. He does not conceal anything (mysticism), he does not mean anything (symbolism), he is merely Dmitri Karamazov, but to be merely a person in Dostoevsky is to join up with all the other people far back. Consequently the tremendous current suddenly flows — for me in those closing words: "I've had a good dream, gentlemen." Have I had that good dream too? No, Dostoevsky's characters ask us to share something deeper than their experiences. They convey to us a sensation that is partly physical — the sensation of sinking into a translucent globe and seeing our experience floating far above us on its surface, tiny, remote, yet ours. We have not ceased to be people, we have given nothing up, but "the sea is in the fish and the fish is in the sea."

There we touch the limit of our subject. We are not concerned with the prophet's message, or rather (if matter and manner cannot be separated) we are concerned with it as little as possible. What matters is the accent of his voice, his song. Hetty might have a good dream in prison, and it would be true of her, satisfyingly true, but it would stop short. Dinah would say she was glad, Hefty would recount her dream, which, unlike

Mitya's, would be logically connected with the crisis, and George Eliot would say something sound and sympathetic about good dreams generally, and their inexplicably helpful effect on the tortured breast. Just the same and absolutely different are the two scenes, the two books, the two writers ...

Now another point emerges. Regarded merely as a novelist, the prophet has certain uncanny advantages, so that it is sometimes worth letting him into a drawing-room even on the furniture's account. Perhaps he will smash or distort, but perhaps he will illumine. As I said of the fantasist, he manipulates a beam of light which occasionally touches the objects so sedulously dusted by the hand of common sense, and renders them more vivid than they can ever be in domesticity. This intermittent realism pervades all the greater works of Dostoevsky and Herman Melville. Dostoevsky can be patiently accurate about a trial or the appearance of a staircase. Melville can catalogue the products of the whale ("I have ever found your plain things the knottiest of all," he remarks). D. H. Lawrence can describe a field of grass and flowers or the entrance into Fremantle. little things in the foreground seem to be all that the prophet cares about at moments — he sits down with them so quiet and busy, like a child between two romps. What does he feel during these intermittencies? Is it another form of excitement, or is he resting? We cannot know. No doubt it is what A. E. feels when he is doing his creameries, or what Claudel feels when he is doing his diplomacy, but what is that? Anyhow, it characterizes these novels and gives them what is always provocative in a work of art: roughness of surface. While they pass under our eyes they are full of dents and grooves and lumps and spikes which draw from us little cries of approval and disapproval. When they have past, the roughness is forgotten, they become as smooth as the moon.

Prophetic fiction, then, seems to have definite characteristics. It demands humility and the absence of the sense of humour. It reaches back — though we must not conclude from the example of Dostoevsky that it always reaches back to pity and love. It is spasmodically realistic. And it gives us the sensation of a song or of sound. It is unlike fantasy because its face is towards unity, whereas fantasy glances about. Its confusion is incidental, whereas fantasy's is fundamental — *Tristram Shandy* ought to be a muddle, *Zuleika Dobson* ought to keep changing mythologies. Also the prophet — one imagines — has gone "off" more completely than the fantasist, he is in a remoter emotional state while he composes. Not many novelists have this aspect. Poe is too incidental. Hawthorne potters too anxiously round the problem of individual salvation to get free. Hardy, a philosopher and a great poet, might seem to have claims, but Hardy's novels are surveys; they do not give out sounds. The writer sits back, it is true, but the characters do not reach back. He shows them to us as they let their arms rise and fall in the air; they may parallel our sufferings but can never extend them — never, I mean, could Jude step forward like Mitya and release floods of our emotion by saying, "Gentlemen, I've had a bad dream." Conrad is in a rather similar position. The voice, the voice of Marlow, is too full of experiences to sing, it is dulled by many reminiscences of error and beauty, its owner has seen too much to see beyond cause and effect. To have a philosophy — even a poetic and emotional philosophy like Hardy's and Conrad's — leads to reflections on life and things. A prophet does not reflect. And he does not hammer away. That is why we exclude Joyce. Joyce has many qualities akin to prophecy and he has shown (especially in the Portrait of the Artist) an imaginative grasp of evil. But he undermines the universe in too workmanlike a manner, looking round for this tool or that; in spite of all his internal looseness he is too tight, he is never vague except after due deliberation; it is talk, talk, never song.

So, though I believe this lecture is on a genuine aspect of the novel, not a fake aspect, I can only think of four writers to illustrate it — Dostoevsky, Melville, D. H. Lawrence and Emily

Bronte. Emily Bronte shall be left to the last, Dostoevsky I have alluded to, Melville is the centre of our picture, and the centre of Melville is *Moby Dick*.

Moby Dick is an easy book, as long as we read it as a yarn or an account of whaling interspersed with snatches of poetry. But, as soon as we catch the song in it, it grows difficult and immensely important. Narrowed and hardened into words, the spiritual theme of *Moby Dick* is as follows: a battle against evil, conducted too long or in the wrong way. The White Whale is evil, and Captain Ahab is warped by constant pursuit until his knight-errantry turns into revenge. These are words — a symbol for the hook if we want one — but they do not carry us much further than the acceptance of the book as a yarn — perhaps they carry us backwards, for they may mislead us into harmonizing the incidents, and so losing their roughness and richness. The idea of a contest we may retain: all action is a battle, the only happiness is peace. But contest between what? We get false if we say that it is between good and evil, or between two unreconciled evils. The essential in *Moby Dick*, its prophetic song, flows athwart the action and the surface morality like an undercurrent. It lies outside words. Even at the end, when the ship has gone down with the bird of heaven pinned to its mast, and the empty coffin, bouncing up from the vortex, has carried Ishmael back to the world — even then we cannot catch the words of the song. There has been stress, with intervals; but no explicable solution, certainly no reaching back into universal pity and love; no "Gentlemen, I've had a good dream." The extraordinary nature of the book appears in two of its early incidents — the sermon about Jonah and the friendship with Queequeg.

The sermon has nothing to do with Christianity. It asks for endurance or loyalty without hope of reward. The preacher, "kneeling in the pulpit's bows, folded his large brown hands across his chest, uplifted his closed eyes, and offered a prayer so deeply devout that he seemed kneeling and praying at the bottom of the sea". And he concludes on a note of joy more terrifying than a menace:

> Delight is to him whose strong arms yet support him, when the ship of this base treacherous world has gone down beneath him. Delight is to him, who gives no quarter in the truth, and kills, bums, and destroys all sin though he pluck it out from under the robes of Senators and Judges. Delight, — top-gallant delight is to him, who acknowledges no law or lord, but the Lord his God, and is only a patriot to heaven. Delight is to him, whom all the waves of the billows of the seas of the boisterous mob can never shake from this sure

Keel of the Ages. And eternal delight and deliciousness will be his, who coming to lay him down, can say with his final breath — O Father! — chiefly known to me by Thy rod — mortal or immortal, here I die. I have striven to be Thine, more than to be this world's, or mine own. Yet this is nothing: I leave eternity to Thee; for what is man that he should live out the lifetime of his God?

I believe it is not a coincidence that the last ship we encounter at the end of the book before the final catastrophe should be called the Delight; a vessel of ill omen who has herself encountered Moby Dick and been shattered by him. But what the connection was in the prophet's mind I cannot say, nor could he tell us.

Immediately after the sermon, Ishmael makes a passionate alliance with the cannibal Queequeg, and it looks for a moment that the book is to be a saga of blood-brotherhood. But human relationships mean little to Melville, and after a grotesque and violent entry Queequeg is almost forgotten. Almost — not quite. Towards the end he falls ill, and a coffin is made for him which he does not occupy, as he recovers. It is this coffin, serving as a life-buoy, that saves Ishmael from the final whirlpool, and this again is no coincidence, but an unformulated connection that sprang up in Melville's mind. *Moby Dick* is full of meanings; its meaning is a different problem. It is wrong to turn the Delight or the coffin into symbols, because even if the symbolism is correct, it silences the book. Nothing can be stated about Moby Dick except that it is a contest. The rest is song.

It is to his conception of evil that Melville's work owes much of its strength. As a rule, evil has been feebly envisaged in fiction, which seldom soars above misconduct or avoids the clouds of mysteriousness. Evil to most novelists is either sexual and social, or something very vague for which a special style with implications of poetry is thought suitable. They want it to exist, in order that it may kindly help them on with the plot, and evil, not being kind, generally hampers them with a villain — a Lovelace or Uriah Heep, who does more harm to the author than to the fellow characters. For a real villain we must turn to a story of Melville's called *Billy Budd*.

It is a short story, but must be mentioned because of the light it throws on his other work. The scene is on a British man-of-war soon after the mutiny at the Nore — a stagy yet intensely real vessel. The hero, a handsome young sailor, has goodness of the glowing aggressive sort which cannot exist unless it has evil to consume. He is not himself aggressive. It is the light within him that irritates and explodes. On the surface he is a pleasant, merry, rather insensitive lad, whose perfect physique is marred by one slight defect, a stammer, which finally destroys him.

He is dropped into a world not without some man-traps, and against whose subtleties simple courage ... without any touch of defensive ugliness, is of little avail; and where such innocence as man is capable of does yet in a moral emergency not always sharpen the faculties or enlighten the will.

Claggart, one of the petty officers, at once sees in him the enemy — his own enemy, for Claggart is evil. It is again the contest between Ahab and Moby Dick, though the parts are more clearly assigned, and we are further from prophecy and nearer to morality and common sense. But not much nearer. Claggart is not like any other villain.

Naturally depravity ... has its certain negative virtues serving as silent auxiliaries ... It is not going too far to say that it is without vices or small sins. There is a phenomenal pride in it that excludes them from anything mercenary or avaricious. In short the depravity here meant partakes nothing of the sordid or sensual. It is serious, but free from acerbity.

He accuses Billy of trying to foment a mutiny. The charge is ridiculous, yet proves fatal. For when the boy is summoned to declare his innocence he is so horrified that he cannot speak, his ludicrous stammer seizes him, the power within him explodes, and he knocks down his traducer, kills him, and has to be hanged.

Billy Budd is a remote unearthly episode, but it is a song not without words, and should be read both for its own beauty and as an introduction to more difficult works. Evil is labelled and personified instead of slipping over the ocean and round the world, and Melville's mind can be observed more easily. What one notices in him is that his apprehensions are free from personal worry, so that we become bigger, not smaller, after sharing them. He has not got that tiresome little receptacle, a conscience, which is often such a nuisance in serious writers and so contracts their effects — the conscience of Hawthorne or of Mark Rutherford. Melville — after the initial roughness of his realism — reaches straight back into the universal, to a blackness and sadness so transcending our own that they are undistinguishable from glory. He says: "In certain moods, no man can weigh this world without throwing in something, somehow like Original

Sin, to strike the uneven balance." He threw it in, that undefinable something, the balance righted itself, and he gave us harmony and temporary salvation.

It is no wonder that D. H. Lawrence should have written two penetrating studies of Melville, for Lawrence himself is, as far as I know, the only prophetic novelist writing today — all the rest are fantasists or preachers: the only living novelist in whom the song predominates, who has the rapt bardic quality, and whom it is idle to criticize. He invites criticism because he is a preacher also — it is this minor aspect of him which makes him so difficult and misleading — an excessively clever preacher who knows how to play on the nerves of his congregation. Nothing is more disconcerting than to sit down, so to speak, before your prophet, and then suddenly to receive his boot in the pit of your stomach. "I'm damned if I'll be humble after that," you cry, and so lay yourself open to further nagging. Also the subject-matter of the sermon is agitating — hot denunciations or advice relating to sex — so that in the end you cannot remember whether you ought or ought not to have a body, and are only sure that you are futile. This bullying, and the honeyed sweetness which is a bully's reaction, occupy between them the foreground of Lawrence's work; his greatness lies far, far back, and rests, not like Dostoevsky's upon Christianity, nor like Melville's upon a contest, but upon something aesthetic. The voice is Balder's voice, though the hands are the hands of Esau. The prophet is irradiating nature from within, so that every colour has a glow and every form a distinctness which could not other-wise be obtained. Take a scene that always stays in the memory: that scene in Women in Love where one of the characters throws stones into the water at night to shatter the image of the moon. Why he throws, what the scene symbolizes, is unimportant. But the writer could not get such a moon and water otherwise; he reaches them by his special path which stamps them as more wonderful than any we can imagine. It is the prophet back where he started from, back where the rest of us are waiting by the edge of the pool, but with a power of re-creation and evocation we shall never posses.

Humility is not easy with this irritable and irritating author, for the humbler we get the crosser he gets. Yet I do not see how else to read him. If we start resenting or mocking, his treasure disappears as surely as if we started obeying him. What is valuable about him cannot be put into words: it is colour, gesture and outline in people and things, the usual stock-in-trade of the novelist, but evolved by such a different process that they belong to a new world.

But what about Emily Bronte? Why should *Wuthering*

Heights come into this enquiry? It is a story about human beings, it contains no view of the universe.

My answer is that the emotions of Heathcliffe and Catherine Earnshaw function differently to other emotions in fiction. Instead of inhabiting the characters, they surround them like thunder clouds, and generate the explosions that fill the novel from the moment when Lockwood dreams of the hand at the window down to the moment when Heathcliffe, with the same window open, is discovered dead. Wuthering Heights is filled with sound — storm and rushing wind — a sound more important than words and thoughts. Great as the novel is, one cannot afterwards remember anything in it but Heathcliffe and the elder Catherine. They cause the action by their separation; they close it by their union after death. No wonder they "walk": what else could such beings do? Even when they were alive their love and hate transcended them.

Emily Bronte had in some ways a literal and careful mind. She constructed her novel on a time-chart even more elaborate than Miss Austen's, and she arranged the Linton and Earnshaw families symmetrically, and she had a clear idea of the various legal steps by which Heatheliffe gained possession of their two properties. Then why did she deliberately introduce muddle, chaos, tempest? Because in our sense of the word she was a prophetess; because what is implied is more important to her than what is said; and only in confusion could the figures of Heathcliffe and Catherine externalize their passion till it streamed through the house and over the moors. Wuthering Heights has no mythology beyond what these two characters provide; no great book is more cut off from the universals of Heaven and Hell. It is local, like the spirits it engenders, and, whereas we may meet Moby Dick in any pond, we shall only encounter them among the harebells and limestone of their own county.

A concluding remark. Always, at the back of my mind, there lurks a reservation about this prophetic stuff, a reservation which some will make more strongly while others will not make it at all. Fantasy has asked us to pay something extra, and now prophecy asks for humility and even for a suspension of the sense of humour, so that we are not allowed to snigger when a tragedy is called Billy Budd. We have indeed to lay aside the single vision which we bring to most of literature and life and have been trying to use through most of our enquiry, and take up a different set of tools. Is this right? Another prophet, Blake, had no doubt that it was right. "May God us keep/From Single vision, & Newton's sleep!" he cried, and he has painted that same Newton with a pair of compasses in his hand, describing a miserable mathematical triangle and turning his back upon the gorgeous and immeasurable water-growths of Moby Dick. Few will agree with Blake. Fewer will agree with Blake's Newton. Most of us will be eclectics to this side or that according to our temperament. The human mind is not a dignified organ, and I do not see how we can exercise it sincerely except through eclecticism. And the only advice I would offer my fellow eclectics is: "Do not be proud of your inconsistency. It is a pity, it is a pity that we should be equipped like this. It is a pity that Man cannot be at the same time impressive and truthful."

For the first five lectures of this course we have used more or less the same set of tools. This time and last we have had to lay them down. Next time we shall take them up again, but with no certainty that they are the best equipment for a critic, or that there is such a thing as a critical equipment.

Chapter 8   Pattern and Rhythm

Our interludes, gay and grave, are over, and we return to the general scheme of the course. We began with the story, and having considered human beings we proceeded to the plot which springs out of the story. Now we must consider something which springs mainly out of the plot, and to which the characters and any other element present also contribute. For this new aspect there appears to be no literary word — indeed the more the arts develop the more they depend on each other for definition. We will borrow from painting first and call it the pattern. Later we will borrow from music and call it rhythm. Unfortunately both these words are vague — when people apply rhythm or pattern to literature they are apt not to say what they mean and not to finish their sentences: it is "Oh, but surely the rhythm ..." or "Oh, but if you call that pattern ..."

Before I discuss what pattern entails, and what qualities a reader must bring to its appreciation, I will give two examples of books with patterns so definite that a pictorial image sums them up: a book the shape of an hour-glass and a book the shape of a grand chain in that old-time dance, the lancers.

Thais, by Anatole France, is the shape of an hour-glass. There are two chief characters, Paphnuce the ascetic, Thais the courtesan. Paphnuce lives in the desert, he is saved and happy when the book starts. Thais leads a life of sin in Alexandria, and it is his duty to save her. In the central scene of the book they approach, he succeeds; she goes into a monastery and gains salvation, because she has met him, but he, because he has met her, is damned. The two characters converge, cross and recede with mathematical precision, and part of the pleasure we get from the book is due to this. Such is the pattern of *Thais* — so simple that it makes a good starting-point for a difficult survey. It is the same as the story of *Thais*, when events unroll in their time-sequence, and the same as the plot of *Thais*, when we see the two characters bound by their previous actions and taking fatal steps whose consequence they do not see. But, whereas the story appeals to our curiosity and the plot to our intelligence, the pattern appeals to our aesthetic sense, it causes us to see the book as a whole. We do not see it as an hour-glass — that is the hard jargon of the lecture-room which must never be taken literally at this advanced stage of our enquiry. We just have a pleasure without knowing why, and when the pleasure is past, as it is now, and our minds are left free to explain it, a geometrical simile such as an hour-glass will be found helpful. If it was not for this hour-glass the story, the plot, and the characters of Thais and Paphnuce would none of them exert their full force, they would none of them breathe as they do. "Pattern", which seems so rigid, is connected with atmosphere, which seems so fluid.

Now for the book that is shaped like the grand chain: *Roman Pictures* by Percy Lubbock.

Roman Pictures is a social comedy. The narrator is a tourist in Rome; he there meets a kindly and shoddy friend of his, Deering, who rebukes him superciliously for staring at churches and sets him out to explore society. This he does, demurely obedient; one person hands him on to another; café, studio, Vatican and Quirinal purlieus are all reached, until finally, at the extreme end of his career he thinks, in a most aristocratic and dilapidated palazzo, whom should he meet but the second-rate Deering; Deering is his hostess's nephew, but had concealed it owing to some backfire of snobbery. The circle is complete, the original partners have rejoined, and greet one another with mutual confusion which turns to mild laughter.

What is so good in *Roman Pictures* is not the presence of the "grand chain" pattern — anyone can organize a grand chain —

but the suitability of the pattern to the author's mood. Lubbock works all through by administering a series of little shocks, and by extending to his characters an elaborate charity which causes them to appear in a rather worse light than if no charity was wasted on them at all. It is the comic atmosphere, but sub-acid, meticulously benign. And at the end we discover to our delight that the atmosphere has been externalized, and that the partners, as they click together in the marchesa's drawing-room, have done the exact thing which the book requires, which it required from the start, and have bound the scattered incidents together with a thread woven out of their substance.

Thais and *Roman Pictures* provide easy examples of pattern; it is not often that one can compare a book to a pictorial object with any accuracy, though curves, etc., are freely spoken of by critics who do not know what they want to say. We can only say (so far) that pattern is an aesthetic aspect of the novel, and that though it may be nourished by anything in the novel — any character, scene, word — it draws most of its nourishment from the plot. We noted, when discussing the plot, that it added to itself the quality of beauty, beauty a little surprised at her own arrival; that upon its neat carpentry there could be seen, by those who cared to see, the figure of the Muse; that Logic, at the moment of finishing its own house, laid the foundation of a new one. Here, here is the point where the aspect called pattern is most closely in touch with its material; here is our starting-point. It springs mainly from the plot, accompanies it like a light in the clouds, and remains visible after it has departed. Beauty is sometimes the shape of the book, the book as a whole, the unity, and our examination would be easier if it was always this. But sometimes it is not. When it is not I shall call it rhythm. For the moment we are concerned with pattern only.

Let us examine at some length another book of the rigid type, a book with a unity, and in this sense an easy book, although it is by Henry James. We shall see in it pattern triumphant, and we shall also be able to see the sacrifices an author must make if he wants his pattern and nothing else to triumph.

The Ambassadors, like *Thais*, is the shape of an hour-glass. Strether and Chad, like Paphnuce and Thais, change places, and it is the realization of this that makes the book so satisfying at the close. The plot is elaborate and subtle, and proceeds by action or conversation or meditation through every paragraph. Everything is planned, everything fits: none of the minor characters are just decorative like the talkative Alexandrians at Nicias' banquet; they elaborate on the main theme, they work. — The final effect is pre-arranged, dawns gradually on the reader, and is completely successful when it comes. Details of the intrigue may be forgotten, but the symmetry created is enduring.

Let us trace the growth of this symmetry.

Strether, a sensitive middle-aged American, is commissioned by his old friend, Mrs. Newsome, whom he hopes to marry, to go to Paris and rescue her son Chad, who has gone to the bad in that appropriate city. The Newsomes are sound commercial people, who have made money over manufacturing a small article of domestic utility. Henry James never tells us what the small article is, and in a moment we shall understand why. Wells spits it out in *Tono Bungay*, Meredith reels it out in *Evan Harrington*, Trollope prescribes it freely for Miss Dunstable, but for James to indicate how his characters made their pile — it would not do. The article is somewhat ignoble and ludicrous — that is enough. If you choose to be coarse and daring and visualize it for yourself as, say, a button-hook, you can, but you do so at your own risk; the author remains uninvolved.

Well, whatever it is, Chad Newsome ought to come back and help make it, and Strether undertakes to fetch him. He has to be rescued from a life which is both immoral and unremunerative.

Strether is a typical James character — he recurs in nearly all the books and is an essential part of their construction. He is the observer who tries to influence the action, and who through his failure to do so gains extra opportunities for observation. And the other characters are such as an observer like Strether is capable of observing — through lenses procured from a rather too first-class oculist. Everything is adjusted to his vision, yet he is not a quietist — no, that is the strength of the device; he takes us along with him, we move.

When he lands in England (and a landing is an exalted and enduring experience for James, it is as vital as Newgate for Defoe; poetry and life crowd round a landing) — when Strether lands, though it is only old England, he begins to have doubts of his mission, which increase when he gets to Paris. For Chad Newsome, far from going to the bad, has improved: he is distinguished, he is so sure of himself that he can be kind and cordial to the man who has orders to fetch him away; his friends are exquisite, and as for "women in the case" whom his mother anticipated, there is no sign of them whatever. It is Paris that has enlarged and redeemed him — and how well Strether himself understands this!

> His greatest uneasiness seemed to peep at him out of the possible impression that almost any acceptance of Paris might give one's authority away. It hung before him this morning, the vast bright Babylon, like some huge iridescent

object, a jewel brilliant and hard, in which parts were not to be discriminated nor differences comfortably marked. It twinkled and trembled and melted together; and what seemed all surface one moment seemed all depth the next. It was a place of which, unmistakably, Chad was fond; wherefore, if he, Strether, should like it too much, what on earth, with such a bond, would become of either of them?

Thus, exquisitely and firmly, James sets his atmosphere — Paris irradiates the book from end to end, it is an actor though always unembodied, it is a scale by which human sensibility can be measured, and when we have finished the novel, and allow its incidents to blur that we may see the pattern plainer, it is Paris that gleams at the centre of the hour-glass shape — Paris — nothing so crude as good or evil. Strether' sees this, and sees that Chad sees it, and when this stage is reached the novel takes a turn: there is, after all, a woman in the case: behind Paris, interpreting it for Chad, is the adorable and exalted figure of Mme. de Vionnet. It is now impossible for Strether to proceed. All that is noble and refined in life concentrates in Mme. de Vionnet and is reinforced by her pathos. She asks him not to take Chad away. He promises — without reluctance, for his own heart has already shown him as much — and he remains in Paris not to fight it but to fight for it.

For the second batch of ambassadors now arrives from the New World. Mrs. Newsome, incensed and puzzled by the unseemly delay, has dispatched Chad's sister, his brother-in-law, and Mamie, the girl whom he is supposed to marry. The novel now becomes, within its ordained limits, most amusing. There is a superb set-to between Chad's sister and Mme. de Vionnet, while as for Mamie — here is Mamie, seen through Strether's eyes.

> As a child, as an "bud", and then again as a flower of expansion, Mamie had bloomed for him, freely, in the almost incessantly open doorways of home; where he remembered her as first very forward, as then very backward — for he had carried on at one period, in Mrs. Newsome's parlous ... a course of English literature reinforced by exams and teas — and once more, finally, as very much in advance. But he had kept no great sense of points of contact; it not being in the nature of things at Woollett that the freshest of the buds should find herself in the same basket with the most withered of the winter apples ... He none the less felt, as he sat with the charming girl, the signal growth of a confidence. For she was charming, when all was said — and none the less so for the visible habit and

practice of freedom and fluency. She was charming, he was aware, in spite of the fact that if he hadn't found her so he would have found her something he should have been in peril of expressing as "funny". Yes, she was funny, wonderful Mamie, and without dreaming it; she was bland, she was bridal — with never, that he could make out as yet, a bridegroom to support it; she was handsome and portly and easy and chatty, soft and sweet and almost disconcertingly reassuring. She was dressed, if we might so far discriminate, less as a young lady than as an old one — had an old one been supposable to Strether as so committed to vanity; the complexities of her hair missed moreover also the looseness of youth; and she had a mature manner of bending a little, as to encourage and reward, while she held neatly together in front of her a pair of strikingly polished hands: the combination of all of which kept up about her the glamour of her "receiving", placed her again perpetually between the windows and within sound of the ice-cream plates, suggested the enumeration of all the names ... gregarious specimens of a single type, she was happy to "meet".

Mamie is another Henry James type; nearly every novel

contains her — Mrs. Gereth in *The Spoils of Poynton* for instance, or Henrietta Stackpole in *The Portrait of a Lady*. He is so good at indicating instantaneously and constantly that a character is second-rate, deficient in sensitiveness, abounding in the wrong sort of worldliness; he gives such a character so much vitality that its absurdity is delightful.

So Strether changes sides and loses all hopes of marrying Mrs. Newsome. Paris is winning — and then he catches sight of something new. Is not Chad, as regards any fineness in him, played out? Is not Chad's Paris after all just a place for a spree? This fear is confirmed. He goes for a solitary country walk, and at the end of the day he comes across Chad and Mme. de Vionnet. They are in a boat, they pretend not to see him, because their relation is at bottom an ordinary liaison, and they are ashamed. They were hoping for a secret week-end at an inn while their passion survived; for it will not survive, Chad will tire of the exquisite Frenchwoman, she is part of his fling; he will go back to his mother and make the little domestic article and marry Mamie. They know all this, and it is revealed to Strether though they try to hide it; they lie, they are vulgar — even Mme. de Vionnet, even her pathos, is stained with commonness.

It was like a chill in the air to him, it was almost

appalling, that a creature so fine could be, by mysterious forces, a creature so exploited. For, at the end of all things, they were mysterious; she had but made Chad what he was — so why could she think she had made him infinite? She had made him better, she had made him best, she had made him anything one would; but it came to our friend with supreme queerness that he was none the less only Chad ... The work, however admirable, was nevertheless of the strict human order, and in short it was marvellous that the companion of mere earthly joys, of comforts, aberrations — however one classed them — within the common experience, should be so transcendently prized ...

She was older for him tonight, visibly less exempt from the touch of time; but she was as much as ever the finest and subtlest creature, the happiest apparition, it had been given him, in all his years, to meet; and yet he could see her there as vulgarly troubled, in very truth, as a maidservant crying for her young man. The only thing was that she judged herself as the maidservant wouldn't; the weakness of which wisdom too, the dishonour of which judgement, seemed but to sink her lower.

So Strether loses them too. As he says: "That, you see, is

my only logic. Not, out of the whole affair, to have got anything for myself." It is not that they have gone back. It is that he has gone on. The Paris they revealed to him — he could reveal it to them now, if they had eyes to see, for it is something finer than they could ever notice for themselves, and his imagination has more spiritual value than their youth. The pattern of the hourglass is complete: he and Chad have changed places, with more subtle steps than Thais and Paphnuce, and the light in the clouds proceeds not from the well-lit Alexandria, but from the jewel which "twinkled and trembled and melted together; and what seemed all surface one moment seemed all depth the next".

The beauty that suffuses *The Ambassadors* is the reward due to a fine artist for hard work. James knew exactly what he wanted, he pursued the narrow path of aesthetic duty, and success to the full extent of his possibilities has crowned him. The pattern has woven itself, with modulation and reservations Anatole France will never attain. But at what sacrifice!

So enormous is the sacrifice that many readers cannot get interested in James, although they can follow what he says (his difficulty has been much exaggerated), and can appreciate his effects. They cannot grant his premise, which is that most of human life has to disappear before he can do us a novel.

He has, in the first place, a very short list of characters. I have already mentioned two — the observer who tries to influence the action, and the second-rate outsider (to whom, for example, all the brilliant opening of What Maisie Knew is entrusted). Then there is the sympathetic foil, — very lively and frequently female — in *The Ambassadors* Maria Gostrey plays this part; there is the wonderful rare heroine, whom Mine. de Vionnet approached and who is consummated by Milly in *The Wings of the Dove*; there is sometimes a villain, sometimes a young artist with generous impulses; and that is about all. For so fine a novelist it is a poor show.

In the second place, the characters, besides being few in number, are constructed on very stingy lines. They are incapable of fun, of rapid motion, of carnality, and of nine-tenths of heroism. Their clothes will not take off, the diseases that ravage them are anonymous, like the sources of their income, their servants are noiseless or resemble themselves, no social explanation of the world we know is possible for them, for there are no stupid people in their world, no barriers of language and no poor. Even their sensations are limited. They can land in Europe and look at works of art and at each other, but that is all. Maimed creatures can alone breathe in Henry James's pages — maimed yet specialized. They remind one of the exquisite deformities who haunted Egyptian art in the reign of Akhnaton —

huge heads and tiny legs, but nevertheless charming. In the following reign they disappear.

Now this drastic curtailment, both of the numbers of human beings and of their attributes, is in the interests of the pattern. The longer James worked, the more convinced he grew that a novel should be a whole — not necessarily geometric like *The Ambassadors*, but it should accrete round a single topic, situation, gesture, which should occupy the characters and provide a plot, and should also fasten up the novel on the outside — catch its scattered statements in a net, make them cohere like a planet, and swing through the skies of memory. A pattern must emerge, and anything that emerged from the pattern must be pruned off as wanton distraction. Who so wanton as human beings? Put Tom Jones or Emma or even Mr. Casaubon into a Henry James book, and the book will burn to ashes, whereas we could put them into one another's books and only cause local inflammation. Only a Henry James character will suit, and though they are not dead — certain selected recesses of experience he explores very well — they are gutted of the common stuff that fills characters in other books, and ourselves. And this castrating is not in the interests of the Kingdom of Heaven, there is no philosophy in the novels, no religion (except an occasional touch of superstition), no prophecy, no benefit for the superhuman at all. It is for the sake of a particular aesthetic effect which is certainly gained, but at this heavy price.

H. G. Wells has been amusing on this point, and perhaps profound. In *Boon* — one of his liveliest works — he had Henry James much upon his mind, and wrote a superb parody of him.

> James begins by taking it for granted that a novel is a work of art that must be judged by its oneness. Some one gave him that idea in the beginning of things and he has never found it out. He doesn't find things out. He doesn't even seem to want to find things out ... He accepts very readily and then elaborates ... The only living human motives left in the novels of Henry James are a certain avidity and an entirely superficial curiosity ... . His people nose out suspicions, hint by hint, link by link. Have you ever known living human beings do that? The thing his novel is about is always there. It is like a church lit but without a congregation to distract you, with every light and line focussed on the high altar. And on the altar, very reverently placed, intensely there, is a dead kitten, an egg-shell, a bit of string ... Like his "Altar of die Dead", with nothing to the dead at all ... For if there was they couldn't all be candles and the effect would vanish ...

Wells sent *Boon* as a present to James, apparently thinking the master would be as much pleased by such heartiness and honesty as was he himself. The master was far from pleased, and a most interesting correspondence ensued. James is polite, reminiscent, bewildered, deeply outraged and exceedingly formidable; he admits that the parody has not "filled me with a fond elation", and regrets in conclusion that he can sign himself "only yours faithfully, Henry James." Wells is bewildered too, but in a different way; he cannot understand why the man should be upset. And, beyond the personal comedy, there is the great literary importance of the issue. It is this question of the rigid pattern; hour-glass or grand chain or converging lines of the cathedral or diverging lines of the catherine wheel, or bed of Procrustes — whatever image you like as long as it implies unity. Can it be combined with the immense richness of material which life provides? Wells and James would agree it cannot, Wells would go on to say that life should be given the preference, and must not be whittled or distended for a pattern's sake. My own prejudices are with Wells. The James novels are a unique possession, and the reader who cannot accept his premises misses some valuable and exquisite sensations. But I do not want more of his novels, especially when they are written by someone else, just as I do not want the art of Akhnaton to extend into the reign of Tutankhamen.

That then is the disadvantage of a rigid pattern. It may externalize the atmosphere, spring naturally from the plot, but it shuts the doors on life and leaves the novelist doing exercises, generally in the drawing-room. Beauty has arrived, but in too tyrannous a guise. In plays — the plays of Racine, for instance — she may be justified, because beauty can be a great empress on the stage, and reconcile us to the loss of the men we knew. But in the novel her tyranny as it grows powerful grows petty, and generates regrets which sometimes take the form of books like Boon. To put it in other words, the novel is not capable of as much artistic development as the drama: its humanity or the grossness of its material (use whichever phrase you like) hinder it. To most readers of fiction the sensation from a pattern is not intense enough to justify the sacrifices that made it, and their verdict is "beautifully done, but not worth doing".

Still this is not the end of our quest. We will not give up the hope of beauty yet. Cannot it be introduced into fiction by some other method than the pattern? Let us edge rather nervously towards the idea of "rhythm".

Rhythm is sometimes quite easy. Beethoven's Fifth Symphony, for instance, starts with the rhythm "diddidy dum", which we can all hear and tap to. But the symphony as a whole has also a rhythm — due mainly to the relation between its movements — which some people can hear but no one can tap to. This second sort of rhythm is difficult, and whether it is substantially the same as the first sort only a musician could tell us. What a literary man wants to say, though, is that the first kind of rhythm, the diddidy dum, can be found in certain novels and may give them beauty. And the other rhythm, the difficult one — the rhythm of the Fifth Symphony as a whole — I cannot quote you any parallels for that in fiction, yet it may be present.

Rhythm in the easy sense is illustrated by the work of Marcel Proust.

Proust's conclusion has not been published yet, and his admirers say that when it comes everything will fall into its place, times past will be recaptured and fixed, we shall have a perfect whole. I do not believe this. The work seems to me a progressive rather than an aesthetic confession, for with the elaboration of Albertine the author is getting tired. Bits of news may await us, but it will be surprising if we have to revise our opinion of the whole book. The book is chaotic, ill-constructed, it has and will have no external shape; and yet it hangs together because it is stitched internally, because it contains rhythms.

There are several examples (the photographing of the grandmother is one of them), but the most important, from the binding point of view, is the "little phrase" in the music of Vinteuil. The little phrase does more than anything else — more even than the jealousy which successively destroys Swann, the hero and Charlus — to make us feel that we are in a homogeneous world. We first hear Vinteuil's name in hideous circumstances. The musician is dead — an obscure little country organist, unknown to fame — and his daughter is defiling his memory. The horrible scene is to radiate in several directions, but it passes.

Then we are at a Paris salon. A violin sonata is performed, and a little phrase from its andante catches the ear of Swann and steals into his life. It is always a living being, but takes various forms. For a time it attends his love for Odette. The love affair goes wrong, the phrase is forgotten, we forget it. Then it breaks out again when he is ravaged by jealousy, and now it attends his misery and past happiness at once, without losing its own divine character. Who wrote the sonata? On hearing it is by Vinteuil, Swann says: "I once knew a wretched little organist of that name — it couldn't be by him." But it is, and Vinteuil's daughter and her friend transcribed and published it.

That seems all. The little phrase crosses the book again and again, but as an echo, a memory; we like to encounter it, but it has no binding power. Then, hundreds and hundreds of pages on, when Vinteuil has become a national possession, and there is talk of raising a statue to him in the town where he has been so wretched and so obscure, another work of his is performed — a posthumous septet. The hero listens — he is in an unknown, rather terrible universe while a sinister dawn reddens the sea. Suddenly for him, and for the reader too, the little phrase of the sonata recurs — half heard, changed, but giving complete orientation, so that he is back in the country of his childhood with the knowledge that it belongs to the unknown. We are not obliged to agree with Proust's actual musical descriptions (they are too pictorial for my own taste), but what we must admire is his use of rhythm in literature, and his use of something which is akin by nature to the effect it has to produce — namely a musical phrase. Heard by various people — first by Swann, then by the hero — the phrase of Vinteuil is not tethered: it is not a banner such as we find George Meredith using — a double-blossomed cherry tree to accompany Clara Middleton, a yacht in smooth waters for Cecilia Halkett. A banner can only reappear, rhythm can develop, and the little phrase has a life of its own, unconnected with the lives of its auditors, as with the life of the man who composed it. It is almost an actor, but not quite, and that "not quite" means that its power has gone towards stitching Proust's book together from the inside, and towards the establishment of beauty and the ravishing of the reader's memory. There are times when the little phrase — from its gloomy inception, through the sonata, into the septet — means everything to the reader. There are times when it means nothing and is forgotten, and this seems to me the function of rhythm in fiction: not to be there all the time like a pattern, but by its lovely waxing and waning to fill us with surprise and freshness and hope.

Done badly, rhythm is most boring, it hardens into a symbol, and instead of carrying us on it trips us up. With exasperation we find that Galsworthy's spaniel John, or whatever it is, lies under the feet again; and even Meredith's cherry trees and yachts, graceful as they are, only open the windows into poetry. I doubt that it can be achieved by the writers who plan their books beforehand, it has to depend on a local impulse when the right interval is reached. But the effect can be exquisite, it can be obtained without mutilating the characters, and it lessens our need of an external form.

That must suffice on the subject of easy rhythm in fiction: which may be defined as repetition plus variation, and which can be illustrated by examples. Now for the more difficult question. Is there any effect in novels comparable to the effect of the Fifth Symphony as a whole, where, when the orchestra stops, we hear something that has never actually been played? The opening movement, the andante, and the trio-scherzo-trio-finale-trio-finale that composes the third block, all enter the mind at once, and extend one another into a common entity. This common entity, this new thing, is the symphony as a whole, and it has been achieved mainly (though not entirely) by the relation between the three big blocks of sound which the orchestra has been playing. I am calling this relation "rhythmic". If the correct musical term is something else, that does not matter; what we have now to ask ourselves is whether there is any analogy to it in fiction.

I cannot find any analogy. Yet there may be one; in music fiction is likely to find its nearest parallel.

The position of the drama is different. The drama may look towards the pictorial arts, it may allow Aristotle to discipline it, for it is not so deeply committed to the claims of human beings. Human beings have their great chance in the novel. They say to the novelist: "Recreate us if you like, but we must come in," and the novelist's problem, as we have seen all along, is to give them a good run and to achieve something else at the same time. Whither shall he turn? Not indeed of help but for analogy. Music, though it does not employ human beings, though it is governed by intricate laws, nevertheless does offer in its final expression a type of beauty which fiction might achieve in its own way. Expansion. That is the idea the novelist must cling to. Not completion. Not rounding off but opening out. When the symphony is over we feel that the notes and tunes composing it have been liberated, they have found in the rhythm of the whole their individual freedom. Cannot the novel be like that? Is not there something of it in *War and Peace*? — the book with which we began and in which we must end. Such an untidy book. Yet, as we read it, do not great chords begin to sound behind us, and when we have finished does not every item — even the catalogue of strategies — lead a larger existence than was possible at the time?

Chapter 9 Conclusion

It is tempting to conclude by speculations as to the future of the novel: will it become more or less realistic, will it be killed by the cinema, and so on. Speculations, whether sad or lively, always have a large air about them, they are a very convenient way of being helpful or impressive. But we have no right to entertain them. We have refused to be hampered by the past, so we must not profit by the future. We have visualized the novelists of the last two hundred years all writing together in one room, subject to the same emotions and putting the accidents of their age into the crucible of the inspiration, and, whatever our results, our method has been sound — sound for an assemblage of pseudo-scholars like ourselves. But we must visualize the novelists of the next two hundred years as also writing in the room. The change in their subject-matter will be enormous; they will not change. We may harness the atom, we may land on the moon, we may abolish or intensify warfare, the mental processes of animals may be understood; but all these are trifles, they belong to history, not to art. History develops, art stands still. The novelist of the future will have to pass all the new facts through the old if variable mechanism of the creative mind.

There is, however, one question which touches our subject, and which only a psychologist could answer. But let us ask it. Will the creative process itself alter? Will the mirror get a new coat of quicksilver? In other words, can human nature change? Let us consider this possibility for a moment — we are entitled to that much relaxation.

It is amusing to listen to elderly people on this subject. Sometimes a man says in confident tones: "Human nature's the same in all ages. The primitive cave man lies deep in us all. Civilization — pooh! a mere veneer. You can't alter facts." He speaks like this when he is feeling prosperous and fat. When he is feeling depressed and is worried by the young, or is being sentimental about them on the ground that they will succeed in life when he has failed, then he will take the opposite view and say mysteriously: "Human nature is not the same. I have seen fundamental changes in my own time. You must face facts." And he goes on like this day after day, alternately facing facts and refusing to alter them.

All I will do is to state a possibility. If human nature does alter, it will be because individuals manage to look at themselves in a new way. Here and there people — a very few people, but a few novelists are among them — are trying to do this. Every institution and vested interest is against such a search: organized religion, the State, the family in its economic aspect, have nothing to gain, and it is only when outward prohibitions weaken that it can proceed; history conditions it to that extent. Perhaps the searchers will fail, perhaps it is impossible for the instrument of contemplation to contemplate itself, perhaps if it is possible it means the end of imaginative literature — which if I understand him rightly is the view of that acute inquirer, Mr. I. A. Richards. Anyhow — that way lies movement and even combustion for the novel, for if the novelist sees himself differently he will see his characters differently, and a new system of lighting will result.

I do not know on the verge of which philosophy or what rival philosophies the above remarks are wavering, but as I look back at my own scraps of knowledge, and into my own heart, I see these two movements of the human mind: the great tedious onrush known as history, and a shy crab-like sideways movement. Both movements have been neglected in these lectures: history because it only carries people on, it is just a train full of passengers; and the crab-like movement because it is too slow and cautious to be visible over our tiny period of two hundred years. So we laid it down as an axiom when we started that human nature is unchangeable, and that it produces in rapid succession prose fictions, which fictions, when they contain 50,000 words or more, are called novels. If we had the power or license to take a wider view, and survey all human and pre-human activity, we might not conclude like this; the crab-like movement, the shillings of the passengers, might be visible, and the phrase "the development of the novel" might cease to be a pseudo-scholarly tag or a technical triviality, and become important, because it implied the development of humanity.